Physical Fitness and the Christian

Fifth Edition

Exercising Stewardship

Pamela Diehl Johnson • L. Delyte Morris

Cedarville University

Kendall Hunt
p u b l i s h i n g   c o m p a n y

This text is dedicated to the members of Cedarville's initial PACL classes in 1986 who used the first edition of the text, as well as to all of the succeeding faculty and students who have helped shape this 5th edition. Our prayer is that you are living the principles of <u>discipline</u>, <u>moderation</u>, and <u>discernment</u> in your body care stewardship and with all God has entrusted to your care.

Cover images © Shutterstock, Inc.
Scripture quotation on front cover from The Holy Bible, English Standard Version®(ESV®), copyright © 2001 by Crossway, a publishing ministry of Good News Publishers. Used by permission. All rights reserved.

Kendall Hunt
publishing company
www.kendallhunt.com
Send all inquiries to:
4050 Westmark Drive
Dubuque, IA 52004-1840

Contents

Chapter 4: **The Cardiorespiratory System: Structure and Function**

Chapter 5: **Conditioning the Cardiorespiratory System**

Chapter 6: **The Musculoskeletal System: Structure and Function**

Chapter 7: **Conditioning for Muscle Strength and Muscle Endurance**

Chapter 8: **Flexibility: Stewardship of our Joints and Connective Tissue**

Chapter 9: **Stress and the Steward**

Chapter 10: **Stewardship through Sound Nutrition**

Chapter 11: **Good Stewardship through Wise Weight Management**

Chapter 12: **Health and the Consumer: Stewardship of Well-being and Resources**

Chapter 13: **So... Now What?**

Appendix A: Introduction to Cedarville University Fitness Center and Nautilus Equipment

Appendix B: Assessing Your Cardiorespiratory Fitness

Appendix C: Target Training Heart Rates for 60%, 75%, 85% Heart Rate Range

Acknowledgments

Textbooks are rarely the result of the authors' efforts alone, and that certainly is true of this text. The Lord's enablement and direction has been clear and evident throughout the revision process, and He has used many people to assist us.

The revisions that form the basis for this fifth edition are based on input from the many students at Cedarville University who have provided us with valuable feedback and student perspective as a result of their experience with the text in the required "PACL" (Physical Activity and the Christian Life) course for which it is used. In addition, the faculty in Cedarville University's Department of Kinesiology and Allied Health have also provided key insights and ideas to help make the text an even more useful tool in their endeavors to provide excellent learning experiences to challenge and equip their students to be good stewards of their lives. Thanks especially to KAH Department Chair Evan Hellwig and faculty members Teresa Clark, April Crommett, Chris Cross, Kathy Freese, Kirk Martin, Brent Newman, Paul Orchard, Jeff Reep, Libby Shearer, and Sandy Shortt. Thanks also to Dean's Assistant Pam Bromer for her part in the production of this manuscript. The final thanks in this section goes to Nancy Ranger, College of Health Professions Dean's Assistant and "proof-reader extraordinaire," for her painstaking efforts in reviewing and correcting the final version of the manuscript. Thank you, thank you, thank you!

Grateful acknowledgment is given to the administrators of Cedarville University who have provided support in accomplishing this revision through the resources they have made available to the faculty and students. Thank you, President Bill Brown, Provost John Gredy, and Academic Vice President Tom Cornman.

Thanks must also be extended to the prayer warriors and donors whom God used to make our fitness center, the Callan Athletic Center, and the Doden Field House a reality. These facilities have provided our students with an attractive locus of application for the principles and knowledge presented in this text not only during their PACL course but throughout their college experience. May God bless you richly for your sacrificial investment in the lives of our students.

Last, but certainly not least, we want to give two other special thanks: to Dr. Cliff Johnson, Pam's husband (and our former Academic Vice President), for his godly understanding, encouragement, patience, and love through the challenging times to complete this revision; and to Dee's dog "Pete" for the many hours left alone so the human could "play" with the silly computer.

Chapter 1

Introduction to Physical Fitness and the Christian

Essential Terms

Body's Trainable Systems

Christian

Eternal Life

Hypokinetic Conditions

Physical Activity

Physical Fitness

Stewardship

Objectives

Upon completion of this chapter, students should be able to:

1. Define, explain, and use effectively the essential terms listed above.

2. Explain the most important decision that needs to be made in life.

3. Apply the definition of physical fitness to life choices, decisions, and activities.

4. Develop or affirm an appreciation of the life-long personal responsibility involved in pursuing physical fitness.

5. Explain the roles of both Scripture and science in the pursuit of the knowledge, attitudes, and values necessary to conduct a God-honoring body care program.

6. Understand the details of a physical fitness program as a stewardship responsibility before God in light of His ownership of our lives.

7. Understand the meaning of stewardship, the role of a steward, and the application of the metaphor to our body care responsibilities.

8. Have an initial awareness of the content and direction of the remainder of the text.

Scripture Verses to Commit to Memory

*John 3:16 "For God so loved the world, that he gave his only Son, that whoever believes in him should not perish but have eternal life."

Romans 3:23 "For all have sinned and fall short of the glory of God."

Romans 6:23 "For the wages of sin is death, but the free gift of God is eternal life in Christ Jesus our Lord."

John 14:6 "Jesus said to him, "I am the way, and the truth, and the life. No one comes to the Father except through me."

The Christian—A Foundational Matter

This text has been written from a Christian theistic perspective or world view. This perspective is based on the presuppositions that God is; that He is Tri-unity; that He has revealed Himself to man through His creation, through His inerrant written word the Bible, and through His Son, the Lord Jesus Christ. We believe that while the physiological and psychological principles and truths that underlie a godly body care program apply to all human beings, the reasons for applying them and the value in doing so make the most sense to CHRISTIANS... that is, believers in Jesus Christ.

It is essential to understand that what you, the reader, decide about Jesus Christ is the most important decision you will ever make about anything in your life. It is far more important than anything you decide about physical fitness, for regardless of how well we care for these physical bodies, they will return to dust (Genesis 3:19), yet we will exist eternally in a "spiritual body" (a most fascinating truth developed in 1 Corinthians 15). The decision you make about what you will do with Jesus Christ and what He has done for you determines where you will spend that eternity and significantly affects how you approach this life here on earth. The decision to accept or reject Jesus Christ results in either eternal life spent in heaven or eternal death spent in hell (See John 3:16, 18, and 36, Mark 16:16, John 5:24–29, and Acts 16:31). It also determines whether you will live this life for and empowered by self, or whether you will live it for and empowered by God.

Christians are believers in the Lord Jesus Christ as the Son of God. They are individuals who, through the work of the Holy Spirit, have recognized their sinful, hopeless condition before a just and holy God. They have confessed their sinfulness to God, and have asked His sinless Son to be their personal Lord and Savior because they understand from Scripture that Christ is the only way to reconcile or "fix" their broken relationship with Jehovah God (John 14:6). Christians understand they have no ability on their own to be accepted by or meet the requirements of a perfect, holy God (Proverbs 14:12, Isaiah 64:6, Romans 3:23). They realize that is why God sent His Son, the Lord Jesus Christ, into the world to be the perfect sacrifice for all who would accept Him as their personal Lord and Savior. Through His death on the cross and His resurrection three days later, He provided for those who believe in Him the privilege of becoming a child of God and of spending eternity with Him—that is, the privilege of having ETERNAL LIFE (John 3:16). With that incredible gift also comes the indwelling of His Holy Spirit who, among other things, guides and empowers in this life (1 Corinthians 6:19, Romans 8:9, 14, 16, Ephesians 3:16).

Thus the Christian has purpose, power, and perspective in this life and the next. We are reminded in 1 Timothy 4:8 that "...for while bodily training is of some value, godliness is of value in every way, as it holds promise for the present life and also for the life to come." So while we offer this textbook as a resource for you to pursue a lifestyle characterized by physical fitness, we urge you first and foremost to consider your condition for eternity—that is, your "fitness" before Jehovah God—and if you have not done so, to accept God's provision of His Son Jesus Christ to make you fit for Him. It is only from the perspective as a child of God that an appropriate view of physical fitness can be achieved. For those of you who are His children, we encourage you to praise Him with every aspect of your life for His indescribable gift to you.

Physical Fitness—What We Mean

The phrase "physical fitness" has been in popular use for several decades now. As with many familiar phrases, there is a vague consensus about its meaning. This, however, is not very helpful when attempting to determine whether or not you have it or how to achieve it. Many people use the phrases "being in shape" or "being in good condition" to explain it. But when those terms are then explained, the variety of answers are fascinating and usually reflect the individual's past successes or failures with achieving some aspect of this somewhat elusive characteristic. It actually is a generalized performance ability that is the result of the current functioning capacities of several of the body's systems.

Even among professionals in physical education, exercise science, and other related fields there are varying definitions offered for this phrase. Most tend to include such ideas as the capacity to perform daily activities with reserve energy, or to engage in sustained physical activity without undue fatigue. The American College of Sports Medicine defines physical fitness simply as "a set of attributes that people have or achieve that relates to the ability to perform physical activity." (ACSM, p. 2)

We would like to propose the following as a useful definition of PHYSICAL FITNESS:

> A capacity to function in each of the body's trainable systems which supports the accomplishment of one's responsibilities and chosen activities, both planned and unplanned, and which is associated with low risk of developing hypokinetic conditions.

As we attempt to develop the application of this definition to daily living, it is important to remember that physical fitness is a dynamic or changing state. The capacity to function that is necessary for each of us changes as we grow, changes as we age, and changes as our life involvements and activities change. The body is designed with a remarkable ability to adapt or change. It can adapt so that it becomes better able to do what it is regularly asked to do. This is often referred to as being able to be conditioned or trained. If we begin by *regularly* (5–7 days a week) walking a given distance (often called conditioning or training), the body will make changes in the trainable structures and functions that support that activity so it can be accomplished more efficiently physiologically. We thus become more "physically fit" to do that activity, as well as any other activities that are similar or that rely on the same structures and functions. We will become more "fit" to walk that distance, and thus will be able to do it more easily. This would even allow us, if we wanted or needed, to do that activity faster or to go farther than we could before.

Conversely, if we stop walking a given amount most days, we will find that the body becomes less and less able to walk significant distances. It adapts to being able to do less and less, thus becomes less "physically fit" to do that activity and any others that rely on those structures and functions in the body. These changes in physical performance ability are often subtle at first and may be masked by "busy-ness" in our lives in a host of pressing but invariably inactive directions. And we can go many days without any apparent need to walk very far or very often because of the growing inactive nature of our lives.

When the deterioration is revealed, though, it is often justified by erroneously attributing it to aging (even by 18 year olds) or lack of athleticism or being busy about the Lord's work. As we shall see, these explanations may have grains of truth in them (the person is older, may not be athletic, and may be very busy in the Lord's work) but that does not make them acceptable reasons for failing to honor the Lord in our body stewardship program. Even writing a book on the Christian and fitness is not an acceptable justification for this sin of omission with regard to providing adequate physical activity in caring for the body.

The principles of conditioning just referenced in discussing the dynamic state of physical fitness will be explored more thoroughly later in the text. The dynamic nature of physical fitness underscores the need for attention to our physical activity levels throughout our lives—young, old, and in between. Attention must be given regardless of the stage in life, the level of athletic giftedness, or the type of ministry into which we are called. All of us have the lifetime responsibility of honoring the Lord with the care we provide the bodies He has given us.

The **body's trainable systems** include the *cardiorespiratory system* (a functional combination of the cardiovascular and respiratory systems) and the *musculoskeletal system* (a functional combination of the muscular and skeletal systems. The quality of the structural and functional characteristics of these systems plays a vital role in the functioning of the entire body, and thus of the entire person. Little we can do in this life is independent of the functioning of these systems, and these systems are interdependent on each other as well as on the other systems of the body. In addition to these systems, the composition of the body plays a key role in the physical fitness of the body. Body composition refers to the relative amounts of fat or adipose tissue compared to the nonfat tissue (muscle, bone, fluid, etc.).

To be "trainable" means to be able to be changed or developed by experiences and/or repeated activities. Every time we are involved in a physical activity that causes our body systems to function beyond the resting situation, acute or temporary changes occur to enable us to do that activity. If the body experiences that situation often enough and at a high enough level (conditioning threshold), it will respond by making chronic or longer lasting changes to handle better that or similar activities. These changes we commonly refer to as "conditioning" or "training." Many view these changes as helping the body become more like it was originally before the fall of Adam and Eve.

The next phrase in the definition, **which supports the accomplishment of one's responsibilities and chosen activities**, acknowledges the fact that the "details" of physical fitness are necessarily different for each of us. They are dependent on what we are responsible to do (Gen. 1:26, Eph. 2:10, 1 Pet. 2:12, 1 Cor. 7–11) and what we have chosen to do. If God has given you the ability to be an Olympic athlete in the pentathlon and to take his Gospel to those who are involved in that, the physical fitness requirements of your responsibilities will necessarily be far beyond that of your friend who has been given a church planting ministry in the Philippines or your sister who is a computer systems analyst. In addition to meeting the demands of your responsibilities, it is necessary that your body care program adequately address the needs of the activities you have chosen to pursue. If your family determines that cross country skiing would be a good recreational activity for the entire family, your needs to develop levels of function in the cardiovascular and musculoskeletal systems will be different from those of the family that chooses to pursue rock climbing or the one that chooses golf. A person who chooses to be involved in cheerleading has significantly different flexibility and strength needs compared to someone who chooses to pursue inline skating.

While much of life is somewhat predictable, some of life is not. While nothing happens that is a surprise to God, things often happen that are a surprise to us. Thus, it is essential that we pursue a level of functioning that will enable us to engage successfully in activities that are **both planned and unplanned**. To be truly physically fit, we need to be prepared to do what we know is coming and yet have a "reserve" available that will enable us to successfully respond to the unknown or the unexpected. The availability of this reserve may mean the difference between life and death, or between using or losing a teachable moment, or between having or wasting a learning opportunity, or between experiencing or missing a "ministry moment" when a seed could be sown, soil could be watered, or the crop could be harvested.

The final aspect of physical fitness is to have a level of functioning that is **associated with low risk of developing hypokinetic conditions**. This aspect of physical fitness is a relatively recent one and is the result of the increasingly inactive nature of our daily lives. The term hypokinetic means that which is less than or deficient in kinetics which is motion. Thus HYPOKINETIC CONDITIONS are problems with the functioning of the body which are primarily or secondarily caused by deficient levels of movement—that is, lack of adequate regular physical activity. More and more information is becoming available regarding the critical role of adequate physical activity in our lives.

Physical Fitness: The Role of Physical Activity

Even a cursory study of the body shows that it is designed for movement. In the typical adult, over 40% of the body weight is muscle tissue, and the primary purpose of muscle tissue is movement. The skeletal system provides the necessary levers for the muscle system so that movement can occur, and the skeletal system is approximately 20% of our body mass. Thus over 60% of what constitutes our physical bodies has as a primary or major function that of movement or physical activity.

Further study reveals that not only is the body designed to be active, it is designed to **need** to be physically active. While any doubt about that should be settled by observing 2 and 3 year olds, do a little study on yourself. Try to sit for an hour without moving (you have to be awake). Most of us will find that we will quickly start longing for movement. Any time we are forced to maintain a static or nonmoving position for any period of time, we experience how good it feels when we finally get to move. Many formal studies ranging from the effects of total bed rest on various body capacities and functions to the effects of various types of conditioning programs have verified this "need to move" and have investigated the most effective means of accomplishing the needed levels of movement.

In addition, the critical role regular PHYSICAL ACTIVITY plays in our health and well-being is becoming more widely acknowledged, especially as the amount of physical activity *required* in our daily lives continues to decrease. Throughout this text, we will use the phrase "physical activity" to mean any movement of the body or a body part caused by the contraction of skeletal muscle tissue which results in a significant increase in energy expenditure above the resting or basal level. This approach to considering physical activity is consistent with definitions commonly used in exercise and physical fitness literature (ACSM, 2; Caspersen et al, p. 126; 2008 *Physical Activity Guidelines*, 2)

The publication in 1979 of *Healthy People: The Surgeon General's Report on Health Promotion and Disease Prevention* [1] led to the publication in 1980 of *Promoting Health/Preventing Disease: Objectives for the Nation*, which was the basis of a decade-long, management-by-objective effort to improve the public health. This 1980 initiative included national health goals and objectives to be achieved by 1990, and was followed in consecutive decades by *Healthy People 2000*, *Healthy People 2010*, and now the current program *Healthy People 2020* (http://www.healthypeople.gov/2020). In each and every version of the initiative, increasing the quantity and quality of physical activity across the age continuum has been identified as an important component of achieving a healthier nation.

In *Healthy People 2020*, twenty-six "Leading Health Indicators" are identified and organized into twelve categories, and "Physical Activity" is one of the twenty-six indicators (included in the "Nutrition, Physical Activity, and Obesity" category). **Table 1.1** lists the fifteen objectives identified in the area of Physical Activity that can help pave the way for the nation's people to become healthier. You will note as you go through this text that the guidelines and recommendations presented throughout are consistent with these objectives, reminding us that good body stewardship is an important component in all of our citizenship responsibilities… as citizens of our nation and as citizens of God's Kingdom.

Table 1.1	Physical Activity Objectives included in Healthy People 2020

PA–1: Reduce the proportion of adults who engage in no leisure-time physical activity.

PA–2: Increase the proportion of adults who meet current Federal physical activity guidelines for aerobic physical activity and for muscle-strengthening activity.

PA–3: Increase the proportion of adolescents who meet current Federal physical activity guidelines for aerobic physical activity and for muscle-strengthening activity.

PA–4: Increase the proportion of the Nation's public and private schools that require daily physical education for all students.

PA–5: Increase the proportion of adolescents who participate in daily school physical education.

PA–6: Increase regularly scheduled elementary school recess in the United States.

PA–7: Increase the proportion of school districts that require or recommend elementary school recess for an appropriate period of time.

PA–8: Increase the proportion of children and adolescents who do not exceed recommended limits for screen time.

PA–9: Increase the number of States with licensing regulations for physical activity provided in child care.

PA–10: Increase the proportion of the Nation's public and private schools that provide access to their physical activity spaces and facilities for all persons outside of normal school hours (that is, before and after the school day, on weekends, and during summer and other vacations).

PA–11: Increase the proportion of physician office visits that include counseling or education related to physical activity.

PA–12: (Developmental) Increase the proportion of employed adults who have access to and participate in employer-based exercise facilities and exercise programs.

PA–13: (Developmental) Increase the proportion of trips made by walking.

PA–14: (Developmental) Increase the proportion of trips made by bicycling.

PA–15: (Developmental) Increase legislative policies for the built environment that enhance access to and availability of physical activity opportunities.

http://www.healthypeople.gov/2020/topicsobjectives2020/objectiveslist.aspx?topicId=33 accessed April 2, 2012

And this is not the only activity at the Federal level giving evidence of the frowing recognition of the critical role physical activity plays in our health. In 2008 the U.S. Department of Health Promotion, issued its first ever *Physical Activity Guidelines for Americans* (www.health.gov/.paguidelines/guidelines/). These *Guidelines* described the characteristics of physical activity that offer substantial health benefits to Americans. The main idea behind the *Guidelines* is that regular physical activity over months and years can produce long-term health benefits and that there is a dose/responce relationship...that is, some is better than none and more is better than some. Table 1.2 presents a summary of the research findings upon which the recommendations uncluded in the *Guidelines* are based.

Table 1.2	The Health Benefits of Physical Activity: Major Research Findings

1. Regular physical activity reduces the risk of many adverse health outcomes.

2. Some physical activity is better than none.

3. For most health outcomes, additional benefits occur as the amount of physical activity increases through higher intensity, greater frequency, and/or longer duration.

4. Most health benefits occur with at least 150 minutes a week of moderate-intensity physical activity, such as brisk walking. Additional benefits occur with more physical activity.

5. Both aerobic (endurance) and muscle-strengthening (resistance) physical activity are beneficial.

6. Health benefits occur for children and adolescents, young and middle-aged adults, older adults, and those in every studied racial and ethnic group.

7. The health benefits of physical activity occur for people with disabilities.

8. The benefits of physical activity far outweigh the possibility of adverse outcomes.

Source: 2008 Physical Activity Guidelines for Americans, p. 7.

Another significant initiative at the national level that was a private-public sector collaborative effort involving almost 300 organizations is the *National Physical Activity Plan (NPAP)* released in May, 2010 (http://www.physicalactivityplan.org.). The NPAP is aimed at creating a national culture that supports physically active lifestyles through the development of a comprehensive set of policies, programs, and initiatives that aim to increase physical activity in all segments of the American population. The *Plan* deals exclusively with physical activity and is aimed at the entire U.S. population. These and other high-level, broadly supported, and well-researched efforts leave little room for doubt that the role of physical activity in developing and maintaining our health is well established...if not necessarily well practiced!!

The public health burden of a sedentary or too physically inactive population is also being recognized globally. Dr. Michael Booth of Australia initiated an effort in 1996 to develop a valid and reliable questionnaire for measuring health-related physical activity. This led to the convening of a working committee of physical activity assessment experts by the World Health Organization in Geneva, Switzerland, the following year. Their efforts resulted in the creation of two questionnaires designed to assess physical activity and sedentary behaviors in various populations. The instruments, known as the International Physical Activity Questionnaires (IPAQ), are available in multiple languages, and can be used in large population studies or in the context of physical activity surveillance. Throughout the first decade of the twenty-first century, researchers and scholars around the world have been testing and utilizing these tools to gain comparable, reliable, and valid information about the physical activity levels within and among various populations toward the goal of assisting in the development of public health policies and programs that can target solutions for physical inactivity and positively influence the health of the nations (www.ipaq.ki.se).

It should be becoming clear that there is strong consensus that physical activity plays a key role in realizing significant health benefits. A careful review of the body of research that is available in this area has been provided by the Physical Activity Guidelines Advisory Committee that was assembled and charged to: "...review existing scientific literature to identify where there is sufficient evidence to develop a comprehensive set of specific physical activity recommendations" (http://www.health.gov/paguidelines/Report/SecretaryLetter.aspx). The results of their efforts provide us with the information in Table 3 regarding the specific health benefits throughout the age continuum of regular physical activity, with a qualitative assessment as to the strength of the research evidence supporting the claimed benefit. This information was published in summary form in the *2008 Physical Activity Guidelines for Americans* publication that was developed from the committee's report.

Table 1.3	Specific Health Benefits Associated with Regular Physical Activity

Children and Adolescents

Strong Evidence	improved cardiorespiratory and muscular fitness
	improved bone health
	improved cardiovascular and metabolic health biomarkers
	favorable body composition
Moderate Evidence	reduced symptoms of depression

Adults and Older Adults

Strong Evidence	lower risk of early death
	lower risk of coronary heart disease
	lower risk of stroke
	lower risk of high blood pressure
	lower risk of adverse blood lipid profile
	lower risk of type 2 diabetes
	lower risk of metabolic syndrome
	lower risk of colon cancer
	lower risk of breast cancer
	prevention of weight gain
	weight loss, particularly when combined with reduced calorie intake
	improved cardiorespiratory and muscular fitness
	prevention of falls
	reduced depression
	better cognitive function (for older adults)
Moderate to Strong Evidence	better functional health (for older adults)
	reduced abdominal obesity
Moderate Evidence	lower risk of hip fracture
	lower risk of lung cancer
	lower risk of endometrial cancer
	weight maintenance after weight loss
	increased bone density
	improved sleep quality

Note: The Advisory Committee rated the evidence of health benefits of physical activity as strong, moderate, or weak. To do so, the Committee considered the type, number, and quality of studies available, as well as consistency of findings across studies that addressed each outcome. The Committee also considered evidence for causality and <u>dose response</u> in assigning the strength-of-evidence rating.
Source: 2008 Physical Activity Guidelines for Americans, USDHHS, 9

There should be no doubt with all of the information available to us from a variety of perspectives that efforts at achieving appropriate levels of physical activity on a regular (daily) basis throughout our lives is a vital component of a God-honoring body care program and is key to achieving and maintaining physical fitness. We are designed to be physically active and to need to be physically active, and that needed movement can be achieved either through the physical activities of our daily responsibilities (although this is rare today) or through planned, structured activities (exercise programs). Through the remainder of this text we will attempt to provide helpful information regarding how this can be accomplished effectively and efficiently.

Physical Fitness and the Christian—Sources of Knowledge

It is important when obtaining information to go to valid, reliable sources. Thus if we are to answer questions like "Why should a Christian be concerned about physical fitness?" or "Isn't concern for the physical body inappropriate for a Christian?", we need to seek those answers from a reliable source. If those answers lead us to the understanding that a Christian should pursue physical fitness, then we need to know where to find the answers to questions like "How do I know what kind of activity is good for me?" and "How much should I do?" Pursuing knowledge requires us to consider briefly how we can know.

The Role of Science

The word "science" is derived from a Latin word which means "to know." Thus science is one way in which man attempts to know things. This "knowledge" is based on several unprovable presuppositions (objective reality or truth, the unity of the universe, and cause and effect) that are accepted by faith. We must understand that science is a process and product of the human mind. It uses a method of "knowing" that can never actually prove anything but can only disprove a given hypothesis or proposed truth. Consensus is achieved after multiple efforts to disprove a hypothesis are unsuccessful; that consensus ultimately assumes the position of knowledge or truth because of its high probability of being true based on man's efforts at knowing.

Specifically, natural science is the systematized body of knowledge about the natural universe, which includes biological science, the systematized body of knowledge of living organisms. God gave man* an incredible mind with which to seek knowledge and develop order in the information he gains. He then is to use it to accomplish the work he has to do here on earth. Adam was given the responsibility of cultivating and keeping the garden of Eden, thus he must have known how to do it (Genesis 2:15). God gave him the responsibility of naming the animals as He brought them before him. In doing this Adam demonstrated an understanding of those animals, as what he said became each animal's name (see Genesis 2:19).

Like Adam, we can understand and know things about the creation, and our bodies are part of that creation. While we do not know everything about how the human body functions (thus we have the "sliding-filament *theory* of muscular

---

*For clarity and ease of reading, the term "man" and masculine pronouns are used throughout the text to refer to all of mankind—both male and female. When reference is intended to be to a specific sex, the terms "male" and "female" are used.

contraction" and the "second messenger hypothesis" of protein hormone action), we do know many things about how they function, what enables them to function better, and what inhibits them from functioning well. Thus science provides important information for us to understand and apply in order to be effective care-givers of our bodies.

The Role of Scripture

The knowledge gained through natural science is limited to what can be known through the use of man's sensory perception. The Christian, while appreciating what he can know and experience through his senses, also knows that there is another source of knowledge and another way of knowing. A Christian knows that there is a reality beyond his own senses, and a way of knowing beyond his own abilities. He knows that God's Word, the Bible, is truth that originates outside of mankind and is independent of mankind for its validity. He knows that "All Scripture is breathed out by God and profitable for teaching, for reproof, for correction, and for training in righteousness, that the man of God may be competent, equipped for every good work." (2 Tim. 3:16, 17). He knows that the Holy Spirit dwelling in him will enable him to understand the truths of Scripture (Ephesians 1:17, 1 Corinthians 2:9–14) since He was the Author of them through chosen men (2 Peter 1:20–21; 2 Timothy 3:16; 2 Peter 3:15).

In light of that knowledge, Christians must turn to Scripture to gain God's perspective of this life and thus how these bodies are to be regarded and kept. Only through Scripture can we gain God's view of these earthly bodies and even of life itself. In the very first book of the Bible we are given a huge clue about what God thinks.

Genesis 1:1 says that "In the beginning God created the heavens and the earth." The rest of the chapter details the process, and lest there be any confusion, the creation of man himself. On the sixth day of creation after the various creatures that live on the land had been created, "God said, Let us make man in our image, after our likeness …So God created man in his own image, in the image of God created he him; male and female he created them." (Genesis 1:26–27). And at the end of that creation endeavor "…God saw every thing that he had made, and behold, it was **very good**" (Genesis 1:31, emphasis mine). Even if we knew nothing else (but we know so much more), just knowing that He made us and we are part of what He called "very good" should give us clear insight regarding our importance. Since our physical bodies are an essential part of "us" in this life, then our bodies are important to Him also.

Scripture must be studied to understand the real purpose of this life and everything we do in this life. It must be studied to gain God's perspective of all that we do as well as to understand His basis for evaluation, since His ways are not our ways (Isaiah 55:8,9; 1 Samuel 16:7). In short, we must know His Word in order to know Him, and we must know Him in order to please Him (Hebrews 11:6, Romans 12:2), since He is what life is all about—its Author, its Sustainer, its Owner, its Reason. In Chapter 2 we will further investigate His Word to more fully understand His perspective of our physical bodies.

Exercising Stewardship—A Meaningful Metaphor

The title of our text presents a play on words with important intent. The phrase "exercising stewardship" is designed to convey our view of the body care responsibilities we have from a Scriptural perspective. God has revealed in Scripture that we are the result of a specific act of creation (Genesis 1:27; 2:7) and that as Christians we are to honor and glorify God with our bodies because we are His (1 Corinthians 6:19, 20; Romans 12:1). We believe this leads us to the conclusion that as Christians we are stewards of our very lives, and thus have stewardship responsibility for our bodies. So how did we reach this conclusion and what does that mean?

A steward by definition is someone who manages the concerns of another, often concerns of a large household or an estate. A synonym for steward might well be manager, a title more commonly used today. Definitions of the term "manage" convey the idea of handling or directing the operations of something with a degree of skill, treating with care, and exercising executive, administrative, and supervisory direction (Merriam-Webster, p. 706, 1154).

Scripture provides further insight in understanding stewards and stewardship. In the Old Testament, a steward was typically a rather superior servant who made decisions, gave orders, and literally acted in the place of his master. (See Genesis 43 and 44, 1 Chronicles 27 and 28, Daniel 1:11 and 16, and Isaiah 22:15–21). The office of steward often presupposed a particularly unique kind of trust on the part of the owner or master who was often a king or ruler of some type. (Hall, pp. 32, 33) To conduct his steward responsibilities effectively, he had to know and understand the owner or master in order to make decisions that would please him, he had to be faithful in carrying out his responsibilities, and he had to know how to conduct the affairs for which he was given responsibility. Thus a good steward knew the owner well, he knew the job well, and he did his duties faithfully.

In the New Testament, Christ used the steward in His parable in Luke 12:42–28. There is an expectation of faithfulness and wisdom on the part of a good steward, and the owner places great trust in him and great responsibility on him. The parable teaches the great retribution that comes to the steward who betrays the trust and is irresponsible, and indicates that the greater the responsibility, the greater the retribution. In Luke 16 Christ again utilizes the steward in a negative parable reference when an unrighteous steward loses perspective and is unfaithful to his master and misuses his position. A passage in the opening verses of 1 Corinthians 4 points out that ". . . it is required of stewards that they be found trustworthy" (verse 2) again making reference to a primary characteristic of a good steward—faithfulness or trustworthiness.

Several important implications can be drawn from the steward metaphor as it is applied to our body care responsibilities. In identifying ourselves as stewards of our bodies, we acknowledge God's ownership of our bodies (1 Corinthians 6:19,20) as well as the fact that God has given us responsibility to care for our bodies (although He continues to be involved in sustaining them as indicated in Colossians 1:17). To be good stewards, we must care for them as He would. We must be faithful or trustworthy in doing so, and we must do so with wisdom and knowledge and understanding.

Exercising stewardship implies doing the activities of a steward. A steward is *active*, and is commended for *doing* his duties and for honoring his master in doing so. While the term "exercise" is commonly used to refer to exerting the body for the sake of developing and maintaining physical fitness, exercising also means "bringing into play or realizing in action," as well as "discharging an official function." Action is key.

The teaching from Christ's parables is that there are significant negative consequences of not being a good steward by wasting or misusing what was put in his care or by lack of appropriate action. The application of that truth to our bodies is readily apparent. To be good stewards of our bodies, we must know the Owner well and must know what He wants us to do. We must obey His directives faithfully and use wisdom in making decisions as we carry out those directives and responsibilities. We must learn well the jobs we have been given to do with regard to caring for these bodies. We must understand that the basis for our evaluation from the Owner will be how *faithfully* we carry out the responsibilities we individually have been given (1 Corinthians 4:2). This perspective should provide significant motivation as we approach the remainder of this text, and more importantly the remainder of our lives, with the goal of hearing from the Owner, "Well done, my good and faithful servant."

An Overview of the Text

In the initial section of the text we will present an overview of what God has to say about the body and our stewardship responsibility before Him in caring for it. This will provide an appropriate foundation for the remainder of the text as we develop the details of a God-honoring physical fitness or body care program. Next, we will present and explain the two major systems that are involved in our ongoing stewardship responsibilities—the cardiorespiratory system and the musculoskeletal system. We will look at the structure and function of the systems and their components, and then investigate the why, what, how, how much, and how often of exercise and conditioning for good stewardship.

Man is a physical, spiritual, and mental/emotional being. He moves, he thinks, he feels, and he has the ability to commune with God. Each aspect of man's being interacts with and is interdependent with every other aspect of man, and as a person he interacts with other people, with creation, and with God. Physical well being can have a positive effect on every other aspect of man's existence, while physical distress can have a negative effect. Spiritual difficulties and disobedience will have not only negative spiritual consequences but can have negative physical and mental consequences (see the Sixth Commandment, Exodus 12; Daniel 4:30–37; 2 Samuel 11, 12; 1 Corinthians 11:30). Psychosomatic illnesses are physical illnesses either caused or worsened by the emotional or mental condition of the individual, demonstrating the powerful effect the mind can have on the body. Scripture reminds us that "a joyful heart is good medicine" (Proverbs 17:22), verifying the positive impact that emotional health can have on the restoration of the body. One of the results of our increasingly inactive lifestyle is the loss of the natural diffusing effect of physical activity on the stress response of the body. The role that regular, structured physical activity can have in addressing the problems associated with chronic stress as well as the role of a healthy spiritual life in dealing with those issues will be presented in Chapter 9.

Our physical lives are dependent upon sufficient and appropriate nutrition. We will review the nutritional needs of the body and present information about how those needs can be met in a God-honoring manner. Along with appropriate nutrition can be met in a God-honoring manner. Along with appropriate nutrition, the good steward must make sure that nutrition is of both the quality and quantity appropriate to maintain the proper weight and body composition. Attention to physical activity levels (energy use), portion sizes, and caloric density of foods (energy intake) are key elements of successful stewardship in weight management.

Our stewardship responsibilities are clearly manifested throughout our multiple roles as consumers, whether we are consuming products, services, or essential resources such as food and water. In the final portions of the text, we will provide information and guidance in several key areas that influence our health.

At the beginning of each chapter, the major objectives of that chapter are listed to give you an overview of its content. Key words and phrases are identified by ALL CAPS to assist you in identifying important terms and ideas as they are initially used in the text. Understanding these concepts and thinking through how they apply in your body stewardship responsibilities is key to your success in this learning experience.

Our Bodies . . . His Gift

The Giver of Life has given to us,
*   these bodies to keep as He would.*
He's made them each different, thus their care must be too,
*   if we are to do what we should.*
He's revealed in His Word, and shown in His world,
*   they're important to Him in His plan.*
He sent His own son to this earth clothed in one,
*   to achieve the salvation of man.*
Your body's a part of the you God has made,
*   the you for whom Christ faced the cross;*
Your body's the temple God's Spirit dwells in,
*   as you take the Good News to the lost.*
To care for our bodies in a God-honoring way .
*   demands that desire in our heart.*
Then discipline must guide, moderation must control,
*   and wisdom must imbue each part.*
The Giver of Life will not ask when we're through,
*   what we weigh or how far we've run*
Nor will He accept the excuses we use, like "too busy,"
*   "too tired," or "no fun."*
Friend, the Giver of Life will not ask how we did,
*   compared to Jenny or Guy.*
The question He'll ask of His stewards is this:
*   "What did you do with what I gave you . . . and why?"*

—Pamela Diehl Johnson

Bibliography and Resources for Further Study

American College of Sports Medicine. *ACSM's Guidelines for Exercise Testing and Prescription*. Philadelphia: Lippincott Williams & Wilkins, 8th Edition, 2010.

Bancroft, Emery H. *Elemental Theology*. Grand Rapids: Zondervan Publishing House, 1960.

Caspersen, C.J., K.E. Powell, and G.M. Christenson, "Physical Activity, Exercise, and Physical Fitness: Definitions and Distinctions for Health-related Research," *Public Health Report*, 1985; 100(2):126-31.

Hall, Douglas J. *The Steward: A Biblical Symbol Come of Age*. Grand Rapids: William B. Eerdmans Publishing Company, 1990.

"International Physical Activity Questionnaire," https://www.ipaq.ki.se or https://sites.google.com/site/theipaq/.

"IPAQ Introduction," http://www.ernaehrungsdenkwerkstatt.de/fileadmin/user_upload/ED-WText/TextElemente/PHN-Texte/koerperAktivitaet/International_Physical_Activity_Questionnaire.pdf.

Meyer, F. B. *Bible Commentary*. Wheaton, IL: Tyndale House Publishers, Inc., 1979.

Mish, Frederick C. (Editor in Chief). Merriam-Webster's Collegiate Dictionary. Springfield, MA: Merriam-Webster, Inc., Tenth Edition, 1993.

Morris, Henry M. *The Biblical Basis for Modern Science*. Grand Rapids, MI: Baker Book House, 1984.

"The National Physical Activity Plan for the U.S," Accessed April 02, 2012. http://www.physicalactivityplan.org.

Nieman, David C. *Exercise Testing and Prescription: A Health-Related Approach*. Mountain View, CA: Mayfield Publishing Company, 5th Edition, 2003.

Physical Activity Guidelines Advisory Committee. 2008. *Physical Activity Guidelines Advisory Committee Report, 2008*. Washington D.C.: U.S. Department of Health and Human Services. Also available at: http://www.health.gov/paguidelines/Report/Default.aspx.

Public Health Service, U.S. Department of Health and Human Services. Healthy People 2010, Vols. I and II, 2nd Edition. Stock No. 017-001-00547-9. Pittsburgh, PA: U.S. Government Printing Office, Superintendent of Documents., 2001. (Also at www.healthypeople.gov)

Ramm, Bernard. *The Christian View of Science and Scripture*. Grand Rapids, MI: Wm. B. Eerdmans Pub. Co., 1955.

Seeley, Rod R., T. D. Stephens, and P. Tate. *Essentials of Anatomy and Physiology*. Dubuque: WCB/McGraw-Hill, 3rd Edition, 1999.

Sharp, G. Thomas. *Science According to Moses: The Foundation of a Biblical World View*. Noble, OK: Creation Truth Publications, Volume I, 1992.

Silvius, John E. *Biology: Principles and Perspectives*. Dubuque, IA: Kendall/Hunt Publishing Company, 1994.

U.S. Department of Health, Education, and Welfare (USDHEW). 1979. *Healthy People. The Surgeon General's Report on Health Promotion and Disease Prevention*. Stock No. 017-001-00416-2. Washington, D. C. U.S. Government Printing Office. Also available at: http://www.eric.ed.gov/PDFS/ED186357.pdf.

U.S. Department of Health and Human Services (USDHHS). 2008. *2008 Physical Activity Guidelines for Americans*. Washington, DC: USDHHS; Accessed April 2, 2012. http://www.health.gov/paguidelines/guidelines/default.aspx.

U.S. Department of Health and Human Services (USDHHS). Office of Disease Prevention and Health Promotion. *Healthy People 2020*. Washington, DC. Accessed April 2, 2012. http://www.healthypeople.gov/2020.

U. S. Department of Health and Human Services. *Physical Activity and Health: A Report of the Surgeon General*. Atlanta, GA: U. S. Department of Health and Human Services, Centers for Disease Control and Prevention, National Center for Chronic Disease prevention and Health Promotion, 1996.

VanTill, Howard J. *The Fourth Day*. Grand Rapids, MI: Wm. B. Eerdmans Pub. Co., 1986.

World Health Organization. *World Health Report on Reducing Risks and Promoting Healthy Life*. 2002. http://www.who.int/whr/2002/en/whr02_en.pdf.

Chapter 2

A Scriptural Perspective of the Body

Objectives

Upon completion of this chapter, students should be able to:

1. Present, discuss, and recognize the importance of a scriptural perspective of the body.

2. Understand the unique contributions of general and special revelation to our understanding of the body.

3. Discuss with knowledge and understanding, and be able to answer questions concerning the six truths from Scripture, with key references, which help develop an understanding of God's perspective of the body.

4. Understand and explain the influence of Greek philosophy as a source of error and confusion with regard to the body being considered evil.

5. Understand the various meanings of the terms "body" and "flesh" in their Greek and Hebrew origins as well as in their current usage and how those multiple meanings can be a source of error and confusion.

6. Explain and answer questions regarding the foundational principles for physical fitness and the Christian presented in the final portion of this chapter.

Scripture Verses to Commit to Memory

1 Corinthians 6:19, 20 Or do you not know that your body is a temple of the Holy Spirit within you, whom you have from God? You are not your own, for you were bought with a price. So glorify God in your body.

Colossians 1:16, 17 For by him all things were created, in heaven and on earth, visible and invisible, whether thrones or dominions or rulers or authorities—all things were created through him and for him. And he is before all things, and in him all things hold together.

Genesis 1:25–27 And God made the beasts of the earth according to their kinds and the livestock according to their kinds, and everything that creeps on the ground according to its kind. And God saw that it was good. Then God said, "Let us make man in our image, after our likeness. And let them have dominion over the fish of the sea and over the birds of the heavens and over the livestock and over all the earth and over every creeping thing that creeps on the earth." So God created man in his own image, in the image of God he created him; male and female he created them.

Ephesians 2:10 For we are his workmanship, created in Christ Jesus for good works, which God prepared beforehand, that we should walk in them.

Romans 11:36, 12:1 For from him and through him and to him are all things. To him be glory forever. Amen. I appeal to you therefore, brothers, by the mercies of God, to present your bodies as a living sacrifice, holy and acceptable to God, which is your spiritual worship.

The Christian and His Body—An Unholy Alliance?

In Scripture man is identified as a being with various aspects—body, mind, and spirit. Psychological research in the last few decades in the area of man's self-concept has led investigators to determine that "Clearly, *body image*—that is, the manner in which we view our body and the mental representation we have of it—forms an integral part of our body esteem and overall self-worth" (Davis, p. 145). This pattern of thinking creates a potential dilemma for the Christian.

As one who has been given a "new nature" as a result of accepting Jesus Christ as personal Lord and Savior, the Christian is often uncertain as to whether concern for the physical body is a lingering attribute of the old sin nature or a legitimate part of his efforts in his new life in Christ. Should the conclusion be drawn from 1 Timothy 4:8, "bodily training is of some value," that greater levels of spirituality could be reached through greater levels of physical inactivity? Or, should efforts be poured into achieving maximal levels of physical proficiency in every area in an attempt to meet the expectations of a perfect, omnipotent God in light of the exhortation in 1 Corinthians 6:20 to "glorify God in your body?"

Careful study of the entire counsel of Scripture will clarify that neither of these extremes is appropriate, and that godly concern for the physical body is an essential component of the God-honoring Christian life. The physical body is not a "necessary evil," dragging down or imprisoning the "good" soul, even though at times this has been promoted within theological circles as a result of the influence of Greek philosophy. But neither is the physical body a means by which we can earn or achieve salvation and eternal life. Efforts to that end are woefully inadequate and result rather in judgment unto eternal death (Revelation 20:12–14).

Our Sources of Knowledge

The body is an essential aspect of man, God's most glorious creation. In order to develop a godly perspective of the body, it is necessary to view the body as God views it. To do that, we must seek information and understanding from what He has revealed to us. God has revealed Himself and His truth to man through both general and special revelation.

> "General revelation includes all means apart from Christ and the Bible; that is, God's revelation through nature (Romans 1:18–21), through His providential dealings with man (Romans 8:28), through his preservation of the universe (Colossians 1:17), and man's moral

nature (Genesis 1:26; Acts 17:29). Special revelation is that which has come through Christ (John 1:18) and through the Bible." (1 John 5:9–12) (Ryrie *A Survey of Bible Doctrine*, p. 37)

From general revelation, which includes natural science as referenced in Chapter 1, we have been able to gain very detailed information about how our bodies function, what their needs are, and what we can do to have them function as they have been designed to function. The remaining chapters in this text rely heavily on knowledge obtained through years of study on the body and its function, knowledge able to be acquired as the result of the general revelation of God. It is also as a result of the ability to investigate, discover, and understand that God has given to man.

In addition, each individual can obtain very specific information about the body's condition and needs directly from it through an incredible internal awareness sometimes referred to as the "wisdom of the body." While the effects of sin on all of our being have likely dulled our sensitivity to this information, it is available and efforts should be made to heighten our receptiveness to it. Thus, much of the information necessary for us to care effectively for our bodies has been provided through general revelation.

Special revelation has been given to reveal God to man more completely, that man might become wise unto salvation (Packer *Knowing God*, p. 15). The written Word (the Bible) and the Living Word (Jesus Christ) were given that we might clearly understand our hopeless position before God, and that we might know of the provision for our redemption through the blood of Jesus Christ (Romans 3:23–26). Upon appropriating that provision, we have the indwelling Holy Spirit to provide the guidance necessary for growing in godliness (God-likeness) and for living a life that will bring honor and glory to God. Through the Scriptures we can know how and why we came into existence, as well as the hope we can have beyond this life. Thus, special revelation gives us God's perspective of this life and provides us with an effective "operator's manual" for the living of it in a manner that honors and pleases Him.

To have a godly perspective of the body, then, it is necessary to gain knowledge and understanding from both general and special revelation. In the next section we will present several truths from Scripture with regard to the worth and significance of the body.

A Godly Perspective of the Body—Truths from Scripture

A premise on which this text is based is that God views man's physical body as having significant worth and value. This, therefore, should be man's view, and evidence of that worth and value should be prevalent in how we care for our bodies throughout our lives. Following are several truths from Scripture which provide support for this belief.

1 **The body was created by a particular act of creation that was direct, special, and immediate. Man is, like all of creation, sustained by both ongoing divine activity and ordained natural laws.**

Genesis 1:26, 27: Then God said, "Let us make man in our image, after our likeness. And let them have dominion over the fish of the sea and over the birds of the heavens and over the livestock and over all the earth and over every creeping thing that creeps on the earth." So God created man in his own image, in the image of God he created him; male and female he created them.

Genesis 2:7: Then the LORD God formed the man of dust from the ground and breathed into his nostrils the breath of life, and the man became a living creature.

Genesis 2:21–22: So the LORD God caused a deep sleep to fall upon the man, and while he slept took one of his ribs and closed up its place with flesh. And the rib that the LORD God had taken from the man he made into a woman and brought her to the man.

Isaiah 43:7: "Everyone who is called by my name, whom I created for my glory, whom I formed and made."

Colossians 1:16–17: For by him all things were created, in heaven and on earth, visible and invisible, whether thrones or dominions or rulers or authorities—all things were created through him and for him. And he is before all things, and in him all things hold together.

Psalm 119:89–91: Forever, O LORD, your word is firmly fixed in the heavens. Your faithfulness endures to all generations; you have established the earth, and it stands fast. By your appointment they stand this day, for all things are your servants.

Nehemiah 9:6: "You are the LORD, you alone. You have made heaven, the heaven of heavens, with all their host, the earth and all that is on it, the seas and all that is in them; and you preserve all of them; and the host of heaven worships you."

Hebrews 1:3: He is the radiance of the glory of God and the exact imprint of his nature, and he upholds the universe by the word of his power. After making purification for sins, he sat down at the right hand of the Majesty on high…

The accounts of creation in Genesis clearly present that man was created by God in a special creative act, unique from that of the rest of creation. According to Genesis, man was created on the sixth day of creation after the animals of the land, and was the result of deliberate forethought on the part of God. After creating man, God saw that everything He had made was "very good" (Genesis 1:31) and He ceased His creative work. He made all of His creation as a manifestation of His attributes, so that man could not have the excuse that he did not know about the true God (Romans 1:20). These bodies, then, are the result of the Creator's direct effort and are a part of God's revelation of Himself to man. If we knew nothing else from Scripture, this alone should connote such worth and significance as to have us in awe of the opportunity and responsibility to care for them.

But there is more. God's active role in sustaining physical life is further evidence of the body's worth. The doctrine of Preservation (sometimes treated as a part of the doctrine of Providence under the attribute of God's sovereignty) presents that God, by a continuous agency, maintains in existence all the things which He has made, together with all their properties and powers. This implies, among other things, that the creation is not self-existent and self-sustaining; and that preservation is not merely a refraining from destroying the creation, but a continuous agency of God by means of which He maintains in existence that which He has created. (Thiessen, pp. 174–176)

In addition to His ongoing, active role in sustaining the creation, God has designed the creation to follow certain natural laws. God has enabled and allowed man to gain knowledge in areas dealing with these ordained natural laws so he might effectively carry out his stewardship role in the creation (including his own body), a responsibility given at creation and continued with additional instructions after the flood (Genesis 1:26, 28; Genesis 9:1–4).

Unfortunately, history shows us that we have not always wisely used the knowledge we have in caring for this earth or these bodies. We sometimes act as if we own the creation rather than have stewardship responsibility for it. A godly perspective of our position and our responsibilities will enable us to accomplish our task appropriately—that of caring for the creation as the Creator would.

> ### 2 Man is, unlike any of the rest of the creation, created "in the image of God," and his body is included in this image bearing role.

> **Genesis 1:25, 26a, 27:** And God made the beasts of the earth according to their kinds and the livestock according to their kinds, and everything that creeps on the ground according to its kind. And God saw that it was good. Then God said, "Let us make man in our image, after our likeness. ..." So God created man in his own image, in the image of God he created him; male and female he created them.

> **Genesis 9:6:** "Whoever sheds the blood of man, by man shall his blood be shed, for God made man in his own image."

The message of Scripture is clear: man has been created in the image and likeness of God. Man's understanding of that message, however, is not so clear. God made the beast of the earth after its kind, the cattle after their kind, and the creeping things after their kind, but He made man after **His** kind. There is much discussion in theological literature regarding the full meaning of being created in the image and likeness of God, and the reader is encouraged to study those presentations. For our concerns here, however, the focus of our attention is whether or not the physical body is included in this concept. We believe it is, although we are quick to emphasize that in doing so we do not believe this necessitates attributing a body to God.

Man was created a total being, material and non-material, and his total being was created in the image of God. Neither of the references in the first chapter of Genesis (verses 26 and 27) presents that only the non-material part of man was to be made in God's image and likeness. Portions of God's instructions to Noah after the flood also support the idea that the physical body is included when reference is made to man in the image of God. Noah was given permission to kill animals for food (Genesis 9:3), but then was warned that any person or any animal that "…sheds man's blood, by man his blood shall be shed; **For God made man in his own image**" (Genesis 9:6, emphasis mine). This seems to reinforce the idea that the body is included in, and actually plays an important part in, our image bearer role. Since killing a person is only destruction of the physical body and that is prohibited by God because man is made in His image, the body must play a part in our image bearing role.

Furthermore, there are only two references in Scripture to beings that are in the image of God. These references are of man, as indicated in the Genesis references, and of the God-man Jesus Christ, referred to as being "the exact imprint of His nature" (Hebrews 1:3). Christ had, before His death, burial, and resurrection, a physical human body, as does man. Upon His resurrection, Christ had a **spiritual** body, and He will exist forever as the God-man in this resurrected body (Acts 1:11; Revelation 5:6). All of mankind will also be given spiritual bodies in which they will spend eternity—some an eternity with the LORD, and some an eternity in hell (see 1 Corinthians 15:22, Revelation 20:12–14, and John 5:28, 29). Thus, both Christ, the absolute and perfect representation of God, and man, a relative and less than perfect representation, are the only beings accorded the role of image bearers of God; and both have bodies as an essential aspect of their being.

It is clear that being created in the image of God has given man an incredible place of standing in the sight of God.

> *Hebrews 2:6–7: It has been testified somewhere, "What is man, that you are mindful of him, or the son of man, that you care for him? You made him for a little while lower than the angels; you have crowned him with glory and honor, and set him over the works of your hands."*

Such an understanding leads to a consideration of the sanctity of life and a great concern on the part of many that human life is not now being appropriately honored. Such practices as the killing of babies by abortions and the killing of the infirm or the aged through euthanasia or "assisted suicide" are clear evidence that the concerns are valid. Believers should strive mightily to change public and personal thinking that leads to activities like these that value human life only when it is convenient or productive or comfortable. (See Sherlock, pp. 172–173.) In addition, however, we must make sure that we are personally demonstrating how much we value the sanctity of life through our daily body stewardship program. We must literally match our talk with our walk and communicate a consistent message about the value of life by the way we honor God in caring for our own.

It is indeed a mystery of God how a being who is both material and non-material can be "in the image" of One Who is, in His essential Being, Spirit (Bancroft, p. 49). As we mature in our knowledge of God, we can more fully grasp the significance of our role as image-bearers and its appropriate manifestation in every area of our lives, including the area of body stewardship. According to G. C. Berkouwer in his text *Man: The Image of God:*

"Scripture's emphasis on the whole man as the image of God has triumphed time and time again over all objections and opposing principles. Scripture never makes a distinction between man's spiritual and bodily attributes in order to limit the image of God to the spiritual as furnishing the only possible analogy between man and God."

Since our image bearer role encompasses all that we are, including our bodies, we should do all that we can to glorify Him in them and through them. How we care for them and use them speaks volumes to others about what our attitudes and beliefs really are toward the One we represent.

3 The believer's body is owned by God and is the dwelling place of the Holy Spirit.

1 Corinthians 6:19, 20: Or do you not know that your body is a temple of the Holy Spirit within you, whom you have from God?-You are not your own, for you were bought with a price. So glorify God in your body.

John 14:15–17: "If you love me, you will keep my commandments. And I will ask the Father, and he will give you another Helper, to be with you forever, even the Spirit of truth, whom the world cannot receive, because it neither sees him nor knows him. You know him, for he dwells with you and will be in you."

Romans 8:9: You, however, are not in the flesh but in the Spirit, if in fact the Spirit of God dwells in you. Anyone who does not have the Spirit of Christ does not belong to him.

Worth and significance are given to the body by the fact of God's ownership of it and the Holy Spirit's residence in it. His ownership makes us stewards of our bodies, and the Holy Spirit's residence gives added motivation and significance to that stewardship responsibility. These bodies must be treated with the care and concern befitting the holy, glorious God since He owns them and after salvation His Holy Spirit resides in them. In order to be a good steward of them, we must be faithful, trustworthy, and dependable in caring for them. The extent to which we know both the Master and the assignment well, and strive to accomplish the assignment in accordance with that knowledge, is the extent to which we can honor and glorify Him in it.

Knowing God means more than having knowledge about God and His truths, although that is an essential part of it. J. I. Packer, in his excellent book *Knowing God*, states that knowing Him must involve making our knowledge about His attributes a matter of:

"meditation *before* God, leading to prayer and praise *to* God... Meditation is the activity of calling to mind, and thinking over, and dwelling on, and applying to oneself, the various things that one knows about the works and ways and purposes and promises of God." (Packer, pp. 18, 19)

As we know Him better, we can be more effective stewards of our bodies, because we will be able to know how He would care for them. It is our challenge to think God's thoughts after Him and to apply those thoughts to our stewardship duties. Knowing Him should cause us to approach the stewardship responsibility of our body with awe that so great and glorious a God would give us such a privilege. Such knowledge should energize us and humble us; it should guide our thoughts, our attitudes, and our actions in caring for our bodies.

The faithfulness of our stewardship efforts will not be determined by other men but by God. Thus, care of our bodies is a very personal responsibility each of us has before God on a moment by moment basis. The results of those efforts are in His hands; the faithfulness is in ours. Our success will be dependent upon our knowledge of Him, our knowledge of our bodies, and the degree of submission to the knowledge of each we achieve in our hearts and lives.

↳ Him + our bodies

4 The physical body is the mode of operation for accomplishing the work man has to do and is the means by which we communicate with and testify to the world, including other believers.

Genesis 1:26–27: Then God said, "Let us make man in our image, after our likeness. And let them have dominion over the fish of the sea and over the birds of the heavens and over the livestock and over all the earth and over every creeping thing that creeps on the earth." So God created man in his own image, in the image of God he created him; male and female he created them.

Ephesians 2:10: For we are his workmanship, created in Christ Jesus for good works, which God prepared beforehand, that we should walk in them.

Matthew 28:19–20: "Go therefore and make disciples of all nations, baptizing them in the name of the Father and of the Son and of the Holy Spirit, teaching them to observe all that I have commanded you. And behold, I am with you always, to the end of the age."

1 Timothy 4:12: Let no one despise you for your youth, but set the believers an example in speech, in conduct, in love, in faith, in purity.

1 Peter 2:11–12: Beloved, I urge you as sojourners and exiles to abstain from the passions of the flesh, which wage war against your soul. Keep your conduct among the Gentiles honorable, so that when they speak against you as evildoers, they may see your good deeds and glorify God on the day of visitation.

The presence of physical labor even before the fall is evidence of the necessity and significance of the body in God's plan for man. Man must have a body to do his work. The fact that at the new birth man is created for good works prepared beforehand for him to do (Ephesians 2:10) presumes and requires the body's existence. These facts also imply the need for us to be adequately prepared to perform the tasks for which we will be held accountable. Adequate preparation includes both capability and availability—we must do that which is within our responsibility to be prepared and available in our bodies, our minds, and our spirits.

God's will for each Christian's life is unique, by virtue of its unique sphere of influence and responsibility, of its special abilities and spiritual gifts, and of its distinctive work and good works for which it is accountable. Each person has been given the specific body necessary to accomplish that work for which he is responsible. Assurance is given in Scripture that the Christian will never be asked to do that which he will not be enabled to do (Philippians 4:13).

As with many aspects of the Christian's life, however, God has given us responsibility and expects us to do our part. Specifically, "our part" of being ready must include godly care of our bodies; that is, keeping them as God would keep them if He were to do it all. The details of a godly body care program are partly determined by the nature of the work that is to be done. A Christian who is a professional tennis player must have a body care program that differs from that of his brother in Christ who serves as a college president. Those details are also partly determined by the characteristics of the body itself. Joni Eareckson Tada, a quadriplegic with a tremendous ministry for the Lord to the disabled and their families, has a body care program that differs significantly from that of her able-bodied friends who assist in her ministry at Joni and Friends, Inc.

In these examples, each person has a unique responsibility before God in effecting a body care program that will honor Him. As we carry out that responsibility, each of us can be confident that we are doing our part to be prepared for whatever role God chooses. The assigning and enabling is God's responsibility; the availability and part of the capability is man's responsibility. It is clear, then, that God has affirmed the importance of the body and its care by the work He has given it to do.

The very name Christian declares that we are "Christ's ones," His representatives in the world. We are to strive to have a walk worthy and fully pleasing to the Lord and His message, the gospel (Philippians 1:27, Colossians 1:10). Our bodies are the medium as well as a part of the message we carry, for the testimony of changed lives speaks loudly to a watching world. Our appearance and our actions send messages to all who observe us, believers and unbelievers alike. We must be careful that the message we send is one befitting the One we represent.

As we carry the message of freedom in Christ from the power and penalty of sin, we must give evidence of that freedom in our lives, or the message cannot be heard (1 Corinthians 9:27). That is why sins such as gluttony, body-worship, adultery, fornication, homosexuality, drunkenness, and slothfulness—all manifest in the body—must not be evident in our lives if we want to share the good news as appropriate messengers (1 Peter 4:3; Galatians 5:19,21,24; 1 Corinthians 6:9–11; Matthew 25:26; Romans 16:18). It is important that, to the extent it is our responsibility, we not allow our bodies or what we do with them to be a hindrance to accomplishing the Lord's work.

Christ often met physical needs to open hearts and minds to His message. Throughout Scripture the Christian is given direction and instruction about how to live the successful Christian life, because it is in this life that he brings honor or dishonor to God. The impact of the physical body is significant. The body can be a stumbling block, or it can be an instrument of righteousness. A God-honoring body care program can assist efforts to the latter.

> **5** **The body, as part of creation, is a means through which God can teach man and accomplish His purposes, through which man can learn of God, and through which man can fulfill his purpose for being: to glorify God.**

Acts 14:15–17: "Men, why are you doing these things? We also are men, of like nature with you, and we bring you good news, that you should turn from these vain things to a living God, who made the heaven and the earth and the sea and all that is in them. In past generations he allowed all the nations to walk in their own ways. Yet he did not leave himself without witness, for he did good by giving you rains from heaven and fruitful seasons, satisfying your hearts with food and gladness."

Romans 1:20: For his invisible attributes, namely, his eternal power and divine nature, have been clearly perceived, ever since the creation of the world, in the things that have been made. So they are without excuse.

Psalm 139:13–16: For you formed my inward parts; you knitted me together in my mother's womb. I praise you, for I am fearfully and wonderfully made. Wonderful are your works; my soul knows it very well. My frame was not hidden from you, when I was being made in secret, intricately woven in the depths of the earth. Your eyes saw my unformed substance; in your book were written, every one of them, the days that were formed for me, when as yet there was none of them.

Romans 11:36, 12:1: For from him and through him and to him are all things. To him be glory forever. Amen. I appeal to you therefore, brothers, by the mercies of God, to present your bodies as a living sacrifice, holy and acceptable to God, which is your spiritual worship.

1 Corinthians 10:31: So, whether you eat or drink, or whatever you do, do all to the glory of God.

Isaiah 43:7: "...everyone who is called by my name, whom I created for my glory, whom I formed and made."

This statement might be misunderstood as suggesting that God talks with man today as He did in biblical times (Genesis 2:16, 3:8–19, 1 Samuel 3:4). This is **not** its intent. What God has determined to say to man has been said in His written Word and through the Living Word Jesus Christ, perfectly, completely, and without error. Part of the thought intended in this statement, however, is acknowledgment of the sovereignty and providence of God. We are reminded in Scripture that He works all things according to the counsel of His will (Ephesians 1:11). God accomplished His purpose in King Nebuchadnezzar's life by causing significant changes in his body:

"Immediately the word was fulfilled against Nebuchadnezzar. He was driven from among men and ate grass like an ox, and his body was wet with the dew of heaven till his hair grew as long as eagles' feathers, and his nails were like birds' claws. At the end of the days I, Nebuchadnezzar, lifted my eyes to heaven, and my reason returned to me, and I blessed the Most High, and praised and honored him who lives forever, for his dominion is an everlasting dominion, and his kingdom endures from generation to generation... (Daniel 4:33–34)

By overcoming his pride and arrogance through dramatic physical changes, God compelled the king to confess the sovereignty and supremacy of God in the affairs of heaven and earth. God providentially uses man's physical body to assist him in understanding and knowing God and God's will for his life.

The New Testament is replete with examples of Christ using the healing of physical afflictions and the meeting of physical needs to teach spiritual truths to recipients and observers alike. (See Matthew 9:27–31, 12:22, 15:30, 21:14; Mark 5:27–34, 6:5, 6:35–43, 6:56; 7:32–37 for some examples.) God may use physical ailments as an opportunity for reflection, as a punishment (see 1 Corinthians 11:30, 31) or as a means of encouraging humility (2 Corinthians 12:7) and an appropriate perspective on the grace of God, as indicated by Paul in regard to his own physical affliction:

Three times I pleaded with the Lord about this, that it should leave me. But he said to me, "My grace is sufficient for you, for my power is made perfect in weakness." Therefore I will boast all the more gladly of my weaknesses, so that the power of Christ may rest upon me. (2 Corinthians 12:8–9)

We also believe that knowledge of the body can give man more understanding and awareness of the Creator. The body's tremendous capacity to adapt, to compensate, and to respond all clearly speak of an all-wise and all-powerful Creator. Thus, even as man studies the creation, the Creator is more clearly revealed because His attributes are evident throughout His creation. The body, as part of that creation, is a significant part of the means by which God can teach us and through which we can know more of Him.

Man was caused by God, and man was caused for God (Colossians 1:16)—to commune with Him, to obey Him, to worship Him, and to glorify Him. Apart from God, man has no cause or purpose for being. Throughout Scripture, man is discussed in his relationship to God as "being a little lower than the angels," indeed a very exalted position. Man was given free will that he might choose to commune, to obey, to shun evil and turn to God, and in so doing to bring glory to Him unique from that of any other part of the creation. Man can worship God by offering himself—body-soul-spirit—to Him. Thus, in light of the gift that life itself is, in light of Who the Giver of that life is, and in light of the price that was paid for our spiritual lives, we ought to do all that we can to "glorify God in your body and in your spirit, which are God's" (1 Corinthians 6:20).

6 The body is an essential part of God's plan: His plan at creation, His plan for man's redemption, and His plan for eternity.

Genesis 2:4, 5, 15: These are the generations of the heavens and the earth when they were created, in the day that the LORD God made the earth and the heavens. When no bush of the field was yet in the land and no small plant of the field had yet sprung up—for the LORD God had not caused it to rain on the land, and there was no man to work the ground,… The LORD God took the man and put him in the garden of Eden to work it and keep it.

Psalm 8:4–6: What is man that you are mindful of him, and the son of man that you care for him? Yet you have made him a little lower than the heavenly beings and crowned him with glory and honor. You have given him dominion over the works of your hands; you have put all things under his feet…

Hebrews 10:10: And by that will we have been sanctified through the offering of the body of Jesus Christ once for all.

1 Peter 2:24: He himself bore our sins in his body on the tree, that we might die to sin and live to righteousness. By his wounds you have been healed.

Romans 3:23–25: For all have sinned and fall short of the glory of God, and are justified by his grace as a gift, through the redemption that is in Christ Jesus, whom God put forward as a propitiation by his blood, to be received by faith. This was to show God's righteousness, because in his divine forbearance he had passed over former sins.

Ephesians 1:7: In him we have redemption through his blood, the forgiveness of our trespasses, according to the riches of his grace…

Romans 8:22–23: For we know that the whole creation has been groaning together in the pains of childbirth until now. And not only the creation, but we ourselves, who have the first fruits of the Spirit, groan inwardly as we wait eagerly for adoption as sons, the redemption of our bodies.

See also 1 Corinthians 15:35-50 for a presentation on the unique aspects for our resurrection bodies.

1 Thessalonians 4:16–17: For the Lord himself will descend from heaven with a cry of command, with the voice of an archangel, and with the sound of the trumpet of God. And the dead in Christ will rise first. Then we who are alive, who are left, will be caught up together with them in the clouds to meet the Lord in the air, and so we will always be with the Lord.

Revelation 20:12, 15: And I saw the dead, great and small, standing before the throne, and books were opened. Then another book was opened, which is the book of life. And the dead were judged by what was written in the books, according to what they had done. … And if anyone's name was not found written in the book of life, he was thrown into the lake of fire.

It is evident in the creation account presented in Genesis that the plan of God was to have a material world prepared that would be a proper and fitting place for man, His crowning piece in the creation. Through the creation He revealed His power, His glory, His supremacy, and His goodness, among other things. All was perfect at the creation, but all of the creation suffered under the consequences of the fall. God, however, in His magnificent grace and mercy provided for the salvation of man and the restoration of heaven and earth (see 2 Peter 3:7, 10, 13 and Colossians 1:20). Since the sin of Adam (and Eve) was in his whole being, the provision of God was to have His Son, Jesus Christ, accept a human body (the incarnation) through which to accomplish His redemptive work for man, including the redemption of his physical body.

Thus, it is by the grace and mercy of God that we can have redemption, through the work of Christ in His body. Through His incarnation, Christ revealed God to men (John 1:18), and provided for all of mankind a clear example for living (1 Peter 2:21). By carrying out the will of God through His death, burial, and resurrection, He provided the appropriate and necessary sacrifice for the sin of all mankind (Hebrews 10:1–14). By this work done in His body, all who accept Christ as their personal Lord and Savior will have their sin removed and His righteousness substituted in its place before God; redemption from the eternal consequence of sin; reconciliation of the relationship with God; propitiation or satisfaction of the righteous wrath of God; as well as judgment of the sin nature, making holy living possible for the believer through the reigning power of the indwelling Holy Spirit.

> "Thus the Incarnation has ramifications in relation to our knowledge of God, to our salvation, to our daily living, to our pressing needs, and to the future. It truly is the central fact of history." (Basic Theology, Ryrie, p. 245)

The importance of the body of Christ in the plan of God cannot be overstated.

In addition, Scripture presents that even our physical bodies have been redeemed by Christ's work so that we will have "spiritual bodies" in which to spend eternity. The passage in 1 Corinthians, Chapter 15 referred to above describes some of the attributes of those bodies, and Christ's own resurrection body gives us a glimpse of what those bodies will be like. It is helpful to note that those bodies, unlike these, are spiritual (yet are visible), are incorruptible, and are eternal. They will be similar to these bodies (v. 36), but different (vv. 39–41). While it is difficult to understand the meaning of all of this, it is important to acknowledge that all of us will have bodies throughout eternity... an impressive indication of the importance of bodies in the plan of God.

Sources of Error and Confusion

In light of the truths from Scripture presented, why is there such confusion and "negative press" about the body among Christians? Certainly the ultimate source of all that opposes God's truth (and all truth) is Satan, the father of lies (John 8:44) and the arch-deceiver (Revelation 20:10). He prefers us to think either that the body is nothing or that it is everything. Either lie will serve his purpose of opposing God. To the extent that he can deceive men, he can interfere with their ability to glorify God. The confusion that he has helped to develop can be unravelled and rendered ineffective in the light of the scriptural truths in the preceding part of this chapter. The following study of some of the apparent sources of confusion can also assist in improving understanding.

Influence of Greek Philosophy

Viewing man as either a body with a soul or a soul with a body instead of a unity of body/soul/spirit is generally attributed to the influence of Greek philosophy. "The human soul is considered by Plato to be an immaterial agent, superior in nature to the body and somewhat hindered by the body in the performance of the higher, psychic functions of human life" (Runes, p. 237). Plato taught that through sense perceptions man could only attain knowledge of the changeable world of bodies (material things). Through the soul, however, he could discover another world, that of immutable (unchanging) essences referred to by Plato as Forms or Ideas. Knowledge of these Ideas was viewed as the only true knowledge, and it could only be attained in Mathematics and especially in Philosophy.

Plato taught that it was important for the soul to seek to rise above dependence on sense perception (characteristic of the young or immature) and strive toward a direct intuition of intelligible essences (characteristic of the mature and intellectually elite). He declared that the soul existed before the body and was born with true knowledge in it, but that due to its burden of bodily cares and interests, it could not easily recall those innate truths (Runes, pp. 237, 238). It is easy to understand how such teachings led to a body-soul dualism, and to the evaluation of the soul as good and the body as bad.

This Platonic view of man has had broad influence both within and without the church. "Platonism was very highly regarded by the Christian Fathers (Ambrose, Augustine, John Damascene and Anselm of Canterbury for instance) and it continued as the approved philosophy of the Christian Church until the 12th century" (Runes, p. 239). This "body = bad, soul = good" thinking was manifested in such unbiblical, extreme, dualistic philosophies and practices as asceticism and gnosticism. The influence of these heresies on the early church is evident throughout the New Testament in such things as the Colossian heresy; problems in the Corinthian church with knowledge, wisdom and sexual practices; and in the concerns addressed in 1 and 2 Timothy and 1 and 2 John.

The dualism Christ taught was that of those who are children of the kingdom and those who are children of the wicked one (Matthew 13:38). However, "The dualism (of Plato and Aristotle) has the consequence for the doctrine of man of identifying the body with evil and of assuming the essential goodness of mind or spirit …The Bible knows nothing of a good mind and an evil body" (Niebuhr, p. 7). The message of Scripture, while sometimes tainted in its interpretation by these pervasive philosophies, nowhere presents the body = bad, soul = good concept. Although the human body is acknowledged as frail and limited, it is never presented as the source of or cause of evil. If it were, Christ could not have been without sin. And He was. "For we do not have a High Priest who cannot sympathize with our weaknesses, but was in all *points* tempted as *we are, yet* without sin." (Hebrews 4:15)

Paul reminded the believers at Colosse that Christ had freed them from the do's and don'ts of asceticism which give only the appearance of wisdom and spirituality but are of no real value in countering the self-centeredness of the old nature (Colossians 2:20–23). He reminded Timothy (1 Timothy 4:1–5) that Christians should live affirmatively, *for* the Lord, rather than turn their backs on the good of creation that God had provided for them. Both exhortations were given in response to ascetic influences in the early church. Both should assist us in developing an appropriate attitude toward the body.

The Use of the Terms "Body" and "Flesh" in Scripture

In order to achieve understanding about the confusion that exists regarding the use of the terms "body" and "flesh" in Scripture, it is necessary to review the meanings of the terms in the English, the Hebrew, and the Greek. The primary definitions for both words in the English dictionary emphasize *the physical exclusively*.

> BODY: "The total organized physical substance of an animal or plant; the physical organism." (Gove, p. 246)

> FLESH: "The soft parts of the body of man or a lower animal; the body parts composed chiefly of skeletal muscle with accompanying fat and connective tissues as distinguished from visceral structures and bone. (Gove, p. 869)

By comparison, the words most often translated "body" in Scripture (O.T.: *basar*; *beten*; *geviyyah*; N.T.: *soma*) all primarily convey the idea of **the whole person, the totality of man** when they are used in reference to man. The Greek term *sarx* which is translated "flesh" conveys similar meanings as the Hebrew *basar*, which is also sometimes translated "flesh". (Wood, pp. 143/4, 370/1) Thus there is already a conflict between what is commonly understood from the English words and what is commonly conveyed by the Hebrew and Greek terms. The English terms primarily convey exclusively the physical, while the Hebrew and Greek commonly convey the whole being.

In addition to this source of confusion, each word has a full range of meanings in each of the languages. "Body" can mean the trunk or torso of a man or animal, the stem of a plant, the main or central part of anything, a dead person, a group of people, or a person. The term "flesh" is variously used to mean meat, the human body, mankind, and all living beings (Gove, pp. 246, 869). The context of each term must be carefully used to discern the meaning accurately.

The Hebrew words translated "body" in the Old Testament, while primarily conveying the whole of man, have contextual meanings ranging from animal musculature to the human womb, the human body, a corpse, living things, and life itself (Richards, p. 135). The New Testament usage of *soma* encompasses such meanings as the physical body (Matthew, 10:28), the total person (Romans 12:1), unregenerate man (Romans 6:6), and the Church (Romans 12:5).

The principal word for "flesh" in the Old Testament is variously used to mean the whole body (Proverbs 14:30), the whole man (Psalm 16:9), mankind in general (Numbers 16:22), and the physical frailty of man (Psalm 16:4) (Wood, p. 370). The New Testament use of *sarx* carries all of the meanings of the Old Testament *basar*, with a few very distinctive meanings occurring in the Pauline epistles. These uses have been the source of much misunderstanding.

In Colossians 2:1 Paul refers to being "in the flesh" and is referring to the whole of his existence (physical and spiritual). This same "in the flesh" phrase is used to refer to the physical body of man (2 Corinthians 10:3), and on several occasions in reference to Christ the God-man in His incarnate form (1 Peter 3:18, 4:1; 2 John 7). While obviously using "flesh" to mean physical body, there is certainly no negative connotation with its use in this way.

In several other passages in the New Testament, however, Paul uses the term "flesh" to convey the idea of being controlled or directed by the natural, sinful, unregenerate nature of man (as contrasted with being controlled and directed by the indwelling Holy Spirit as a result of the new birth). An example of this meaning being conveyed by the "in the flesh" phrase can be seen in Romans 8:8, "So then, those who are in the flesh cannot please God." In other passages such phrases as "after the flesh" (Romans 8:4; 2 Peter 2:10) and "according to the flesh" (2 Corinthians 10:3) are used to convey the same idea of being controlled by the old nature, as are phrases like the "lust of the flesh" (Galatians 5:16), "works of the flesh" (Galatians 5:19–21), and "desires of the flesh" (Ephesians 2:3).

This review of the range of meanings for the different terms demonstrates the necessity of careful, Spirit-led study of context and intended word meanings when reading about the body in Scripture. It is important to note that nowhere in Scripture does God communicate that **only** the physical part of man is sinful, or that **especially** the physical aspect is so. The contrast repeatedly drawn is not between body and spirit, flesh and soul, material and non-material, but between the centers of control—man's old nature or God's Holy Spirit.

Foundational Principles for Physical Fitness and the Christian

We have reviewed several truths from Scripture that support the premise that a godly perspective assigns worth and significance to the body. We have also reviewed some of the sources of error regarding the role and importance of the body. In light of these truths it seems appropriate for the following principles to permeate and shape our efforts in physical fitness.

1. Care of the body is an important and essential task shared by man with God. It is part of man's God-given stewardship responsibility, and as such must be done with wisdom and diligence. God is our Master and our standard. The responsibility should fill us with awe, an awe that both motivates and humbles us in our efforts.

2. A godly body care program must be that which God would do if He assumed full responsibility. Thus, it must be grounded in our knowledge of Him and His values. As such, it must be characterized by discipline, moderation, and wisdom, and accomplished by His grace.

3. The degree to which we are faithful and wise in discerning and conducting a godly body care program is the degree to which we will be physically prepared to do the work He has for us to do. Lack of wisdom and faithfulness may have a bearing on the quality or quantity of time we have on earth, and thus on the quality and quantity of works we can do for Him. Several of the Proverbs describe health and long life as benefits of wisdom and fear of the Lord (Proverbs 3, 4, 9, 10).

   My son, do not forget my teaching, but let your heart keep my commandments, for length of days and years of life and peace they will add to you.... Be not wise in your own eyes; fear the

LORD, and turn away from evil.It will be healing to your flesh and refreshment to your bones.

(Proverbs 3:1–2, 7–8 ESV).

4. However, having a physically fit body will NOT cause God to love us more. Nothing we can do in our bodies will cause God to love us more or less. He loves us with a perfect love, a love that is not earned or lost, a love that does not grow or diminish, because He is Love (1 John 4:8). Thus, His love does not depend on us or what we do, but on Him and Who he is. We must not place our value system on God by thinking that the more physically fit we are, the more He will love us. That is man's way, and God's ways are not man's ways.

For my thoughts are not your thoughts, neither are your ways my ways, declares the LORD. For as the heavens are higher than the earth, so are my ways higher than your ways and my thoughts than your thoughts.

(Isaiah 55:8–9 ESV)

Efforts to achieve or maintain physical fitness must not be works to earn His love or favor. Rather, they should be efforts to demonstrate our love and appreciation for Him for Who He is and for all He has done for us.

5. Godliness is not conferred by or synonymous with physical fitness. A physically fit body is not automatically more pleasing to God. A physically fit body is not automatically more useful to God than an unfit one. As the Lord reminded Samuel when he was reviewing the sons of Jesse to select Saul's replacement, "Do not look on his appearance or on the height of his stature, because I have rejected him (Eliab). For the LORD sees not as man sees; man looks on the outward appearance, but the LORD looks on the heart" (1 Samuel 16:7).

Some achieve high levels of fitness because they worship their bodies; others do so primarily to achieve the acclaim of man, and the rewards of this world. The condition of the heart that promotes these purposes is not pleasing or honoring to God. We please Him when we love Him with a godly love. We love Him when we through faith obey Him by keeping His commands and walking in the light of His Word. By this we can glorify Him. Thus, it is God's work to choose whom He will use and how; it is our work to be prepared and available, fit for His use.

Summary

It has been our desire in this chapter to provide opportunity for you to begin looking at your bodies as God looks at them. We have endeavored to lead, develop, challenge, and reinforce your thinking in this area through portions of God's word as well as through discussions based on it.

A godly perspective of the mortal body must acknowledge both its significance and its insignificance. We are reminded in 1 Timothy 4:8 that the benefits of bodily training are limited and transient—limited in what they can accomplish, and temporary in their effect. Our lives are compared to a vapor (James 4:14) and our days are compared to grass (Psalm 103:15). Yet the Psalms also declare: "When I look at Your heavens, the work of Your fingers, the moon and the stars, which You have set in place, what is man that You are mindful of him, and the son of man that You care for him? Yet You have made him a little lower than the heavenly beings, and crowned him with glory and honor" (Psalm 8:3–5). We are image bearers of the God of the Bible. We have been fearfully and wonderfully made, and have been given the privilege of stewardship responsibility for the creation. As we are able to perceive and comprehend these truths through the enabling of the Holy Spirit, we are truly able to glorify God in our bodies.

The remainder of this text is intended to provide the information and knowledge, gleaned from general revelation and presented in the light of special revelation, necessary to develop a godly body care or physical fitness program. The information in this text must be studied and applied in conjunction with your knowledge of your own body and your growing knowledge of God. It should be used to the end that you may be found a faithful steward, of whom it can be said, "Well done." We encourage you to continue developing your thinking in this area as you proceed through the text, and truly, throughout the rest of your life.

Bibliography and Resources for Further Study

Bancroft, Emery H. *Elemental Theology*, 4th Edition. Grand Rapids, MI: Zondervan Publishing House, 1977.

Begg, Alistair. *What Angels Wish They Knew: The Basics of True Christianity*. Chicago, IL: Moody Press, 1998.

Berkouwer, G. C. *General Revelation*. Grand Rapids, MI: Wm. B. Eerdmans Publishing Company, 1955.

Berkouwer, G. C. *The Image of God*. Grand Rapids, MI: Wm. B. Eerdmans Publishing Company, 1962.

Brand, Paul and P. Yancey. *Fearfully and Wonderfully Made*. Grand Rapids, MI: Zondervan Publishing House, 1980.

Brand, Paul and P. Yancey. *In His Image*. Grand Rapids, MI: Zondervan Publishing House, 1984.

Davis, Caroline. "Body Image, Exercise, and Eating Behaviors" Chapter 6 in Fox, Kenneth R. (Editor). *The Physical Self: From Motivation to Well-Being*. Champaign, IL: Human Kinetics, 1997.

Fox, Kenneth R.(Editor). *The Physical Self: From Motivation to Well-Being*. Champaign, IL: Human Kinetics, 1997.

Gove, Philip (Editor in Chief). *Webster's Third New International Dictionary of the English Language Unabridged*. Springfield, MA: Merriam-Webster Inc., Publisher, 1993.

Hall, Douglas John. *The Steward: A Biblical Symbol Come of Age*. Grand Rapids, MI: Wm. B. Eerdmans Publishing Company, 1990.

Hastings, James. *Dictionary of the New Testament of Christ and the Gospels*. Vol. 1. Grand Rapids: Baker Book House, 1973.

Heller, Alfred. *Your Body, His Temple*. Nashville, TN: Thomas Nelson Publishers, 1981.

Henry, Matthew. *Commentary on the Whole Bible*. Edited by Leslie F. Church. Grand Rapids, MI: Zondervan Publishing House, 1961.

Hiebert, Dennis. "Glorifying God in the Body," *Dialog* (Minnesota), Vol. 24 (Spring 1985), pp. 133–135.

Jamieson, Robert, A. Fausset, and D. Brown. *Commentary Critical and Explanatory on the Whole Bible*. Grand Rapids, MI: Zondervan Publishing House, 1984.

McGrath, Alister E. *Christian Theology: An Introduction*, 2nd Edition. Malden, MA: Blackwell Publishers Inc., 1997.

Niebuhr, Reinhold. *The Nature and Destiny of Man*. Vol 1. New York, NY: Charles Scribner's Sons, 1964.

Packer, J. I. *Knowing Christianity*. Downers Grove, IL: InterVarsity Press, 1995.

Packer, J. I. *Knowing God*. Downers Grove, IL: InterVarsity Press, 1973.

Richards, Lawrence O. (Editor). *Expository Dictionary of Bible Words*. Grand Rapids, MI: Zondervan Corporation, 1985.

Runes, Dagobert D. *Dictionary of Philosophy*. Ames, IA: Littlefield, Adams, and Co., 1958.

Rodin, R. Scott. *Stewards in the Kingdom: A Theology of Life in All Its Fullness*. Downers Grove, IL: InterVarsity Press, 2000.

Ryrie, Charles C. *Basic Theology*. Chicago, IL: Moody Press, 1986.

Ryrie, Charles C. *The Ryrie Study Bible, New King James Version*. Chicago, IL: Moody Press, 1985.

Ryrie, Charles C. *The Ryrie Study Bible Expanded Edition, King James Version*. Chicago, IL: Moody Press, 1994.

Ryrie, Charles C. *A Survey of Bible Doctrine*. Chicago, IL: Moody Press, 1972.

Sherlock, Charles. *The Doctrine of Humanity: Contours of Christian Theology*. Downers Grove, IL: InterVarsity Press, 1996.

Swenson, Richard A. *More than Meets the Eye: Fascinating Glimpses of God's Power & Design*. Colorado Springs, CO: NavPress, 2000.

Swindoll, Charles R. *The Bible: Applying God's Word to Your Life*. Nashville, TN: Broadman Press, 1986.

Swindoll, Charles R. *Growing Deep in the Christian Life*. Portland, OR: Multnomah Press, 1986.

Taylor, Alfred E. *Platonism and Its Influence*. New York, NY: Cooper Square Pub., Inc., 1963.

Thiessen, Henry Clarence. *Introductory Lectures in Systematic Theology*. Grand Rapids, MI: Wm. B. Eerdmans Publishing Company, 1949.

Vine, W. E. (Edited by Merrill F. Unger, William White, Jr.). *Vine's Complete Expository Dictionary of Old and New Testament Words with Topical Index*. Nashville, TN: Thomas Nelson, 1996.

Wood, D. R. W. (Revision Editor). *New Bible Dictionary*, 3rd Edition. Downers Grove, IL: InterVarsity Press, 1996.

Zion, Leela C. "Body Concept as It Relates to Self Concept." *The Research Quarterly*, Vol. 36 (December 1965): 490–495.

Chapter 3

Principles of Physical Conditioning for Good Stewardship

Essential Terms

Conditioning Curve	*Lifespan*
Discernment	*Moderation*
Discipline	*Physical Fitness*
Duration (Training)	*Progressive Overload*
Frequency (Training)	*Reversibility*
Homeostasis	*Specificity*
Intensity (Training)	*Stewardship*
Life Expectancy	*Training Threshold*

Objectives

Upon completion of this chapter, students should be able to:

1. Define, explain, and effectively use the terms listed above.
2. Know and understand the principles of training as articulated in this chapter.
3. Recognize examples of each principle as used in an appropriate and Godly body care program.
4. Know what has occurred with regard to lifespan and life expectancy since the Exodus.
5. Explain the concept of homeostasis with regard to physical conditioning.
6. Explain why the Believer should place a priority on being a good steward of his/her body.

Our Responsibility for Our Bodies

Because God is the great I AM and the body's Creator-Designer, only He has perfect knowledge and understanding of it. So, only He is capable of providing a perfect program for its care. But, He didn't choose to do that. Instead, He entrusted that responsibility to us. He has, by common grace, allowed mankind to gain a great deal of knowledge and understanding of the body and how it functions.

Using that, together with other principles of science, man has been able to increase his LIFE EXPECTANCY (the average number of years that those born in a specific year, in a given country, can expect to live) markedly. In 1900, someone born in the United States had a life expectancy of 49 years. By the year 2000, that number had increased to 72.5 years for males and 79 years for females (Healthy People, 2010).

LIFESPAN, on the other hand, (the average maximum length of life) has remained essentially unchanged since the Exodus. The human organism without congenital defect, and given good nutrition, environment and a healthful lifestyle has the God-implanted vigor to live about 120 years, the age Moses attained. The life expectancy increase we've seen is due to man's ability to use the knowledge and tools God's grace has provided to enable more people to reach greater ages, particularly in the late twentieth century. Improved living conditions, better nutrition, immunization against many childhood infections and improved diagnostic/treatment procedures (of which anti-infective drugs have likely had the greatest impact on the most people) have greatly decreased infant mortality, and enabled successful treatment of many life-threatening conditions at all ages.

Epidemiological studies show that now our major health threats are related to lifestyle. That is, we aren't as healthy as we could be because of choices we make. How we eat, sleep, exercise, deal with stress, etc. has greater influence on how well we function than do infectious agents or health care services/policies. More than at any time in Post-Fall human history, we control the level of well-being we enjoy. We need to be obedient stewards of the bodies God has given us.

Godly Body Stewardship

Obedient, Godly stewardship of the body… What does that mean? As explained in Chapters 1 and 2, we believe that we've been made stewards of God's creation, including the body. As Believer-Stewards, we have a very special relationship with the Owner/Master; with the privilege of that relationship comes great responsibility and accountability. What's required of a steward? "Moreover it is required in stewards that one be found faithful" (1 Cor. 4:2). This wonderfully complex God-created organism, the body in which we will live our lives and through which we will accomplish whatever ministries He gives us, has been placed in our care.

As good stewards, it is our on-going responsibility to be faithful in keeping our bodies in the best possible functioning condition so that their limitations are not due to neglect or carelessness on our part. Although we shouldn't take undue pride in our physical accomplishments (1 Cor. 4:7—"For who makes you differ from one another? And what do you have that you did not receive? Now if you did indeed receive it, why do you glory as if you had not received it?"), neither should we be lazy or careless in how we take care of ourselves.

Our care of our bodies needs to be characterized by DISCIPLINE, MODERATION, and DISCERNMENT. DISCIPLINE is self-control; in this context, it means using rational, sensible control in what and how much we eat, how we use our time, planning exercise into our schedules, being sure to get adequate sleep, avoiding use of alcohol, nicotine or other substances, etc. The discipline we exercise should be directed and led by the Holy Spirit. "Discipline without direction is drudgery" (Whitney); we don't discipline ourselves in these matters just to prove we can be hard on ourselves, or for reasons of pride, but we do it so we may honor God in our bodies.

MODERATION is the avoidance of extremes in all aspects of our lives. Extremes with regard to diet, exercise, or any aspect of self-care oppose and destroy the dynamic balance that characterizes all of creation. By avoiding extremes, one is less likely to get caught up in "fads" like bizarre diets, food supplement regimens or extreme workouts. If we practice moderation, we won't over-emphasize care of our physical bodies at the cost of neglecting our spiritual and academic responsibilities.

DISCERNMENT is wise, knowledge-based judgement. We need to use discernment as we make lifestyle choices. We won't always be able to choose an optimal diet, or have the amount of time we'd like for physical exercise, but we can choose the *best* of the options available.

If these qualities of discipline, moderation and discernment characterize our care of our bodies, we will be effective, faithful stewards of them. **That** is what is required of us.

How Are You Doing As A "Faithful Steward"?

Ask yourself a few questions about how you currently take care of the body God has given you. We suggest these for a start; you can add others.

1. Do you eat breakfast most days?
2. Do you eat vegetables other than corn and potatoes on a regular basis? → starch
3. Do you eat raw fruits several times a week?
4. Do you average at least a half-hour of vigorous physical exercise on most days?
5. When you shop for food, do you read labels?
6. Do you have a daily routine that you follow most days?
7. How well do you cope with life's everyday ups and downs? freaking w/traffic
8. Do you know how to evaluate nutritional supplements?
9. Do you know what's meant by "alternative medicine?"
10. Do you get 7–8 hours sleep most nights?

Principles of Conditioning: The Concept

As a living organism, the body has the capacity to respond and adjust to change. To maintain life, a state of dynamic balance or HOMEOSTASIS must be maintained. When something upsets that balance (a stimulus or a stressor), the body has a variety of mechanisms it can use to re-establish homeostasis. If it does so successfully, all is well. If it cannot re-establish the dynamic balance, the organism will ultimately die. While this is an oversimplified explanation of homeostasis as it occurs in the human body, it is adequate to provide the foundation needed to understand what happens during exercise as the body makes immediate, temporary adjustments to meet demands. Slower, longer lasting adjustments occur when the exercise is repeated in a systematic fashion. These more persistent adaptations are referred to as training or conditioning effects.

There are four principles that should guide our efforts to condition the body; these are based on the body's ability to respond and adapt to exercise stimuli. These principles are: **progressive overload**, **specificity**, **reversibility**, and the **conditioning curve**. These principles have been developed based on understanding gained through study of the body's response to exercise. We recognize that there is still much to be learned about the body's adaptive responses. We believe that understanding these principles, and applying them to one's life with discipline, moderation, and discernment should help one to exercise appropriate body stewardship.

Principle of Progressive Overload

To improve the functional condition of the body, the body must be "pushed"; that is, it must be caused to work harder than it normally does. This needs to be done in an orderly, systematic way, within identifiable ranges of "harder". This is the principle of progressive overload, and is based on the ability of the body to respond and adapt to change.

When we exercise, the body responds by making the changes needed to keep all the cells working as they are designed to work. The heart beats faster and more forcefully so that more blood circulates to the working cells. The vessels in the working areas of the body dilate to allow more blood to flow into areas of need. More blood flow means more oxygen to the cells, allowing the cells to function properly. Since cells are functioning at a higher level of intensity, more oxygen is required; a dynamic balance is achieved because oxygen is being delivered faster.

When we exercise on a regular basis, the body makes more lasting adaptations to facilitate oxygen delivery and optimize cell function. When we condition our bodies, we repeatedly create a situation that requires a new state of homeostasis. Our bodies have the capacity to make lasting adjustments so that homeostasis is more easily achieved when exercise demands are made. These changes not only improve our ability to meet demands imposed by work, environment or other stressors, but they also make the body more efficient at maintaining resting homeostasis. In this improved state of function, the body has a greater reserve capability to meet everyday demands or the cumulative effects of small exertional challenges, or even major exertional challenges.

A certain level of work intensity, or challenge, is needed to stimulate the body to initiate the kinds of changes at the tissue level which will result in improved function. That degree of intensity or level of work is known as the THRESHOLD STIMULUS. As training continues and tissue adaptation occurs, the threshold is raised, and new work intensities are applied. That is PROGRESSIVE OVERLOAD; that is, gradually increasing the work the body is asked to do.

The INTENSITY, then of an exercise effort is simply the challenge the body is asked to meet; in strength training, it is the resistance to be overcome; in cardiorespiratory training, it is increasing speed or going up an incline rather than remaining on the level. The DURATION is the length of time an exercise is done, or the number of repetitions done; FREQUENCY refers to the number of times/day or times/week that workouts are done. Any or all of these variables may be manipulated to achieve progressive overload.

Principle of Specificity

The changes that occur in the body as a result of systematic conditioning are specific in a multitude of ways. Responses are specific to the body part being exercised, and to the energy production system being utilized, as well as the positions and movements being employed. When one does bench presses with the arms, the triceps, deltoids and pectoral muscles get stronger. Biceps and brachioradialis muscles in the arms or quadriceps in the legs do not. If one does flexibility exercises for the left shoulder, it becomes more flexible, but the muscles surrounding the joint don't become stronger, nor does the right shoulder become more flexible. Strength exercises improve strength only. Flexibility exercises do not improve cardiorespiratory endurance; they improve flexibility. Doing exercises or activities that do not require additional transport of oxygen to tissues will not improve one's ability to transport oxygen. Conditioning is specific!

While this principle seems quite obvious, it is regularly violated in practice. Some "aerobic" exercise programs are a compilation of flexibility and strength exercises, and actually have minimal beneficial effect on the cardiovascular system. Conditioning is very specific. You must know what muscle group or body system an exercise or activity actually utilizes to know what benefits you can expect. This kind of knowledge and understanding protects you from the quackery that is rampant in the health and fitness industry. It will also help you with faithful and successful stewardship.

Principle of Reversibility

Just as the body makes adjustments that we call "conditioning" it becomes "deconditioned" if regular exercise is discontinued. Training effects are REVERSIBLE. When exercise is stopped for even short periods of time, training effects are gradually lost. The degree of loss varies, but on average, 10 weeks without exercise will cause training gains to be lost completely.

This principle provides a firm foundation for the importance of developing and maintaining a healthful and active lifestyle **after** college. All of the conditioning experienced by even the best of college athletes will not provide health benefits later in life if an appropriate level of physical activity is not maintained.

What can one do in the case of illness or injury? If at all possible, the best answer may be an alternate form of exercise. For example, pedaling a stationary bike rather than jogging, or swimming rather than jogging, biking or walking. The important thing is to maintain activity at some level, as health allows. In this way, a portion of conditioning gains can be maintained.

Principle of the Conditioning Curve

The human body is very responsive to demands made upon it; that is why we can condition it. However, the **degree** of response to a given stimulus also changes. When a sedentary person begins an exercise program, the TRAINING THRESHOLD, or minimum work intensity needed to bring about improvement, is very low. Improvement, i.e. "training effect," occurs rapidly. However, as one continues to exercise and to accrue training benefits, the training threshold is raised, and improvement comes in smaller increments.

The person who is already well-conditioned encounters "diminished returns" with regard to the improvement achieved relative to the effort expended. It is true that, the more fit one is, the harder one must work to raise that functional level. It is this "exaggerated return versus diminished return" observed that we identify as the CONDITIONING CURVE.

Why should we be mindful of this principle? We think it helpful to know that, in almost any situation, our bodies are capable of making adaptation. It is encouraging for the sedentary, perhaps overweight individual just starting an exercise program to know that he/she will see obvious changes, and that the effort expended needs only to be moderate.

Is this principle discouraging to the already well-conditioned person? We don't think it should be. We think it can be helpful for the more fit person to understand that more effort is needed to move to a higher level of function than to maintain the present level. This allows one to make an informed choice about the role of physical conditioning in one's life, in light of other responsibilities and priorities.

Bibliography and Resources for Further Study

Fox, Edward L., Richard Bowers, and Merle Foss. *The Physiological Basis of Physical Education and Athletics.* 4th Ed. Saunders, 1988.

McArdle, William, Frank Katch, and Victor Katch. *Exercise Physiology: Nutrition, Energy, and Human Performance.* Lippincott: Williams & Wilkens, 2009.

U.S. Department of Health and Human Services; U.S. Department of Agriculture, *Dietary Guidelines for Americans: Healthy People* 2020, U.S. Government, 2010.

Swindoll, Charles R. *The Bible: Applying God's Word in Your Life.* Broadman Press, 1988.

Terry, Patricia H. *Made for Paradise=God's Original Plan for Healthy Eating, Physical Activity, and Rest.* New Hope Publishing, 2007.

Wilmore, Jack, David Costill, and W. Larry Kenney. *Physiology of Sport and Exercise.* 4th ed. Human Kinetics, 2008.

Chapter 4

The Cardiorespiratory System: Structure and Function

Essential Terms

Aerobic	Heart Rate
Alveoli	Hemoglobin
Anaerobic	Mitral Valve
Aorta	Pulmonary Artery
Aortic Valve	Pulmonary Veins
Arteries	Pulmonic Valve
Arterioles	Respiration
Atrium	Stroke Volume
Bicuspid Valve	Systole
Blood Pressure	Trachea
Bronchi	Tricuspid Valve
Capillaries	Vascular
Coronary Arteries	Veins
Cardiac Output	Ventricle
Diastole	Venules
Erythrocytes	

Objectives

Upon completion of this chapter, students should be able to:

1. Define, explain, and effectively use the terms listed above.

2. Accurately describe the structure of the heart.

3. Accurately trace the flow of blood from its return to the right atrium to its ejection into systemic circulation.

4. Identify the forces responsible for systolic and diastolic blood pressures, respectively.

5. Accurately describe and discuss the interactive roles of the vessels, blood and the respiratory structures in delivery of oxygen to tissues.

6. Correctly identify structural and functional differences among capillaries, veins and arteries.

7. Explain the role of the coronary arteries.

8. Define "cardiac output" and describe how its distribution varies from rest to strenuous exercise.

9. Describe the adaptations of the cardiovascular and respiratory systems to exercise.

10. Describe and discuss the meaning of one's responsibilities for Godly stewardship of the cardiorespiratory system.

Purpose of the Cardiorespiratory System

The majesty and wisdom of the body's Master Designer is vividly revealed in the intricate and exquisite function of the cardiorespiratory system. The heart, lungs, airways, blood and blood vessels all work together masterfully to accommodate the changing oxygen needs of the billions of cells in the body. Whether one is sleeping restfully or engaging in a vigorous tennis match, the optimally functioning cardiorespiratory system can adjust and meet the tissues' oxygen needs.

The cardiorespiratory system, like all the body's systems, was made to support physical work, and to be kept in good functional condition by physical work. Our stewardship responsibilities include insuring that the cardiorespiratory system is adequately "worked" on a regular basis throughout life. For most of us, that means that we have to deliberately plan for exercise, because our normal life activities are inadequate to keep the system in optimal functioning condition. Obviously, the intensity of the "work" is guided/determined by factors like health, age, and the purpose or goals of conditioning.

In this chapter we will review the structure and function of the various components of the cardiorespiratory system, and the adaptations that occur in response to activity.

Structure of the Cardiorespiratory System

Humans are AEROBIC beings; that is, we depend on oxygen to live. While most of our cells can function for brief periods of time without oxygen (ANAEROBICALLY), ultimately each must have a regular supply of oxygen or die. The cardiorespiratory system consists of those structures which provide that regular oxygen supply. Although this is a phenomenal task, the healthy system is perfectly designed to accomplish it.

The Heart

The heart is a muscular four-chambered pump about the size of an adult fist that is located in the center of the chest, immediately behind the sternum (breastbone). It weighs less than a pound and is composed of a very specialized muscle, the myocardium. The myocardium is a type of striated muscle tissue found nowhere else in the body. It is similar to skeletal muscle, but the fibers are arranged differently. Instead of parallel bundles, as in skeletal muscle, the fibers are arranged in

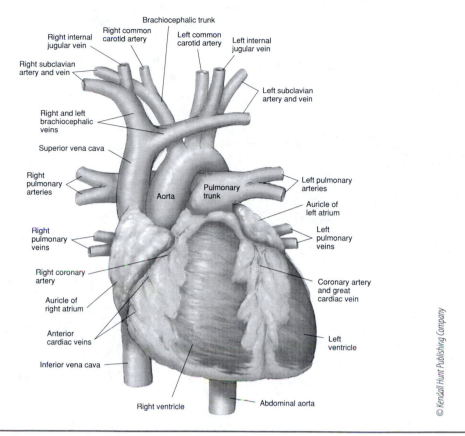

Figure 4.1 | Anterior view of the heart

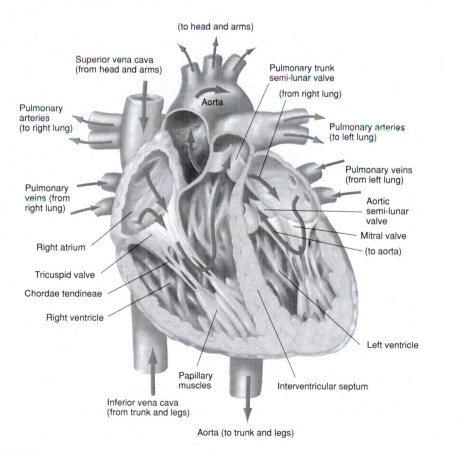

Figure 4.2 | Anterior view of the heart (internal)

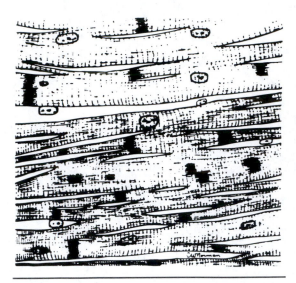

Figure 4.3 | Cardiac muscle.

a lattice-like pattern; when one cell is stimulated to contract, the impulse spreads throughout the interconnected fibers of the myocardium. As a result, the heart muscle contracts with a rhythmic "squeezing" action.

The four-chambered pump is actually two pumps situated side by side and working together. Each side has an upper chamber called an ATRIUM (plural: atria) and a lower chamber called a VENTRICLE. The atria are collecting or receiving chambers, and have minimal pumping responsibility; their muscular walls are fairy thin. The ventricles, though, are primarily pumping chambers; they receive the blood from the atria and then, by contracting, send it out to their respective areas.

The RIGHT VENTRICLE pumps the blood received from the right atrium to the lungs. The right side of the heart is responsible for sending the blood to the lungs; this is called "pulmonary circulation." The LEFT VENTRICLE pumps the blood it receives from the left atrium to the entire body through a very large vessel called the AORTA. This blood is freshly oxygenated, having just returned from the lungs; the process of pumping it out to the body's organs is "systemic circulation." More force is needed to power systemic circulation, so the myocardium of the left ventricle is usually fairly thick.

The atria and ventricles are separated by one-way valves so that blood can circulate in only one direction through the heart. The valve between the right atrium and right ventricle is called the TRICUSPID VALVE. The one between the left atrium and the left ventricle is called the BICUSPID or MITRAL VALVE.

The right side of the heart is responsible for pulmonary circulation. The right atrium receives blood from the venous system throughout the body, passes it through the tricuspid valve to the right ventricle, which sends it through the PULMONIC VALVE and into the PULMONARY ARTERY, and finally to each lung. The blood that comes to the right atrium has been flowing through the tissue capillary beds. Some of the oxygen has been removed by the tissues, and carbon dioxide (a product of tissue work) has been deposited in it. This oxygen-depleted blood is then sent by the right ventricle to the lungs for re-oxygenation and carbon dioxide removal. Freshly oxygenated blood is returned to the left atrium from the lungs through the PULMONARY VEINS. Pulmonary circulation is then complete.

The left side of the heart is responsible for systemic circulation. The newly oxygenated blood is received by the left atrium and passed through the mitral valve to the left ventricle. The left ventricle then contracts and sends this oxygen-rich blood throughout the body, sending it through the AORTIC VALVE and into the AORTA, the largest artery of the body.

Appropriately, the heart itself is the first organ to receive freshly oxygenated blood. Vessels that supply the myocardium, the CORONARY ARTERIES, branch from the aorta just as it exits the heart. These arteries branch, spread and penetrate through the myocardium, so that all parts of the heart have an on-going supply of blood rich in oxygen.

The Vascular System

The tubular network of vessels that carry the blood is called the VASCULAR SYSTEM. It can be compared to a pipeline that supplies every cell in the body with oxygen-bearing blood, and then returns blood to the heart to be sent to the lungs for re-oxygenation, and upon its return, pumped into systemic circulation. This "pipeline" is made up of ARTERIES, ARTERIOLES, VENULES, and VEINS.

Arteries carry blood away from the heart. Their walls are connective tissue and smooth muscle, and are thick enough to withstand the considerable force with which the heart propels blood into them. Their thickness is also great enough that diffusion of gasses or other substances does not occur between arterial blood and surrounding tissue.

Arterioles are small arteries with thinner walls, composed mostly of smooth muscle tissue. These expand or contract to regulate blood flow to body tissues. These branch again-and-again, to smaller and thinner-walled vessels. These finally end in a microscopic network of vessels, the capillary beds.

The capillary beds are the sites in the vascular system where substance exchanges (oxygen, carbon dioxide, nutrients, etc.) occur. The tiny vessels that form these networks are CAPILLARIES. The walls of these vessels are only single layers of endothelial cells. These thin walls allow oxygen and other nutrients to diffuse out of the blood and into adjacent cells, while carbon dioxide and other metabolic waste products can do the reverse. The propulsive force of the heart is gradually reduced by the repeated branching of arteries into ever-smaller diameters; by the time the capillaries are reached, there is minimal force, so the filmy, delicate structure of the capillaries is not a problem.

There are trillions of capillary networks throughout all the body tissues. Although microscopic, the network regulates very effectively the amount of blood flowing to a specific area of tissue, according to tissue needs. This is accomplished by contraction or relaxation of a ring of smooth muscle, the PRE-CAPILLARY SPHINCTER. In this way, the body tissues that need the most oxygen and other materials at a given time get it.

Gas, nutrient and metabolic waste having been exchanged, the capillary beds empty into VENULES, or tiny veins. These have walls of endothelial cells and connective tissue. These in turn lead to larger diameter VEINS, whose walls have a smooth muscle layer as well as endothelium and connective tissue. Veins have less smooth muscle in their walls than arteries, since the blood they carry is under very little pressure. Many of the larger veins have one-way valves in their walls to assist in the return of blood to the heart against gravity. Venous blood return from the legs is greatly assisted by the squeezing of leg muscles as we move around; that is one of the multitude of reasons for regular exercise.

Because of its wondrous design, the vascular system is capable of selective distribution of blood flow according to changing tissue needs. For example, blood flow to the skeletal muscles can vary from about 15% of the total CARDIAC OUTPUT (the amount of blood the heart pumps into systemic circulation per minute) at rest to 85% of the total during vigorous exercise. This massive re-distribution takes time to accomplish, and underscores the need for warm-up and gradual increase in exercise intensity during a workout. A return to the normal resting distribution also takes time, and thus the need for a cool-down period after vigorous exercise.

Table 4.1	Distribution of Cardiac Output	
Rest		**Strenuous Exercise**
20–25%	Liver and digestive system	3–5%
4.5%	Heart	4–5%
20%	Kidneys	2–4%
3–5%	Bones	0.5–1%
15%	Brain	3–4%
5%	Skin	2–3%
15–20%	Skeletal Muscles	80–85%
5–10%	Fatty Tissue	1%

Adapted from: Per-Olaf Astrand and Kaare Rodahl, Textbook of Work Physiology: Physiological Bases of Exercise, 3rd Edition. New York: McGraw-Hill Book Co. 1986, p. 152.

The Blood

The blood itself is really an organ of the cardiorespiratory system. Blood has many roles. It is a key element in the immune system (disease resistance), in the temperature regulation mechanism, and in the general growth and maintenance of body tissue. Its role as oxygen carrier is the one most critical to the function of the entire system.

Blood is a suspension of several cell-types in a liquid that is primarily water with nutrients, electrolytes and other substances dissolved in it. ERYTHROCYTES or red blood cells are the cellular components responsible for oxygen transport. The red cells contain HEMOGLOBIN, an iron-rich protein compound with a high affinity for oxygen. Oxygen chemically combines with hemoglobin when it diffuses from the air sacs (ALVEOLI) into the blood in the capillary beds of the lungs. It is carried in the blood to the capillaries of the muscles or other body tissues, where it is exchanged for carbon dioxide. Carbon dioxide is a waste product produced by cell metabolism.

No matter how strong and efficient the heart, nor how compliant the vascular system, if the blood has too few red cells, or if they are deficient in hemoglobin, oxygen availability to the tissues is reduced. This condition is called "anemia" and it is characterized by exaggerated fatigue in response to even minimal exercise. This underscores the fact that the blood must be considered an essential part of the cardiorespiratory system. To draw an analogy: our nation has a great system of interstate highways; however, if there were not sufficient, good trucks to transport goods to markets, we consumers would not have our needs met.

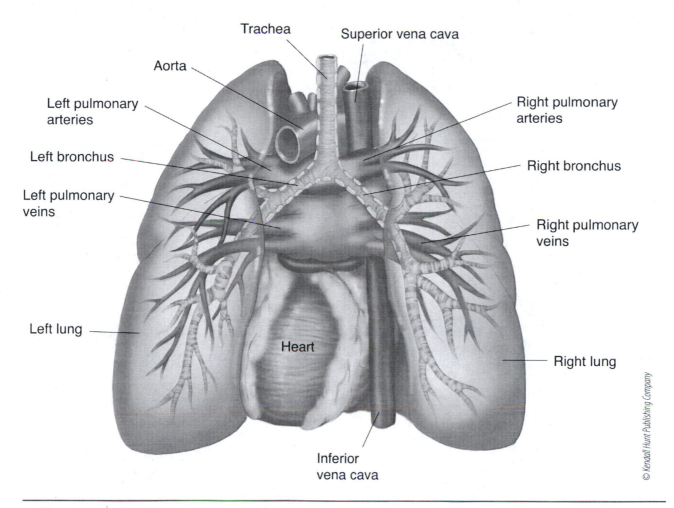

Trachea   Superior vena cava

Aorta

Left pulmonary arteries

Left bronchus

Left pulmonary veins

Left lung

Heart

Inferior vena cava

Right pulmonary arteries

Right bronchus

Right pulmonary veins

Right lung

Figure 4.4 | The Lungs

The Airways and Lungs

We have blood with hemoglobin to carry oxygen, vessels to carry the blood to the tissues, and the heart to pump the oxygen-carrying blood to all the body's tissues. However, we must have a means of getting the oxygen to where it can be absorbed into the blood. The air we breathe contains about 21% oxygen; to get the air into the body and into the blood, we have the exquisitely designed organs of respiration, the airways and lungs.

The lungs are two spongy organs in the thorax, on either side of the heart. They are made up of more than 300 million tiny air sacs, the ALVEOLI. Lung tissue is very highly vascularized, with tiny ALVEOLAR CAPILLARIES wrapping around each of the air sacs. This capillary-alveolar interface is where oxygen is passed into the blood, and carbon dioxide taken from the blood. The vast number of alveoli give the average adult lungs a tremendous surface area for gas exchange about 50–100 sq. meters, or an area the size of half a tennis court (McArdle, p. 217).

Incoming air passes over the mucous membranes of the nasal passages, and into the trachea, or windpipe. In these areas it is filtered, warmed and humidified. It then passes into the right and left BRONCHI, each of which supplies a lung. These large airways branch into structures ever smaller in diameter, called BRON-CHIOLES. Bronchioles terminate in alveolar ducts, which are totally surrounded by microscopic alveoli. The blood vessels that carry blood into the lungs also branch

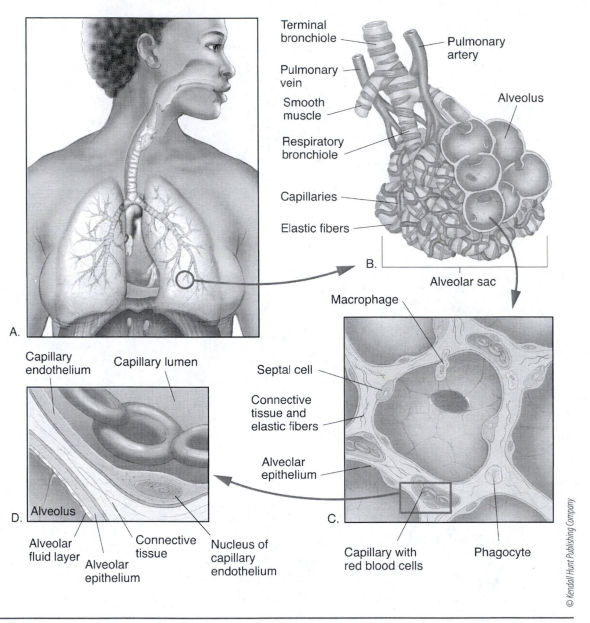

Figure 4.5 | Pulmonary Circulation

into ever smaller ones, terminating in alveolar capillaries, which surround each of the air sacs.

The "floor" of the chest or thoracic cavity is a muscle called the diaphragm. The intercostal muscles are between the ribs. During "inspiration," the ribs are spread and lifted by the intercostals, and the diaphragm is pulled down, increasing thoracic volume and allowing air to come rushing in. During "expiration" the intercostals relax, allowing the ribs to return to their resting positions; the diaphragm rises, making the thoracic diameter smaller, forcing air out. The process of bringing air into specialized structures so that oxygen can be loaded into red blood cells, and so that carbon dioxide can be taken from the cells and exhaled is termed "external respiration." The oxygen waste product-exchange at the tissue level is termed "internal respiration."

Function of the Cardiorespiratory System

The heart, vessels, lungs and blood work together to supply tissues with the oxygen they need. At rest, approximately five liters of blood per minute is sent into the systemic circulation. As mentioned before, this is called CARDIAC OUTPUT. Its amount is the product of the number of times per minute that the heart beats (HEART RATE) and the amount of blood pumped at each heart beat (STROKE VOLUME). During exercise the tissues need much more oxygen, and thus a much greater blood supply. The larger blood supply or cardiac output is produced by large increases in both heart rate and stroke volume.

The blood is circulated to body tissues under significant pressure. This pressure is the result of the heart's pumping force, the diameters of the vessels, and the volume of blood. The pressure that drives the blood to the organ systems is termed BLOOD PRESSURE, and is expressed by two numbers using the pressure measurement of millimeters of mercury (mm.Hg.).

The larger number represents the pumping force of the left ventricle; the smaller number represents the pressure present in the arteries between contractions of the left ventricle. The contraction phase of the heart's functioning is called SYSTOLE, so the blood pressure that results from it is called SYSTOLIC BLOOD PRESSURE. The filling phase of the heart's functioning is known as DIASTOLE, so the pressure in the arterial system at that time is the DIASTOLIC BLOOD PRESSURE.

At rest, normal adult systolic pressure ranges from 90 to 130 mm.Hg; normal diastolic pressures are typically 60 to 90 mm.Hg. During exercise, the heart pumps with greater force, so systolic pressure increases dramatically. It may go as high as 200 to 225 mm.Hg. The arteries, however, are able to expand and accommodate the greatly increased volume of blood being sent through them. For this reason, diastolic pressure during exercise changes very little if at all.

Adaptations to Exercise

When one performs an activity that requires a large increase in oxygen supply to tissues, blood flow must increase. Numerous adjustments are made to cause the increase in systemic blood flow or cardiac output. The heart beats faster, and the strength of ventricular contraction increases so that the amount of blood ejected per beat, or STROKE VOLUME, is greater. These changes can increase cardiac output to a level four or five times greater than the resting level.

To accommodate the increased blood flow, arteries dilate and capillary beds in working tissues open. Pulmonary ventilation (breathing rate) is increased, maximizing the oxygen available to red cells in the lungs' capillary beds. At the tissue level, increased temperature facilitates biochemical processes which assist the "unloading" of oxygen from the blood, as well as the "loading" metabolic by-products into the blood for its return to the heart and lungs.

These kinds of adaptations to exercise occur in everyone; they are the means our Creator chose to allow us the diversity we enjoy in the kinds of physical work we can do. However, there are some differences between persons whose cardiorespiratory systems are better conditioned and those whose systems are "normal" but less well-conditioned. The major difference is in the cardiac output that can be achieved during exercise. There are also differences in the nature of adjustments made to increase systemic circulation and in the muscle cells' ability to extract and use oxygen.

In any person with normally functioning heart and lungs, heart rate and stroke volume increase markedly during exercise. However, the better conditioned person has a more significant increase in stroke volume and a proportionately smaller increase in heart rate. This demonstrates that the heart of a better-conditioned person is more efficient. That is, it increases its output with fewer pumping strokes, because the ventricular walls of the well-conditioned heart are stronger. The pulse rate of a person whose cardiovascular system is well-conditioned is lower than that of a less conditioned person during exercise as well as at rest.

Following is an example of a well-conditioned heart's response to a work assignment compared to that of a heart that is healthy, but not as well conditioned.

This shows the greater efficiency of the well-conditioned heart muscle compared with the one that is less well-conditioned. In both cases, the assignment is accomplished, but with greater ease by the better conditioned heart.

Assignment: Circulate to the Body Cells Approximately 5000 Milliliters of Blood/Minute

The well-conditioned heart is strong enough to pump 85 milliliters at each beat; it must beat 59 times each minute to get the job done ($85 \times 59 = 5015$ mls./min.).

The less-conditioned heart is able to pump 65 milliliters at each beat, thus having to beat 77 times per minute to accomplish the same work ($65 \times 77 = 5005$ mls./min.).

Table 4.2	Cardiovascular Disease Risk Analysis Overview

A well-functioning cardiovascular system is essential in supporting the physical activity that is at the core of physical fitness and therefore, good health. There are various risk factors each of us has to a different degree that indicate our vulnerability to heart disease and stroke. Risk scores calculated from the following information are based on statistical data from the literature and are estimates only. They are not intended to be diagnostic; the significance of a specific risk factor varies with the individual. Factors included are those known to be associated with cardiovascular disease; age has been omitted, since the vast majority of this profile's users will be under age 25. The Questionnaire in Table 4.3 can be used to do a risk analysis estimate based on these risk factor categories.

Family History	Cardiovascular disease does have a hereditary component. The degree to which this represents genetic predisposition rather than similar environmental influences is unclear. Close relatives with early heart attacks/strokes suggests that cardiovascular disease "runs in the family."
Exercise	Those who engage in aerobic exercise on a frequent and regular basis have fewer heart attacks and strokes than those who do not.
Personal Health History	A personal history of diabetes, heart abnormality, rheumatic fever, or high blood pressure puts one at greater risk for cardiovascular disease.
Blood Pressure	Resting blood pressure that is elevated indicates a somewhat higher than normal risk for cardiovascular disease. An extremely low systolic pressure may also carry increased risk.
Exposure to Tobacco	It is known that tobacco use has a negative effect on the cardio-respiratory system; this is most true for the user, but second-hand smoke also has a significant deleterious effect.
Diet	One's use of foods high in fat, salt, and cholesterol effects cardiovascular risk.
Stress and Tension	Emotional stress not properly managed increases one's risk of cardiovascular disease.
Gender	It is well-substantiated that males of all ages are at greater risk than females for cardiovascular disease.

Table 4.3	Cardiovascular Risk Analysis Questionnaire

1. **FAMILY HISTORY**: Add the number for the item(s) that is/are true for you.

Parent or sibling who had a heart attack under age 50	5
Parent or grandparent who had a heart attack after age 50	2
Both parents have (or had) high blood pressure	3
One parent has (or had) high blood pressure	2
Parent(s) or sibling(s) treated for high cholesterol or triglyceride levels	3
Parent or sibling who had a stroke under age 50	5
Parent or grandparent who had a stroke after age 50	2
No history of any of the above	0

TOTAL _____

2. **EXERCISE**: How often do you engage in aerobic exercise (jogging, brisk walking, cycling, racquetball, etc.) for at least 20 consecutive minutes?

Once a week or less	4
Twice a week	2
Three times a week	1
Four or more times a week	0

TOTAL _____

3. **PERSONAL HEALTH HISTORY**: Add any that are true for you.

Diabetic with poor control of blood sugar level	4
Diabetic with good control of blood sugar level	2
Being treated for high blood pressure	3
Have been treated for heart disease or cardiac abnormality	4
Have had rheumatic fever	2
No history of diabetes, high blood pressure or heart problems	0

TOTAL _____

4. **BLOOD PRESSURE**: Have your blood pressure taken at rest. Add the point values for your systolic and diastolic readings.

Systolic _____   Diastolic _____

Systolic		Diastolic	
140 or higher	3	95 or higher	3
130–139	2	90–94	2
121–129	1	81–89	1
91–120	0	80 or below	0

TOTAL _____

5. **EXPOSURE TO TOBACCO**: Add the one that applies to you.

Current tobacco user (in any form)	5
Ex-tobacco user (regular user)	2
Non-smoker, but high exposure to smoke at home or work	1
No tobacco use of any kind; no significant smoke exposure	0

TOTAL _____

6. **DIET**: Add all that are true for the way you typically eat.

Red meat (beef, pork, veal or lamb) 5 or more times/week	4
Red meat 3-4 times/week	3
Fast foods (burgers, fries, pizza) 3 or more times/week	3
Six or more eggs/week	2
More than one 12-oz. Soft drink/day	2
Bacon, ham, or processed cold cuts >3 times/week	3
Add extra salt to foods at the table	1

TOTAL _____

7. **STRESS AND TENSION**: Which is most typical of you?

Nearly always in a hurry; impatient; become annoyed or angry easily	3
Often impatient and tense; sometimes annoyed by inconvenience	2
No more tense or anger-prone than most people I know	1
An easy-going "laid-back" kind of person	0

TOTAL _____

8. **GENDER**: Male 3   Female 1   TOTAL _____

Sum your scores for the eight sections, and evaluate your risk level, using the scale below.

Grand Total _____

Low risk	Less than 10 points
Moderate risk	11–25 points
High risk	26–35 points
Very high risk	36 or more points

Summary

Stewardship of the cardiorespiratory system involves keeping it in optimal functioning condition, so that it can support the body in everyday work efforts, recreational involvements, and the occasional emergency that may arise. The optimal functioning of the cardiorespiratory system is the ability to support the body in its work efforts for an extended period of time without becoming exhausted, and to have a reserve for unusual demands. It reflects the ability of the body to obtain and utilize large amounts of oxygen rapidly and efficiently.

Oxygen is the "currency" with which the body pays for the energy expenditure required for physical activity. Thus, the ability of the cardiorespiratory system to supply the currency and the ability of the cells to use it together determine the amount of work that can be done. In the next chapter we will discuss how the oxygen delivery and use can be made better and more efficient by sound conditioning.

Bibliography and Resources for Further Study

Blair, Steven N. "1993 C.H. McCloy Lecture: Physical Activity, Physical Fitness and Health." *Research Quarterly for Exercise and Sport*, Dec. 1993, pp. 365–396.

Faulkner, J.A., and T.P. White, "Adaptation of Skeletal Muscle to Physical Activity." *Exercise, Fitness and Health: A Consensus of Current Knowledge* (Editors: Bouchard, Shephard, Stephens, Sutton and McPherson). Champaign, IL: Human Kinetics, 1990, pp. 265–279.

Fletcher, G. F., and S. N. Blair, et al. "Statement on Exercise: Benefits and Recommendations for Physical Activity Programs for All Americans." *Circulation*, July, 1992. pp. 340–344.

McArdle, William, Frank Katch, and Victor Katch. *Exercise Physiology*. 4th Ed. Williams & Wilkins, 1996.

McArdle, William, Frank Katch, and Victor Katch. *Exercise Physiology: Nutrition, Energy, and Human Performance*. 7th Ed. Lippincott: Williams & Wilkins, 2009.

Public Health Service, U.S. Department of Health and Human Services. "Physical Activity and Fitness" in *Healthy People 2010, Vols. I and II*. 2nd Ed. Stock No. 017-001-00547-9. Pittsburgh PA: U.S. Government Printing Office, Superintendent of Documents, 2001. (Also at *www.healthypeople.gov*.)

U.S. Department of Health and Human Services; U.S. Department of Agriculture, *Dietary Guidelines for Americans: Healthy People 2020*, U.S. Government, 2010.

Wilmore, Jack, David Costill, and W. Larry Kenney. *Physiology of Sport and Exercise*. 4th ed. Human Kinetics, 2008.

Chapter 5

Conditioning the Cardiorespiratory System

Essential Terms

Aerobic Capacity	*Intensity*
Age Predicted Maximum Heart Rate	*Mode*
Duration	*Pulse Rate*
Frequency	*Resting Heart Rate*
Heart Rate Reserve	*Training Heart Rate*

Objectives

Upon completion of this chapter, students should be able to:

1. Define, explain, and effectively use each of the essential terms listed above.

2. Explain the purpose of the cardiorespiratory system with regard to physical work.

3. Explain the reasons for conditioning the cardiovascular system.

4. Cite key factors for the improvement of aerobic capacity.

5. Calculate his/her individual training heart rate, using 60% as a minimum and 75% as an optimum for active college-age individuals.

6. Identify activities that have value as aerobic conditioning activities.

7. Explain what one needs to do to maintain aerobic fitness.

8. Explain precautions necessary to exercise safely in weather extremes—severe cold or severe heat and/or humidity.

Introduction

The purpose of the cardiorespiratory system is to deliver oxygen to the body tissues at the rate and in the amount needed to support their work level. This is true whether they are at rest or at their highest metabolic rate. The purpose of cardiorespiratory conditioning is to improve that system's ability to accomplish its task. The amount of oxygen the cardiorespiratory system can deliver and the tissues can use is called AEROBIC CAPACITY. Every living person has an aerobic capacity, but that capacity, aerobic fitness, and cardiorespiratory endurance are all terms used to describe the functional capability of the cardiorespiratory system.

An optimally functioning cardiorespiratory system can efficiently and effectively meet the body's oxygen demands. A person with better aerobic capacity can work easier, faster, and longer than one with a lesser capacity. As good stewards, we have the responsibility and challenge of caring for and strengthening the cardiorespiratory system He has given us.

Assessing Aerobic Capacity

As mentioned earlier, aerobic capacity and cardiorespiratory fitness are really interchangeable terms. The true measure of how well the cardiorespiratory system functions is the amount of oxygen that body tissues actually take from the blood that is brought to them. This can be estimated very accurately in the physiology laboratory, using standardized procedures and sophisticated equipment. Fortunately, researchers have learned that aerobic capacity can be estimated with acceptable accuracy (for personal fitness purposes) using simple field tests. These tests have been validated against measurements made under controlled laboratory conditions.

We suggest you take the opportunity to see where you are now with regard to cardiorespiratory fitness. The field test options we recommend are the 1.5 mile run, the 1 mile jog, or the 1 mile walk. The 1.5 mile run evaluation is based on the premise that the more oxygen the body is able to take in and use, the faster you can cover this distance. It also assumes you are physically able to utilize running as an appropriate form of aerobic activity and that you have some experience doing so. The 1 mile jog and the 1 mile walk tests assume that, for whatever combination of reasons, running is not the best activity to use to assess your cardiorespiratory fitness. Both of these tests utilize the principle that the time it takes to cover this distance (keeping an even pace throughout and giving your best effort), coupled with a measure of how hard the heart had to work to support the activity (indicated by heart rate at the end) gives an indication of cardiorespiratory fitness. The faster you cover the distance with a lower heart rate, the better your cardiorespiratory fitness.

Cooper found that, for people who are already active in aerobic pursuits, the times for a 1.5 mile run correlated very well with laboratory measurement of oxygen use (Cooper, "A Means of Assessing O_2 Uptake," pp. 201–204). However, many people, even college students, do not have a good beginning base of aerobic activity. For them, the notion of going out and running a mile and a half not only sounds unpleasant, it probably is! Fortunately, several researchers (Kline, Porcari, et al., and Rippe, et al.) found that estimates of oxygen use based on time for a mile walk together with ending heart rate agreed closely with laboratory measurements of oxygen consumption.

We suggest that persons currently involved in sports or activities like jogging, soccer, roller-blading or the like take the 1.5 mile run test. It will give you a realistic estimate of your current aerobic fitness level. If you have not been regularly participating in some form of aerobic exercise, or if you have an injury or other condition that makes running inadvisable, do the one-mile walk or jog. The validity of each test is dependent on your giving your best effort. Instructions and tables for evaluation are included in the appropriate references identified at the end of this chapter.

We encourage you to do a pre-assessment prior to beginning your cardiorespiratory conditioning programming, and then do a post-assessment using the same test after you have completed at least 12 weeks of your program so you can evaluate your progress. We believe you will find this a very rewarding experience!

Improving Aerobic Capacity

When systematically challenged, the body adapts in ways that make it better able to meet the demands made. Only by being made to work a little harder than usual will the body increase its oxygen-delivering ability. This "going beyond the usual" is the "principle of overload" that was discussed earlier. The process of systematically and regularly challenging the cardiorespiratory system is known as cardiorespiratory or aerobic conditioning.

When one develops a program for improving aerobic condition, there are four items to consider. They are: the MODE of exercise, i.e., what activity will be done; the INTENSITY of the exercise, or what demand is to be made on the systems; the DURATION of a workout session, and the FREQUENCY of workouts.

The MODE of exercise chosen for aerobic conditioning should be one that is enjoyable, easily accessible, and that brings into play the large muscle groups of the back and legs. Ideally, involve as much of the body's musculature as possible. All conditioning sessions don't need to involve the same activity; vary your workouts to keep them interesting and fun! Ideal activities include: brisk walking, jogging, hiking over varying terrain, cycling, skating (ice or roller), cross-country skiing, and swimming. Sports activities can be good aerobic workouts, provided you have sufficient skill to be in near-continuous activity. Some excellent activities include: racquetball, badminton (played well), tennis, basketball, soccer, lacrosse, field hockey, handball, and volleyball. Golf can be a good aerobic activity, provided you walk the course and carry the clubs.

The degree of demand made on the cardiorespiratory system is the INTENSITY of the activity. This needs to be individualized, and modified as one's level of conditioning changes. The easiest and most accessible means of monitoring exercise intensity is by pulse rate. We'll describe that in detail just a bit further along.

The DURATION of an exercise session, in order to stimulate improvement, is about 25–30 minutes. The preponderance of research supports this duration as what is needed for the average healthy person to improve aerobic condition. However, there are those who maintain that they just don't have that much time to devote to aerobic exercise, particularly when you add a 10 minute warm-up and stretching period to the beginning of the session, and a 5–10 minute cool-down period at the end. A group of experts were assembled to develop a clear "public health message" on physical activity. The result was: "Every U.S. adult should accumulate 30 minutes or more of moderate-intensity physical activity on most, preferably all, days of the week." (Pate, et al.) Moderate intensity was described as energy expenditure equal to that of brisk walking.

So, to the question of whether we need 30 continuous minutes of activity, or whether we may accumulate a total of 30 minutes throughout the day, it seems appropriate to suggest use of the "Activity Pyramid" shown in Figure 5.1.

Modeled after the nutrition pyramid, this plan encourages one to use those activities that are part of everyday life as a "base," and to maximize their aerobic value. Put extra walking into your day. Walk to your classroom building rather than riding (you don't have to worry about getting a parking space!) In a department store, take the stairs to upper levels rather than the escalator or elevator. When you do drive, park a distance from the entrance you will use, so that you have a little walk. It's not hard to accumulate 30 minutes of aerobic activity if one makes those choices.

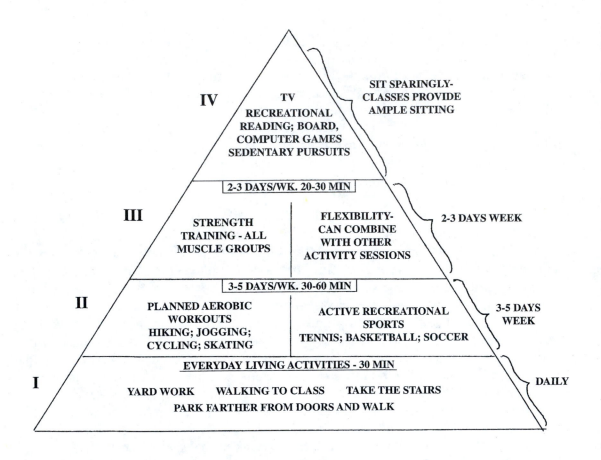

Figure 5.1 | The Activity Pyramid; Adapted from Park Nicollet Health Source Institute for Research and Education.

The second level of the pyramid includes planned workout and sports sessions. The third includes leisure activities as well as strength and flexibility building sessions. This seems like an easy and organized approach to planning exercise into life. If you have not come from a habit of regular exercise, organization is important. Only by developing and following a plan will you succeed in making exercise a part of your daily life.

The FREQUENCY of aerobic workouts is just the number of aerobic exercise sessions per week. Research supports 3 to 5 sessions/week as the desired range for planned, vigorous aerobic exercise sessions; in other words, these are not the accumulated minutes of daily activity, but time set aside for aerobic exercise. Fewer than three sessions may not bring about any improvement in condition; more than five may cause fatigue or injury. Remember though, that on those days you don't have a planned session, you should still accumulate 30 minutes of moderate intensity activity.

Individualizing Exercise Intensity

Exercise intensity needs to be individualized and must be modified as one's level of conditioning changes (principles of specificity and progressive overload). Fortunately, the PULSE RATE provides an easily accessible means of monitoring cardiorespiratory exercise intensity because each "pulse" is caused by a contraction of the heart. The radial pulse, found on the thumb side of the wrist, can be used to determine how hard the heart is working. The carotid pulse, located just to either side of the trachea (windpipe) in the neck, is easier for some people to find. Care must be taken when using the carotid pulse to monitor exercise. The finger pressure over the pulse should be light and steady. Pressure that is too firm may interfere with the proper flow of blood to the brain, and any massaging action over the pulse has the potential to cause a change in heart rhythm. For these reasons, it is recommended that the ability to find and monitor the radial pulse be developed.

Determining Pulse Rate

1. Locate the radial pulse with the index and middle fingers of the other hand. Press fairly firmly along the thumb side of your wrist. If you don't find your pulse right away, keep searching... it's there. Once you locate it, note exactly where you feel it most strongly, and practice locating it several times.

2. When you can find your pulse dependably, watch the second hand of a clock or watch, and count the beats in a 10-sec. time period. Multiply this by 6 for your heart rate in beats per minute, the common reference unit used for heart rate.

3. Practice doing this until you can find and count your pulse quickly and accurately. This is essential when you want an estimate of your heart rate during exercise. An accurate count is impossible to get **during** vigorous exercise, but a 10-second count during a pause in the workout gives an excellent estimate. Because the pulse slows so abruptly when exercise is interrupted, an **immediate** count is essential to accuracy: hence, the importance of being able to locate the pulse quickly.

You can know whether your workout is intense enough to challenge your cardiovascular system appropriately by determining your own training heart rate and periodically monitoring your pulse rate during the workout. If your pulse is below your training rate, the pace of the exercise needs to be increased; if your pulse is several beats above your training rate, you will be more comfortable and still achieve benefit if you slow down a bit.

Determination of your target or training heart rate must take into account two very important variables: age and present level of cardiovascular conditioning. The maximum number of times per minute that the heart can beat declines as age increases; this is reflected in the calculation procedure that follows. Also, resting pulse rate declines as the efficiency of the heart increases. Therefore, resting pulse in included in the calculation, to reflect present condition.

The difference between your age-predicted maximum heart rate and your resting rate is termed your HEART RATE RESERVE. A study in 1957 by the Finnish physiologist Karvonen suggested that to improve cardiovascular fitness significantly, an exercise heart rate must be achieved equal to at least 60% of the HEART RATE RESERVE plus resting rate. More recently, researchers have found that an exercise heart rate of 75% of HEART RATE RESERVE plus the resting rate is a safe and very effective TRAINING THRESHOLD for healthy, active individuals (Getchell, p. 72).

To determine your training heart rate, follow the steps below:

1. Determine your AGE-PREDICTED MAXIMUM HEART RATE by subtracting your age in years from 220. The figure 220 is a constant value that can be used to determine a very good estimate of maximum heart rate for healthy adults. The value was derived from actual maximum heart rate determinations on large numbers of people across a wide age range.

    AGE-PREDICTED MAXIMUM HEART RATE = 220 **minus** AGE IN YEARS

2. Calculate your HEART RATE RESERVE by subtracting your resting pulse from your estimated maximum heart rate. To obtain your resting pulse, count it in the suggested manner after you have been resting quietly for a minimum of 10 minutes.

    HEART RATE RESERVE = MAXIMUM HEART RATE **minus** RESTING HEART RATE

3. Determine your TRAINING HEART RATE by taking 60% of your heart rate reserve (if you are just beginning an exercise program, use 60%; if you are regularly active already, use 75%), and adding to it your resting heart rate. This value, rounded to the nearest whole number, is the heart rate you need to maintain through most of your workout, in order to improve cardiovascular condition.

    TRAINING HEART RATE = (.60 OR .75 × HEART RATE RESERVE) + RESTING HEART RATE

Most people find it more useful to convert this from beats per minute to beats per 10 seconds. To do this, divide your training heart rate by 6.

EXAMPLE: An 18 year old whose resting heart rate is 80 beats per minute.

MAXIMUM HEART RATE = 220 − 18 = **202**

HEART RATE RESERVE = 202 − 80 = **122**

TRAINING HEART RATE:

        If using 75% of heart rate range . . .
        (.75 × 122) + 80 = 91.5 + 80 = 171.5 or 172 beats/minute
            Expressed in beats/10-sec.: 172/6 = 28.6 or **29** beats/10 seconds
        If using 60% of heart rate range . . .
        (.60 × 122) + 80 = 73.2 + 80 = 153.2 or 153 beats/minute
        Expressed in beats/10-sec.: 153/6 = 25.5 or **26** beats/10 seconds

When this 18-year-old goes out to do an aerobic workout, he or she should warm up for 5–10 minutes, then begin the vigorous activity chosen for the workout. At some point during the second five minutes of vigorous activity, a **10**-second heart rate should be obtained. If the rate obtained is below the training heart rate of either 29 or 26, the pace should be increased. If the pulse obtained is more than two or three beats **above** the target rate, the pace should be slowed because the work level is probably more intense than can be sustained for the necessary 25 to 30 minutes.

After 25–30 minutes of activity at or near the training rate, one should cooldown gradually, with five minutes of activity at a leisurely pace. The activity should be one that uses the same muscles as were involved in the vigorous phase of the workout. Typical cool-down activities are walking, slow cycling, and leisurely swimming.

The warm-up and cool-down phases of a conditioning session are important and should not be ignored. Warm-up gives the body opportunity to make the adjustments necessary to meet the demands of exercise gradually. The cardiorespiratory and muscular systems cannot shift instantly into high gear. Also, the possibility of muscle and/or tendon injury is greatly reduced by stretching and by raising muscle tissue temperature and capillary-bed blood flow prior to demanding work.

A Summary of Cardiorespiratory Conditioning

In order to be successful, your aerobic conditioning plan should:

1. Use a form of activity that involves as much muscle mass as possible, like walking, jogging, cycling, skating, swimming, or a vigorous sport.

2. Include planned sessions of 25 to 30 minutes of activity, plus 30 accumulated minutes of moderate intensity activity daily.

3. Bring one's pulse rate into the training range, and sustain it there for 25–30 minutes (planned sessions).

4. Include planned sessions 3 days/week for minimum benefit, or 5 days/week for optimum benefit.

5. Use a 5–10 minute warm-up and stretching period at the beginning, and at least a 5 minute cool-down at the conclusion of the session.

Maintaining Aerobic Fitness

Many functions of the body are dynamic; they respond to what they experience. The functioning of the cardiorespiratory system is no exception. The level of aerobic fitness we have is initially determined by genetics and then by the amount and type of activity we have. Once an appropriate level of aerobic fitness is achieved, it must be used to be maintained. As we indicated previously, our sedentary life responsibilities have dictated that this requires planned, deliberate exercise of the cardiorespiratory system.

Research indicates that aerobic fitness is lost fairly quickly if conditioning activities are stopped. Even within one week significant deconditioning occurs. Within 1 to 2 months, the gains made in a conditioning program are completely lost (Fox, et al., p. 361). An extreme example of the effects of inadequate activity to maintain aerobic fitness were reported in Saltin's classic bed-rest study in which he evaluated the effects of 20 days of bed rest on five college-age men. He found a 27 percent decrease in maximal oxygen use ability. A level of work that required a heart rate of 145 beats per minute before the 20 days of bed rest required a heart rate of 180 beats per minute after the period of inactivity. There was a 7 percent reduction in blood volume and a significant decrease in the stroke volume, suggesting loss of strength and power in the heart muscle (Astrand, pp. 441–442).

The need for regular, appropriate activity to maintain aerobic fitness is evident. For most people two or three 30-minute workouts per week with the heart rate in the training range (60%–75%) will adequately maintain aerobic fitness. This should be in addition to the 30 minutes a day of physical activity that is part of regular lifestyle activities.

Topics of Importance Regarding Cardiovascular Conditioning

We have reviewed the key concepts of cardiovascular or aerobic conditioning in an attempt to provide you with a clear factual understanding. Now we will attempt to answer several questions that are frequently asked about this aspect of physical conditioning. If you have questions we have not included, or if you don't understand some of the answers given, ask your instructor.

Cardiovascular Fitness—Top Priority in Fitness

Cardiovascular fitness is just one aspect of total physical fitness, according to the definition given earlier in the book. However, this kind of exercise seems to receive a lot more popular attention than any other type. Does that mean this is the most important component of physical fitness?

> While it's important to maintain a balance in your exercise program, as in all aspects of your Christian walk, in a sense, cardiovascular fitness is the most important. This is because oxygen delivery and utilization are the foundation for **all** physical work. Everyone needs enough muscular strength for work, with a reserve for emergencies. Depending on your sport and recreational interests, strength may or may not be significantly important. Likewise, while free and easy movement requires flexibility of the spine and joints, there is little value in being overly flexible; in fact, it can be a detriment. Some may find that study, and possibly work, leave little time for personal exercise; if this is the case, the time available would be best used in strengthening the cardiovascular system.

Risks of Cardiovascular Conditioning

Should I have a thorough physical examination, including some sophisticated tests of heart function, prior to starting an exercise program? How important is it to have a treadmill electrocardiogram before starting an exercise program? Several people have had fatal heart attacks while jogging, and college basketball players have died after a workout with a lot of running. Does this kind of exercise put too much strain on the heart?

How necessary it is to have a physical examination or a treadmill electrocardiogram depends on your age, health history, and what you've been doing prior to beginning exercise. You should be examined and have a physician's approval if:

1. You have a history of rheumatic fever, a significant heart murmur, myocardial infarction (heart attack), hypertension (high blood pressure), diabetes, or respiratory disease.

2. You have had a significant illness, or major surgery, in the 3 months prior to the beginning of your exercise program.

3. You take any prescription medicines that alter heart rate or blood pressure.

4. You are 30 or more pounds over the weight suggested for your height, or 15 or more pounds below the suggested weight.

5. You are 35 years old, and have been quite sedentary in the last year.

6. You are 40 or more years old, and have not had a physical within the year.

For the young, healthy person with no history or symptoms of heart disease, a treadmill test is not recommended. When this testing procedure first became available, it was hailed as an ideal pre-exercise screening test for latent heart disease. However, experience has shown that its best use is in evaluating persons with symptoms of heart disease. While it can be used to estimate one's present aerobic fitness level, this estimate can be made from field tests with nearly identical accuracy and none of the expense.

A sound heart will not be damaged by engaging in aerobic exercise in the manner we have described. Those who have suffered sudden cardiac arrest while exercising have been found, at autopsy, to have had significant underlying abnormalities or disease of the cardiovascular system. Some had begun exercise in their mid-thirties or forties, after many years of sedentary living, smoking and/or poor diet, all of which left their mark on the heart and vessels.

It would be foolish for a healthy person to forego the benefits and pleasure of aerobic exercise for fear of suffering a heart attack. Anyone with any doubt about the safety of aerobic exercise for them should, of course, consult a physician.

Will jogging or a lot of vigorous walking cause joint damage, particularly to the knees and ankles?

If you have not significantly injured your knees or ankles, do not have degenerative joint disease or arthritis, are not markedly overweight, and wear good shoes, it is very unlikely you will damage your joints. If you already have significant joint damage due to injury or arthritis, you need to choose another form of aerobic exercise or modify the distance you cover in a workout.

For example, if your activity has been jogging, you might substitute brisk walking; cycling and swimming are also appropriate alternatives, provided you have the time they require. One caution: it would be wise to avoid extreme distances; by extreme, we mean those in excess of 70–80 miles/week. There is not enough data at this time on people who have conditioned at this level for an extended time period to know what the musculoskeletal effects may be.

Benefits of Cardiovascular Conditioning

What kinds of benefits can one expect to achieve by taking the time and effort to plan for regular aerobic exercise?

Improved cardiovascular efficiency and a greater capacity for endurance exercise are proven, measurable benefits. Aerobic exercise burns lots of calories, and so is a valuable aid in weight reduction and maintenance programs. Many who make aerobic exercise a part of their daily lives find the feeling of vigorous well-being and joy in living they experience to be of even greater value than those effects that **can** be quantified. Additionally, many find exercises helpful in moderating their responses to emotional stress. (Folkins and Amsterdam, pp. 289–291)

Will aerobic exercise protect one from heart disease, or increase longevity?

Data are now published which show that a physically active lifestyle is indeed associated with decreased mortality from heart disease, and with length of life. (Blair, et al., p. 2395) However, one cannot predict the future for an individual. To say that because you regularly jog or do some other aerobic activity, you will live longer, would be misleading. Our days, their number, and what they hold are the Lord's. We can't know what He will allow to come into our lives, nor the time span He has allotted for our earthly walk. He does, however, give us the freedom to choose how we will live day-to-day, and the lifestyle we develop for ourselves certainly affects the quality of our days. It's our responsibility to be good stewards of the intricately wonderful bodies we've been given. Stewardship involves doing those things that will help the body to function optimally. Regular exercise is essential to optimal cardiovascular function.

Research has given us a great deal of insight regarding the combination of factors that increase the statistical risk for heart disease. Factors like obesity, high levels of triglycerides and low density lipoprotein cholesterol in the blood, and chronically high stress levels are decreased by regular aerobic exercise. High density lipoprotein cholesterol, which tends to reduce heart disease risk, tends to be increased by exercising aerobically. Thus, exercise can reduce statistical risk for atherosclerosis and coronary artery disease. We suggest that your purpose for exercise be rooted in meeting your stewardship responsibilities, and in enhancing your quality of life and joy in living it. The risk reduction you may achieve will be as the Lord wills.

Conditioning in Hot or Cold Weather

Going out to walk or jog sounds fine in the mild, pleasant days of fall or spring. What does one do in the cold of winter and the heat of summer?

With some common sense modifications, you can continue to exercise as usual. In winter, you can usually exercise very comfortably if you dress in loose layers, wear a knit cap and mittens, and come inside immediately after your workout. A jogger will be quite comfortable most days wearing shorts, sweatpants, socks, shoes, tee-shirt, sweatshirt, knit ski cap, and mittens. If the wind is sharp, the addition of a light-weight nylon or Gore-tex windbreaker and a woolen scarf covering the nose and mouth increases comfort. A walker may need another layer of clothing, since walking doesn't generate quite the heat that jogging or running does. These cautions should be observed when exercising outdoors in cold weather.

1. If the effective temperature (taking wind velocity into account) is below 0°F., find an indoor alternative workout for that day.

2. Be sure to cover your head and your hands on cold days; a great deal of heat is lost if these are not covered. Also, on very cold, windy days, be aware of the possibility of frostbite. The ears, nose, cheeks and fingers are especially vulnerable. Cover them!

3. If you have any form of cardiovascular disease, or asthma that is aggravated by cold air, find an indoor alternative workout on days when the effective temperature is below 15°F.

For most people, exercising in hot weather is a greater problem than exercising in the winter. This is because exercise raises body temperature, and the air temperature is also high, making it difficult for the body to lose its excess heat. Our most effective cooling mechanism is sweating. As moisture evaporates from the skin, excess heat is lost. The high humidity typical of Midwestern and eastern summers slows the evaporation process, and makes it difficult to dissipate excess heat.

You can exercise safely in the heat if you observe the following guidelines:

1. The water lost in sweat **must** be replaced. If the workout is more than 25–30 minutes long, drink at least 1/2 cup of water every 15 minutes. If you are playing tennis, drink water at each court change, **whether you feel thirsty or not**. Be sure to drink water frequently in the 2–3 hours following a vigorous workout, when you have perspired heavily.

2. You do not need to be particularly concerned about replacing the salt lost in perspiration. Salting your food at meals is quite adequate replacement. Our salt need is 0.2 gm./day; yet typically we take in 2–10 gms. daily in our diet. Regardless of what you may have heard about taking salt tablets to offset losses during exercise, don't do it unless it is ordered by a physician.

3. Expensive electrolyte replacement solutions are not superior to plain water for use during exercise. Plain cool water is well-absorbed and is less likely to cause gastrointestinal disturbances than the commercially prepared solutions.

4. Plan your workout for the cooler portions of the day—early morning or evening.

5. Wear light clothing for hot weather exercise. Long pants and long-sleeved shirts should **not** be worn for vigorous exercise during hot weather. Excessive clothing hinders evaporation of perspiration, and hence cooling.

6. When the temperature is greater than 85°F, and relative humidity is greater than 90%, it would be wise to postpone your workout, or to do something less vigorous, i.e., walk rather than jog.

Aerobic Exercise at High Altitudes

We are a very mobile people; it's not unusual to travel to high altitude vacation spots to hike, or ski or to compete in athletic events. When we go to altitudes above 7500 feet we quickly learn that physical exertion seems more difficult. We get out of breath more quickly than usual; fatigue sets in sooner, and competitive performance in any activity requiring sustained running or fast walking declines. Should we be alarmed?

A healthy person who experiences this need not become alarmed, but needs to understand the effects of increased altitude. The difference between sea level and Denver or Pike's Peak is a factor called the partial pressure of oxygen (PO_2). The greater the altitude, the lower the PO_2; the lower the PO_2, the more difficult it is for oxygen to be loaded onto hemoglobin and carried to body tissues. It is the decrease in the blood's saturation with oxygen that produces the breathlessness and early fatigue one encounters on running, climbing a hill, or similar exertions.

The answers to this problem are:

1. realize that you will experience early fatigue when you fly to Denver and go out to jog or play tennis soon after arrival; and

2. realize that your body will adapt or acclimatize to altitude fairly rapidly.

Endurance athletes (middle-and-long distance runners, soccer players, basketball players, tennis players, for example) who go to a competition at a high altitude location need to plan early arrival, in order to allow time for physiological adjustment. As a general rule, two weeks are needed to fully adapt to altitudes up to 7500 feet; higher altitudes require a longer period of adaptation. Locations that are less than 5000 feet above sea level don't cause any deficits in oxygen saturation, and so don't require acclimatization.

The physiological adaptations that occur are numerous, complex, and beyond the scope of this course. What is important to know is that you will need to "back off" the intensity of your aerobic exercise during the early days of your stay, and that your cardiorespiratory system will adapt.

Another thing to remember is that the air is drier at high altitudes, which can cause dehydration. Be sure to drink plenty of water before, during and after workouts.

Are There Times When I Should Skip an Aerobic Workout?

I desire to honor the Lord with my body care program. Are there times when I should NOT do my aerobic workout?

Certainly! When you are ill, listen to your body. Forego aerobic workouts until any fever is gone, and you feel better. If you have been treated by a physician, or had surgery, ask about a reasonable time for resuming regular workouts. When you have an injury, it only makes sense, and is good stewardship, to allow the injured body part to rest and heal. You may be able to substitute an alternate activity for your usual mode of exercise (for example, swimming or cycling for walking or running).

Exercise for Individuals with Asthma or Diabetes

What if I have asthma, and have always been excused from physical education classes? Should I do aerobic exercise?

Yes, you should; however, you will need to find the appropriate level and mode of exercise, and be aware of environmental conditions, making adjustments accordingly. The "wheezing" and breathing difficulty of asthma is caused by constriction of small air passages or bronchioles in the lungs. Asthma varies from person-to-person in severity, frequency of attack, and specific conditions that trigger attacks. Most persons who have chronic asthma can control symptoms with oral bronchodilating medication taken regularly as prescribed, supplemented by aerosol inhalants used prior to exercise. Those with "exercise-induced" asthma usually can prevent/alleviate their symptoms through use of aerosol bronchodilators alone.

If your asthma is triggered by dust, high pollen counts, or temperature extremes, there are likely to be times when you will have to exercise indoors, use a different activity for your workout, or work out at a different time of day. Your attitude should be one of working with your asthma, and determining the level of exercise you can tolerate and what modifications are necessary, rather than one of avoiding exercise. Remember that walking is an effective form of aerobic exercise; rarely is asthma so severe that a young adult cannot do this.

But what about exercise for the diabetic?

Regular aerobic exercise is essential for the diabetic because it can help counter some of the cardiovascular effects of the disease process. Most diabetics find that exercise lessens their insulin requirement. Discuss your exercise program with your physician, and get his/her specific advice regarding diet and insulin adjustments. It may take a while to "fine tune" your food intake and insulin dosage, but the benefits you will derive from regular exercise will more than make it worthwhile.

Good Shoes—An Important Investment

What kind of shoes do I need for my exercise program?

You need shoes that are appropriate for the activities you are doing. A good pair of tennis shoes should be used for racquet sports. Basketball shoes can also be used for volleyball. For jogging and brisk walking, you will need shoes made for jogging. These have mid-soles with added shock-absorbing capability for the thousands of times

Figure 5.2 | Jogging shoe.

your feet strike the ground. They also have excellent support for your arches. The heel counter is very firm to keep your heel from slipping sideways or rotating when you put your foot down. Jogging shoes are made with leather or nylon uppers (the outer covering of the shoe). We suggest nylon or combination nylon/leather uppers because they wear better and aren't damaged as much as an all-leather shoe when you run through a rainstorm.

Good jogging shoes are a significant investment, since most cost $60.00 or more. This looks a bit better when you consider that with reasonable care the fitness walker/jogger can use one pair for 2 to 3 years. Some suggestions to help with your initial shoe purchase:

1. Buy your shoes from a sporting goods store, or a store catering to joggers and runners, and buy shoes made by a well-known maker of running shoes. Looking through the shoe advertisements in Runner's World magazine (available in most libraries) prior to shoe shopping will help you become familiar with the various companies and the shoes they make.

2. Have size measurements taken while you are standing; wear the socks you will use for exercise. Be sure the shoe "feels good" on your foot. Walk around the store in it. (Stay on the carpet!)

3. The heel should fit snugly, and there should be plenty of room for your toes. Allow at least 1/4 inch beyond your toes. Be sure the toe box is high enough, so that the shoe won't rub blisters on the tops of your toes. Shoes vary considerably in this regard; check carefully.

4. If you are heavy, or have arthritis, or any other musculoskeletal problem, buy a shoe with a very thick mid-sole. These help to absorb shock, and lessen the possibility of adding to your joint problems.

The "Stitch in the Side"

What is the cause for the "stitch" or pain in the side that sometimes occurs while running?

While there are many theories as to its cause, "side stitch" remains somewhat a mystery. Two theories that seem most plausible are that the pain is caused by: (1) decreased blood flow to intra-abdominal organs, due to the working muscles taking most of the blood supply; and (2) stretching of connective tissue that holds intra-abdominal organs in place, and the resulting irritation to the nerves in the connective tissue.

Regardless of cause, it does occur. What to do about it? It will stop if you stop jogging and walk for awhile; most people who have become joggers have found that as their conditioning improved, "side stitch" disappeared.

What Kind of Aerobic Exercise Should I Choose?

What's the best kind of exercise for me to use for aerobic fitness?

When this book was first written, jogging was the most often recommended form of aerobic exercise; it was easy, beneficial, required a manageable amount of time, and had been popularized by the work of Kenneth Cooper. Now, more people are walking for exercise; some of them started out as joggers/runners, and found that time and aging joints "caught up with them." Is walking enough to improve cardiorespiratory condition? Happily for those who don't enjoy jogging, the answer is "yes." A University of Massachusetts study found that 30 minutes of brisk walking on a flat surface was an adequate stimulus to improvement. (Porcari, McCarron, et al., p. 129)

Some have begun to use weights in the hands and/or around the ankles to increase the "work" of walking. Is this a good thing? It depends on your goals. If you want to use walking as your mode of exercise, and you want to increase the intensity of the workout, weights may be just the thing for you. It causes you to burn more calories in the workout, so if fat reduction is one of your goals, weights increase the value of each workout. The best way to use weights is to carry them in your hands, or to use a weighted vest. We discourage ankle weights because their positioning at the end of a long body lever magnifies stresses at the knee, and may increase the risk of overuse injury.

The use of sport activities, particularly by the college-age population, is encouraged. The caveat though, is that one must have skill in the chosen activity. Tennis is a good aerobic workout for the intermediate to advanced player, who keeps the ball in play, and moves about the court. It isn't a good workout for the beginner, who spends most of the time chasing tennis balls. Take advantage of the college environment and learn to play tennis and racquetball! They are great lifetime activities.

Does Aerobic Exercise Have to Be "Hard" to Be Beneficial?

I've heard the phrase "No pain, no gain." Does it have to hurt and be hard to be helpful?

A few pages ago we defined and explained the concept of a "training threshold." This is the heart rate that we have to reach and maintain during the aerobic workout in order to stimulate improved function of the cardiorespiratory system. While all that we explained is true, it is also true that aerobic, large-muscle activity of any degree is better than none at all.

In the example used, the calculated training threshold was 172 beats/minute; the person who has been sedentary may find it difficult and unpleasant to maintain that heart rate for more than a few minutes. He or she may decide that exercise is just too "hard" and find excuses for remaining sedentary. Here we would "set aside" science and encourage activity that raises the heart rate, like walking at a moderate pace, cycling at a moderate pace, etc. that the individual can continue for 25–30 minutes at a time. So what if the training heart rate isn't attained; the person is moving, the heart is getting some exercise stimulus, and most importantly, the exercise isn't perceived as "hard" or unpleasant.

Table 5.1	Relative Values of Selected Sport Activities for Improving or Maintaining Cardiorespiratory Fitness		
Activity	Value	Activity	Value
Archery	Poor	Karate	Fair
Backpacking	Good	Lacrosse	Good to Excellent
Badminton	Fair to Good	Racquetball	Fair to Good
Baseball/Softball	Poor to Fair	Skating/Blading	Fair to Good
Basketball (full court)	Good	Skiing (Downhill)	Poor to Fair
Bowling	Poor	Skiing (Cross-Country)	Good to Excellent
Canoeing	Fair to Good	Soccer	Good to Excellent
Field Hockey	Good to Excellent	Tennis (Singles)	Fair to Good
Golf	Poor	Tennis (Doubles)	Fair
Handball	Good	Volleyball	Fair to Good
Ice Hockey	Good to Excellent	Wrestling	Fair to Good

There is actually some scientific support for the idea that even low intensity exercise has value. Blair and his associates did a study of the relationship of physical activity level and mortality from all causes. This was a prospective study involving several thousand healthy men and women. They found that the greatest drop in mortality was seen in those who moved from a sedentary lifestyle to one that included moderate physical activity. While the study showed that mortality rate declined as the level of physical activity and fitness increased, it was not a perfect relationship. In other words, more intense activity was not greatly superior to a lower intensity of exercise. (Blair, et al., "Physical Fitness and All-Cause Mortality," JAMA 262(17): 1989)

So, the answer is "No, exercise does not have to be 'hard' to be good." Getting some activity, at a level one finds fairly easy and enjoyable is far superior to attempting a difficult workout, finding it unpleasant, and never wanting to do it again! Certainly if one's goal is to develop an optimum fitness level, or condition for a sport, it's necessary to challenge the body's systems to a greater degree.

Bibliography and Resources for Further Study

American College of Sports Medicine. *Guidelines for Exercise Testing and Prescription*, 6th Edition. Philadelphia: Lippincott, Williams and Wilkins, 2000.

Blair, Steven N., H. Kohl, R. Paffenbarger, et al. "Physical Fitness and All-Cause Mortality," *JAMA* Vol. 262(17), Nov. 3, 1989, pp. 2395–2401.

Bowers, Richard, and Edward Fox. *Sports Physiology,* 3rd Ed. Dubuque: Wm. C. Brown Publishers, 1992.

Cooper, Kenneth H. "A Means of Assessing Maximal O_2 Uptake," *JAMA* Vol. 203, pp. 201–204, 1968.

Cooper, Kenneth H. *The Aerobics Program for Total Well-being*. New York: M. Evans Co., Inc., 1982.

Cooper, Kenneth H. *Antioxidant Revolution*. Atlanta: Thomas Nelson Publishers, 1994.

Corbin, Charles, Ruth Lindsey, Greg Welk. *Concepts of Physical Fitness*, 10th Ed. Boston: McGraw-Hill, 2000.

Dolgener, Forrest, L. Hensley, J. Marsh, and J. Fjelstul. "Validation of the Rockport Fitness Walking Test in College Males and Females." *Research Quarterly for Exercise and Sport*, Vol. 65 (2), June 1994, pp. 152–158.

Getchell, Bud, Alan Mikesky, and Kay Mikesky. *Physical Fitness—A Way of Life*, 5th Ed. Needham Heights, MA: Allyn & Bacon, 1992.

Harris, Dan (Editor). *Fitness and Exercise Sourcebook*. Omnigraphics, Inc., 1996.

Jackson, Andrew, and Robert Ross. *Understanding Exercise for Health and Fitness*, 3rd Ed. Dubuque: Kendall/Hunt Publishing Co., 1997.

Kline, G.M., J.P. Porcari, R. Huntermeister, et al. "Estimation of VO2 max From A One Mile Track Walk, Gender, Age and Body Weight." *Medicine and Science in Sports and Exercise*, Vol. 19, 1987, 253–259.

McArdle, William, Frank Katch, Victor Katch. *Exercise Physiology—Energy, Nutrition and Human Performance*, 4th Ed. Baltimore: Williams & Wilkins, 1996.

The National Physical Activity Plan for the U.S. Accessed April 02, 2012 http://www. physicalactivityplan.org.

Pate, Russell, Michael Pratt, Steven Blair, et al. "Physical Activity and Public Health," *JAMA* Vol.273(5), Feb. 1, 1995, pp. 402–407.

Physical Activity Guidelines Advisory Committee. 2008. *Physical Activity Guidelines Advisory Committee Report*, 2008. Washington D.C.: U.S. Department of Health and Human Services. Also available at: http://www.health.gov/paguidelines/Report/Default.aspx.

Powers, Scott and Stephen Dodd. *Total Fitness: Exercise, Nutrition and Wellness*, 2nd Ed. Boston: Allyn & Bacon, 1999.

Rippe, James, Ann Ward, William Haskell, et al. "Walking for Fitness," *The Physician And Sportsmedicine*, Vol. 14(10) Oct. 1986, pp. 145–159.

Rippe, James, Ann Ward, John Porcari, Patty Freedson, "Walking for Health and Fitness." *JAMA* Vol 259(18) May 13, 1988, pp. 2720–2724.

U.S. Department of Health, Education, and Welfare (USDHEW). 1979. *Healthy People. The Surgeon General's Report on Health Promotion and Disease Prevention*. Stock No. 017-001-00416-2. Washington, D. C. U.S. Government Printing Office. Also available at: http://www.eric.ed.gov/PDFS/ED186357.pdf.

U.S. Department of Health and Human Services (USDHHS). 2008. *2008 Physical Activity Guidelines for Americans*. Washington, DC: USDHHS. Accessed April 2, 2012. http://www.health.gov/paguidelines/guidelines/default.aspx.

U.S. Department of Health and Human Services (USDHHS). Office of Disease Prevention and Health Promotion. *Healthy People 2020*. Washington, DC. Accessed April 2, 2012. http://www.healthypeople.gov/2020.

Chapter 6

The Musculoskeletal System: Structure and Function

Essential Terms

Aerobic ATP Production ✓   Ligaments ✓

Anaerobic ATP Production ✓   Motor Unit ✓

ATP ✓   Muscle Fiber/Cell ✓

Atrophy ✓   Muscle Tendon ✓

Hypertrophy ✓   Osteoporosis ✓

Hypokinetic ✓   Plastic Elongation ✓

Joint ✓   Strength ✓

Lactic Acid ✓

Objectives

Upon completion of this chapter, students should be able to:

1. Define, explain, and effectively use the essential terms listed above.

2. Accurately identify the primary role of the musculoskeletal system as well as the other roles fulfilled by the bones and muscles.

3. Understand the vital role of movement for the proper functioning of the body.

4. Describe the relationship between physical activity and health.

5. Understand the relationship between a muscle's strength and its endurance.

6. Discuss the major components of a muscle cell and identify the unique property of muscle tissue.

7. Explain strength and understand its determinants.

8. Understand the role of ATP in muscle contraction, and be familiar with the situations in which it is produced aerobically or anaerobically.

9. Identify the factors that affect muscle size.

10. Understand the effect of conditioning and de-conditioning on muscle tissue.

11. Know the effect of exercise and lack of exercise on bone tissue.

12. Understand the typical differences between male and female bones.

13. Identify the changes in cartilage as a result of activity and also conditioning.

14. Understand the role of warm-up in joint and muscle-tendon health.

15. Know the roles of ligaments and muscle tendons, and the effect of conditioning on them.

The Purpose of the Musculoskeletal System

The musculoskeletal system is composed of skeletal muscles, muscle tendons (which connect muscle tissue with bone), the bones of the skeletal system, and ligaments, the connective tissue which joins the bones of the skeleton together at the various joints. The primary and most obvious role of this system is that of movement—willful, purposeful movement. Even a superficial study of the human body gives evidence that it was designed for movement. In most individuals, muscle tissue comprises from 35 to 45 percent of the body mass.

A more thorough analysis of the body reveals that not only is the body designed with movement as a primary purpose, it is designed with movement as a primary need. The body **must** move to function properly. While movement for survival is rather obvious in such instances as jumping out of the way of an oncoming car or withdrawing the hand from a hot stove, movement is also necessary for survival of the body in more subtle ways.

Evidence of the body's need for movement is easily gathered from extreme examples such as the results of bed-rest studies and various clinical conditions like casts and paralysis. Evidence is also available, however, from observation of what is happening to the physical health and well-being of people in technologically advanced cultures where less than 30% of the population is involved in work involving physical labor.

The primary health concerns in high technology cultures, which certainly includes the United States, involve HYPOKINETIC conditions. These are health problems contributed to or caused by inadequate regular activity ("hypo"—less than, deficient in; "kinetic"—of motion). There is a growing body of evidence demonstrating that the lack of sufficient physical activity in our lives due to the increased sedentary nature of our daily living habits poses a serious threat to the health of our bodies, ultimately causing major deterioration in normal body functioning. Conditions such as coronary artery disease, high blood pressure (hypertension), strokes, obesity, depression, osteoporosis, low back syndrome, and some cancers have all been strongly linked with insufficient physical activity. In both *Healthy People 2010* and *2020,* goals include a reduction in the incidence of osteoporosis. This reinforces the importance of maintaining good bone health throughout life and the key role bone health plays in quality of life. The identification of muscular strength, muscular endurance, and flexibility as areas needing increased attention in Goal #22 of *Healthy People 2010* reinforces the critical role of the entire musculoskeletal system in maintaining "healthy people." (U.S. Department of Health and Human Services)

Roles of the Musculoskeletal System

Since regular, appropriate activity is so critical to the optimal functioning of the whole person, diligent and knowledgeable care must be given the musculoskeletal system so that it can consistently provide the needed movement. Movement for physical, psychological, intellectual, and even spiritual wellness is dependent on a sound, healthy musculoskeletal system.

In addition to being the basis of the body's capacity to move, the bones and muscle tissue fulfill other essential functions for the body. Following are some of the less obvious, but no less essential, functions fulfilled by the bones and muscles:

Bones

- provide the framework and underlying form for the body

- provide protection for vital organs such as the brain, heart, and lungs

- compose a complex lever system that efficiently converts the forces produced by muscle tissue into useful movement for the body

- produce red blood cells as signalled by the body

- store calcium, phosphorous, and iron

Muscles

- are the major calorie-consuming tissues in the body

- assist in regulating body temperature

- assist in returning blood to the heart through the venous system

- provide protection for organs and structures in abdominal cavity

- help maintain the posture of the body (necessary for proper functioning)

- contribute to a sense of well-being and healthy self-concept through their tone

It is readily apparent that the musculoskeletal system contributes significantly to the functioning capacity of the body, and must receive a place of priority in our body stewardship efforts.

Muscles

There are over 600 skeletal muscles in the body, most of which are paired in two ways. For most, there is a muscle on the left side of the body which corresponds with one on the right side. In addition, each muscle or muscle group that causes one action (referred to as the agonist) is paired with a muscle or muscle group that causes the opposite action (referred to as the antagonist). (See Figures 6.1, 6.2.) Each muscle is composed of several bundles of muscle cells, called muscle fibers. The arrangement of these bundles of fibers, and the resulting shape of the muscle is that which can best accomplish the task within the body for which it was

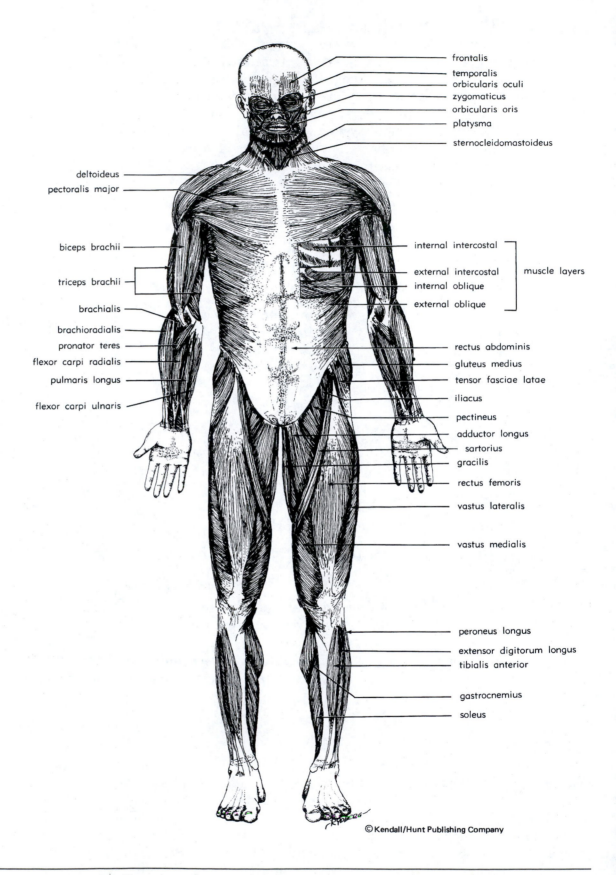

frontalis
temporalis
orbicularis oculi
zygomaticus
orbicularis oris
platysma
sternocleidomastoideus

deltoideus
pectoralis major

biceps brachii

triceps brachii

brachialis
brachioradialis
pronator teres
flexor carpi radialis
pulmaris longus
flexor carpi ulnaris

internal intercostal
external intercostal
internal oblique
external oblique

muscle layers

rectus abdominis
gluteus medius
tensor fasciae latae
iliacus
pectineus
adductor longus
sartorius
gracilis
rectus femoris
vastus lateralis
vastus medialis

peroneus longus
extensor digitorum longus
tibialis anterior
gastrocnemius
soleus

© Kendall/Hunt Publishing Company

Figure 6.1 | Human muscular system, anterior view.

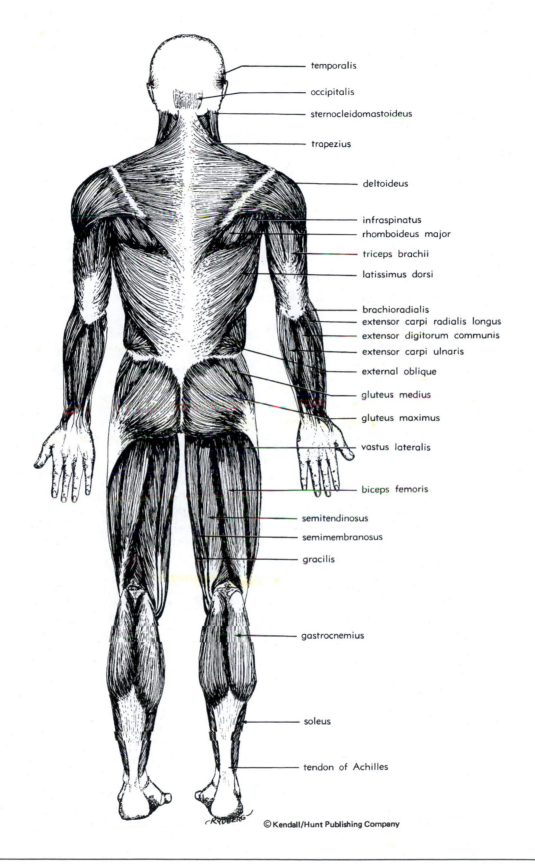

temporalis

occipitalis

sternocleidomastoideus

trapezius

deltoideus

infraspinatus

rhomboideus major

triceps brachii

latissimus dorsi

brachioradialis

extensor carpi radialis longus

extensor digitorum communis

extensor carpi ulnaris

external oblique

gluteus medius

gluteus maximus

vastus lateralis

biceps femoris

semitendinosus

semimembranosus

gracilis

gastrocnemius

soleus

tendon of Achilles

© Kendall/Hunt Publishing Company

Figure 6.2 | Human muscular system, posterior view.

designed. Connective tissue surrounding each of the cells and each of the bundles blends together at each end of the muscle to form the muscle tendon. This strong, inelastic band of connective tissue is continuous with the outer layer of the bone (periosteum). The tendon transfers the force produced by thousands of contractile elements within hundreds of thousands of muscle cells in the muscle to the bone, causing movement.

Most muscle fibers are connected to the central nervous system by one motor nerve which carries the nerve impulse necessary to cause the fiber to contract. This one motor nerve, however, may connect with as few as ten or as many as two thousand muscle fibers within a given muscle, depending on the degree of precision possessed by that muscle. The motor nerve and all of the muscle fibers it connects is referred to as a MOTOR UNIT. When the body requires different amounts of force from a muscle, it can call upon fewer or more motor units, or smaller or larger motor units. If a particular motor unit is fatigued, other motor units within the muscle that innervate the same total number of muscle fibers can be recruited to do the work. That is a major reason why a stronger muscle has more endurance than a weaker muscle: it has more motor units to recruit when those doing the work become fatigued.

A muscle cell is composed of 75 percent water and 25 percent solid materials, of which 20 percent are protein contractile filaments (actin and myosin). Muscle cells range in length from 1 mm. to 400 mm., and range in diameter from just .01 mm. to .1 mm. Their unique property is that of contractility: their protein filaments can interact and cause the cell to shorten or contract. The energy molecule necessary for this to occur is ATP (adenosine triphosphate).

The amount of force that a muscle can produce (its STRENGTH) is based on the number of chemical interactions that can occur between the cells' protein filaments. The number of interactions and the rate at which they can occur is based on the amount of ATP available, the level of various enzymes (chemical catalysts), and the number of protein filaments. These things are determined by genetics, nutrition, androgen (male hormone) levels, and amount of regular exercise (conditioning).

Muscle cells have the ability to produce ATP three different ways, depending primarily on how much ATP is needed and how fast. If large amounts are needed quickly, they must be supplied ANAEROBICALLY, or without the processing of oxygen. Muscle cells have two ways of doing this. The fastest way is by using the energy available in molecules of phosphocreatine to directly combine ADP and phosphate to make ATP. This requires no oxygen directly and can occur very rapidly, but has a very limited capacity.

The other method of making ATP without oxygen directly (anaerobic) involves a process called "anaerobic glycolysis," or the metabolizing of glycogen or glucose to the point of producing pyruvic acid. In this process, ATP molecules are formed. If the cell is unable to immediately oxidize a given pyruvic acid molecule, it is then reduced metabolically to the substance known as LACTIC ACID. While this process is relatively fast, it is not as fast as the phosphocreatine source, but faster at producing ATP's than the aerobic method. This method of producing ATP's has a greater capacity than the method which utilizes phosphocreatine, but less than the AEROBIC method.

If relatively smaller amounts of ATP are needed for a long period of time, they are supplied AEROBICALLY, or through the processing of oxygen. This is the typical situation in the muscle at rest or during relatively low, prolonged, force-production efforts (maintaining posture, walking, holding a book, or any of the other activities referred to as aerobic).

Some cells naturally have a greater aerobic ability (red or slow-twitch fibers), and some have a greater natural anaerobic ability (white or fast-twitch fibers). Most of us have a fairly even distribution of these types of muscle fibers in the muscles throughout our body. However, postural muscles like the soleus in the lower leg have predominantly red fibers, and the orbicularis oculi, a muscle involved in blinking, has 85% white fibers for its short, fast efforts. Total body fiber type variations are found in some elite endurance athletes whose unusually high percentages of red fibers throughout their bodies help insure success in their events.

Response of Muscle Tissue to Exercise

As was indicated, the size of a muscle cell and therefore of the entire muscle is determined initially by genetic code and then by nutrition, androgen levels, and exercise. The typical American diet can adequately provide the necessary nutrients for the growth and development of muscle tissue. Only rarely in extremely long and strenuous muscular efforts would additional protein foods need to be added to the diet. While strength development exercise programs can cause a significant increase in muscle strength, the actual increase in muscle size (as well as the potential for increase in muscle size) is strictly regulated by genetics and androgen levels. Exercise cannot make you something you were not designed to be; it can only enhance what you are.

Muscle tissue is a very dynamic tissue. Its state of functioning is primarily dependent on its use. If it is required to produce more force than usual over a period of time (conditioning), it responds by making changes that increase its ability to produce force. If it is required to produce less force than usual for a period of time, it responds with changes that decrease its ability to produce force. Thus, conditioning causes a muscle to get stronger; inactivity causes a muscle to get weaker.

The nerve that stimulates the muscle cell has a trophic or growth affect on it. Studies have shown that fiber type (slow or fast-twitch) is determined by the nerve that stimulates it. It is reasonable that the increased nerve stimulation that takes place when the cell is exercised at greater levels causes the training response in the cell to occur.

As the cell gets stronger, it gets firmer. Thus we find that a trained muscle has better tone or firmness. Depending on the type and amount of exercise, as well as on the androgen levels in the body, the muscle will also experience HYPERTRO-PHY which is an increase in size. The decrease in size that occurs when a muscle is inadequately used or immobilized is called ATROPHY. Muscles respond to training by becoming stronger, firmer, and especially in males, significantly larger. Muscles respond to inactivity by becoming weaker, softer, and smaller. The idea that "if you don't use it, you'll lose it" most definitely applies to muscle tissue.

Bones

The 206 bones that compose the skeletal system begin in the embryo as flexible cartilage and are found in the octogenarian as a somewhat brittle, non-resilient structure. Bones, even more than muscle tissue, are in a constant state of flux. They are composed of tough, pliable collagen fibers forming a matrix in which crystalline salts, primarily calcium and phosphate, are deposited. These combine to form a tissue that has great tensile and compressional strength. "…bones are constructed in exactly the same way that reinforced concrete is constructed. The steel of reinforced concrete provides the tensile strength, while the cement, sand, and rock provide the compressional strength. Indeed the compressional strength of bone is greater than that of even the best reinforced concrete, and the tensile strength approaches that of steel in reinforced concrete" (Guyton & Hall, p. 989).

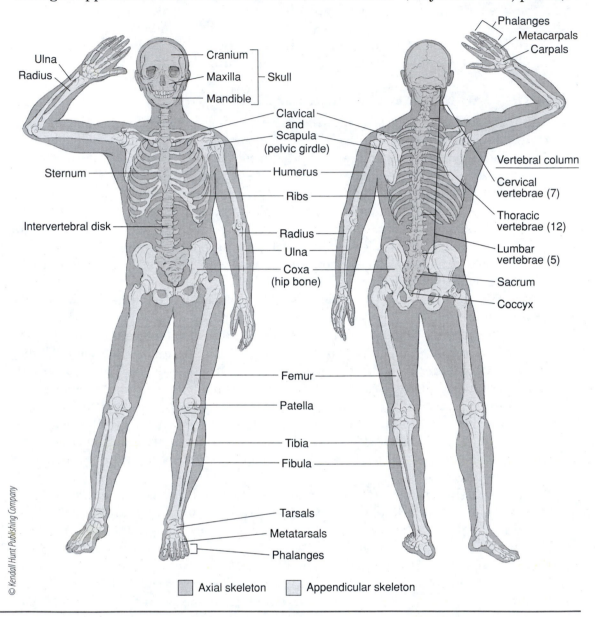

Figure 6.3 | Human skeleton.

Response of Bone Tissue to Exercise

Like muscle, bone is also responsive to the activity that it experiences. "Increased weight bearing will result in thickness of the bone and density of the shaft... The maintenance of the normal mineral metabolism of the bones... depends upon the longitudinal pressure on the long bones brought about by the stress of gravity on the upright, ambulatory human frame" (Astrand and Rodahl, p. 277). Regular exercise accelerates the rate of bone deposition, and elimination of regular weight bearing leads to disuse osteoporosis, or a loss of bone density because of insufficient activity to stimulate bone growth. Excessive stress can also lead, in a fascinating demonstration of the rule that moderation is best, to loss of mineral density in the bone which can result in stress fractures (Malone, et al., p. 21).

Osteoporosis

One of the goals stated in *Healthy People 2020* is the prevention of illness and disability stemming from OSTEOPOROSIS, or loss of mineral density in bone. This condition affects 13–18% of women and 3–6% of men over the age of 50. In the United States, that means 4–6 million women and 1–2 million men are affected. The primary health consequence of osteoporosis is hip fracture; 1 in 3 women and 1 in 17 men will experience hip fracture secondary to osteoporosis. An average of 24% of hip fracture patients age 50 and older die in the year following the fracture, with men having a higher death rate than women (*Healthy People 2010*, p. 2–5).

Preservation of bone mineral density requires attention to both diet and physical exercise. A diet that is adequate in both calories and calcium is needed for strong bones, as is vigorous exercise. This is true throughout life, but especially so during childhood and adolescence. Bone tissue is particularly responsive to exercise in late childhood and adolescence; about 60% of one's final skeletal mass is acquired during this time. Maximizing weight-bearing exercise, along with appropriate diet during this time seems an effective strategy for osteoporosis prevention (Shaw and Snow, p. 102).

Physical activity strengthens bone both by weight bearing against gravity, and by the pull of working muscles on their bony attachments. To be effective in increasing bone mass, exercise must be greater than the skeleton is accustomed to; that is, it must be overloaded. Participation in high-resistance, low-repetition exercise, such as weight training, has been shown beneficial even in the elderly (Shaw and Snow, p. 104).

Loss of bone density will occur in everyone to a degree. It is greater in females, and is accelerated by estrogen loss at menopause. Persons of small stature and/ or of Asian or Northern European descent are at increased risk. These individuals need not accept osteoporosis as inevitable, but do need to implement a preventive strategy that includes attention to both diet and exercise.

Joints

Joints are formed where two or more bones of the skeletal system come together. There are six different types of moving (diarthrodial) joints in the body, each designed to support different types of movement. (See Tables 6.1, 6.2 and Figure 6.4). Most moving joints are surrounded by a fibrous joint capsule lined with a synovial membrane that covers everything except the ends of the bones. The bone ends are covered with a smooth cartilage, and the synovial membrane secretes a lubricating fluid into the joint space each of which helps minimize friction in the joint. Some joints, like the knee, have a fibrous cartilage disc between the two bone surfaces which acts as a shock-absorbing agent. This cartilage also helps insure perfect contact between the moving joint surfaces throughout all of the points in the range of motion.

Table 6.1	Joint and Joint Actions in the Body	
Joint	Joint Type(s)	Movements
Neck	Pivot, Gliding	Flexion, extension, rotation, lateral bending
Trunk	Fibrous joints	Flexion, extension, rotation, lateral bending
Shoulder joint	Ball and socket	Flexion, extension, rotation, abduction, adduction, horizontal abduction and adduction
Elbow	Hinge	Flexion, extension
Wrist	Gliding	Flexion, extension
Hip	Ball and socket	Flexion, extension, rotation, abduction, adduction, horizontal abduction and adduction
Knee	Hinge	Flexion, extension
Ankle	Hinge	Plantar flexion, dorsiflexion
Thumb	Saddle	Flexion, extension, abduction, adduction
Finger/hand	Condyloid	Flexion, extension, abduction, adduction

Table 6.2	Definitions of Joint Actions
Joint Action	Definition
Flexion	Decreasing the angle between two bones
Extension	Increasing the angle between two bones
Hyperextension	Overextension (moving beyond full extension)
Plantar Flexion	Moving the sole of the foot downward
Dorsi Flexion	Moving the top of the foot upward
Abduction	Moving away from middle of body or part
Adduction	Moving toward midline of body or part
Lateral bending	Bending spinal column to side
Rotation	Turning about the vertical axis of the bone

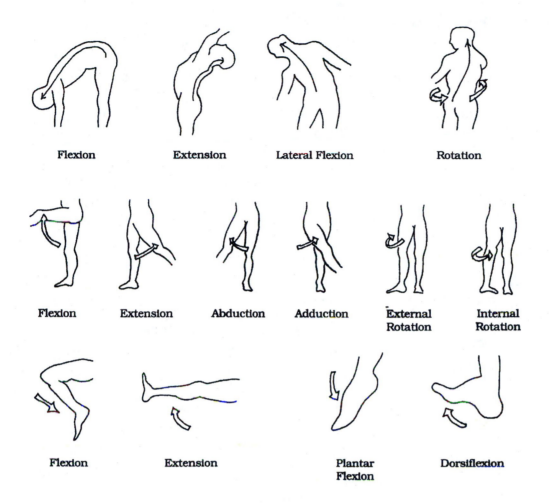

Flexion Extension Lateral Flexion Rotation

Flexion Extension Abduction Adduction External Rotation Internal Rotation

Flexion Extension Plantar Flexion Dorsiflexion

Figure 6.4 | Body movements.

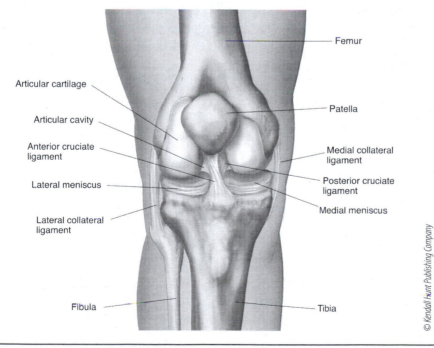

Femur

Articular cartilage

Patella

Articular cavity

Anterior cruciate ligament

Medial collateral ligament

Lateral meniscus

Posterior cruciate ligament

Medial meniscus

Lateral collateral ligament

Fibula

Tibia

© Kendall Hunt Publishing Company

Figure 6.5 | Synovial joint.

Response of Joints to Exercise

Regular, dynamic motion of the joints causes the joint cartilage to be better nourished and thus healthier (Astrand, p. 284). Studies have shown that during activity, the cartilage in the joint gradually swells. In response to increased regular activity (conditioning), the cartilage actually grows thicker. Each of these changes causes an increase in the contact surface area, resulting in less pressure per unit of surface area, which in turn makes the joint structures less susceptible to injury. This demonstrates the importance of proper warm-up before each exercise effort as well as the benefits of regular activity with regard to joint health.

Connective Tissue

Muscle Tendons

Muscle tendons are the combined extensions of the connective tissue surrounding all of the muscle fibers and bundles of fibers. Tendons are fibrous, non-elastic tissue which join muscle tissue to bone. They are the connective tissue link between the force-producing muscle cells and the movement-effecting lever system, the skeleton. Many muscle tendons cross joints and thus affect both the stability and the flexibility of the joints. Tendons become thicker and denser as the muscle tissue becomes stronger.

Ligaments

Ligaments are composed of connective tissue similar in composition to that of tendons. Ligaments connect bone with bone, sometimes alone and sometimes in conjunction with a joint capsule. Ligaments play a primary role in the stability and flexibility of joints. If they are caused to undergo an extreme stretch, which might occur in joint sprains and dislocations, they experience what is referred to as PLASTIC ELONGATION and will never resume their original length. This can cause joint instability and lead to accelerated joint deterioration and arthritis unless muscle-tendon units are strengthened to help compensate for the loss of ligament support.

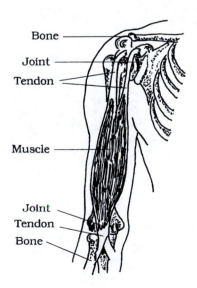

Figure 6.6 │ A typical muscle showing major anatomic structures.

Table 6.3	Summary of Effects of Conditioning on the Musculoskeletal System
Component	**Effect of Conditioning**
Muscles	Increased muscle strength
	Increased muscle endurance
	Decreased fat surrounding muscle
	Increased muscle size (hypertrophy), especially in males
	Increased ability to "burn" calories
	Increased muscle tone or firmness
Bones	Increased density
Joints	Increased cartilage thickness
Connective Tissue	Increased thickness and tensile strength

Joint Capsules

The joint capsule is a fibrous capsule which surrounds the ends of adjoining bones. It defines the joint area and contains the joint fluids. It is often strengthened by ligaments and is lined with a synovial membrane, a specialized tissue which secretes lubricating fluid (synovium) into the joint.

Summary

Stewardship of the musculoskeletal system involves keeping the muscles, bones, joints, and connective tissues in the best possible condition. Since regular, appropriate movement is so critical to the functioning of the entire body, wise and diligent care of the musculoskeletal system is foundational to good body stewardship. Although the details will vary among individuals since each of us has a specific role with specific requirements to fulfill, we are all subject to the same natural laws that God has designed into the body for its preservation. The next two chapters will review how to practice good stewardship of the musculoskeletal system in light of these natural laws.

Bibliography and Resources for Further Study

ASCM, (Walter Thompson, ED) (Ed.) *ACSM's Guidelines for Exercise Testing and Prescription*, 8th Edition. Philadelphia, PA: Lippincott Kluwer Williams & Wilkins, 2010.

Astrand, Per-Olof, and K. Rodahl. *Textbook of Work Physiology: Physiological Bases of Exercise*, 3rd Edition. New York: McGraw-Hill Book Co., 1986.

Baechle, Thomas R. and Roger Earle, Eds. *Essentials of Strength Training and Conditioning / National Strength and Conditioning Association*, 3rd Edition. Champaign, IL: Human Kinetics, 2008.

Corbin, Charles B., Ruth Lindsey, and Greg Welk. *Concepts of Physical Fitness: Active Lifestyles for Wellness*. 16th Edition. Dubuque, IA: McGraw-Hill Humanities, 2010.

Delavier, Frederic. *Strength Training Anatomy*. 3rd Edition., Human Kinetics, 2010.

Guyton, Arthur C. *Textbook of Medical Physiology*, 9th Edition. Philadelphia, PA: W.B. Saunders, 1996.

Jackson, Allen W., J. R. Morrow Jr., D. W. Hill, and R. K. Dishman. *Physical Activity for Health and Fitness: An Individualized Lifetime Approach*. Updated Edition. Champaign IL: Human Kinetics, 2004.

McArdle, William D., Frank I Katch, and Victor L. Katch. *Essentials of Exercise Physiology*, 2nd Edition. Baltimore, MD: Lippincott Williams & Wilkins, 2000.

Malone, Terry R, Thomas McPoil, and Arthur J. Nitz. *Orthopedic and Sports Physical Therapy*, 3rd Edition. St. Louis, MO: Mosby-Year Book, Inc., 1997.

Nieman, David C. *Exercise Testing and Prescription*, 5th Edition. Mountain View, CA: Mayfield Publishing Co., 2003.

Physical Activity Guidelines Advisory Committee. *2008. Physical Activity Guidelines Advisory Committee Report*, 2008. Washington D.C.: U.S. Department of Health and Human Services. Also available at: http://www.health.gov/paguidelines/Report/Default.aspx.

Salem, George and J. E. Turman, Jr. "Neuromuscular Function and Adaptation to Exercise." In *Clinical Exercise Testing and Prescription: Theory and Application*, S. O. Roberts, R. A. Robergs, and P. Hanson, Eds. New York: CRC Press, 1997.

Shaw, Janet M., and Christine Snow. "Osteoporosis and Physical Activity." In *Toward a Better Understanding of Physical Fitness & Activity*, Charles Corbin and Robert Pangrazi, Eds. Scottsdale, AZ: Holcomb Hathaway, Publishers, 1999.

U.S. Department of Health and Human Services (USDHHS). 2008. *2008 Physical Activity Guidelines for Americans*. Washington, DC: USDHHS. Accessed April 2, 2012. http://www.health.gov/paguidelines/guidelines/default.aspx.

U.S. Department of Health and Human Services. *Healthy People 2010: Understanding and Improving Health*. 2nd ed. Washington, D.C. U.S. Government Printing Office, November 2000.

U.S. Department of Health and Human Services (USDHHS). Office of Disease Prevention and Health Promotion. *Healthy People 2020*. Washington, DC. Accessed April 2, 2012. http://www.healthypeople.gov/2020.

Chapter 7

Conditioning for Muscle Strength and Muscle Endurance

Essential Terms

Anabolic Steroids ✓   Isokinetic Exercise ✓

Creatine ✓   Isometric Exercise ✓

Concentric Contraction ✓   Isotonic Exercise ✓

Delayed Onset Muscle Soreness (DOMS) ✓   Muscle Tone ✓

Eccentric Contraction ✓

Objectives

Upon completion of this chapter, students should be able to:

1. Define and correctly use the terms above.

2. Explain why muscle strength and endurance are important to optimal well-being.

3. Identify factors that affect muscle strength and muscle endurance.

4. Appropriately apply the principles of training to muscle conditioning.

5. Safely and effectively use strength training equipment

6. Commit to an ongoing program of personal muscle conditioning.

Why Muscle Conditioning?

It is a common, and mistaken, idea that muscle conditioning is only needed by athletes, body builders, or those whose jobs require heavy muscular work. Women have tended to view strength training as "just for men"; they have feared that muscle conditioning would cause them to develop a "masculine" looking physique. Men have thought that a few weeks of strength training would give them an "Adonis-like" appearance.

All of those ideas are untrue. The fact is that everyone needs strong muscles for reasons that have nothing to do with appearance or athletic performance. Women *will not* develop thick, bulky musculature as result of strength training, though they will greatly increase in strength. Men will develop more visible musculature than women, but not necessarily that of a Greek statue as a result of strength training. The muscle size and definition they develop greatly depends on their hereditary body type and subcutaneous fat.

Everything you do, from carrying your luggage into the dorm or lugging those heavy textbooks to class, to playing your favorite sport, requires muscle strength. If your muscles are weak, then tasks require a greater percentage of your strength capacity every time you do them. Over the course of the day, that adds up to significant fatigue. The stronger your muscles, the smaller is the proportion of their strength capacity that is required by your daily activities. Thus you are not worn-out by your everyday tasks. You are more likely to have energy remaining for sports, recreation and, yes… more effective study.

Obviously, stronger muscles help you to perform better in all kinds of movement tasks. There are some other advantages to strengthening your skeletal muscles. One of those is the *prevention of injury*. Not all of our joints are equally stable from a structural standpoint; in our knee joint for example, God chose the design that maximizes our mobility, agility and ability to jump. Knowing that the bony structure of such a joint is such that it is prone to torque injury, He provided muscles which, if they are strong, greatly reduce the likelihood of injury. Similarly, our vertebral column is a marvel of mobility. However, back pain is an extremely common complaint, even among young people; it most often is brought on by lifting or twisting in a way that the muscles that stabilize the column are not prepared to handle. Strengthening those muscles minimizes the risk of injury.

With increases in muscle strength there is a degree of increase in the amount of muscle tissue one has. That is advantageous because it increases one's rate of metabolism. That is of particular importance in weight management; our metabolism is the rate at which we burn calories in the maintenance of basic life processes. So, by increasing our muscle mass, we somewhat increase our calorie-use even at rest, which aids in weight control.

The cellular changes that occur when skeletal muscle is strengthened also afford the advantage of *improvement in our ability to efficiently use glucose*. The cell's insulin receptor sensitivity increases, allowing the cells to efficiently use sugars derived from the foods we eat, and keeping blood sugar within a normal range. Since a below-par glucose metabolism places one at risk for diabetes, this is definitely an advantage.

Finally, since muscles are anchored to bones, when they work stresses are transferred to the bones. God built into bones the ability to adapt to increased mechanical forces by increasing their mineral and collagen (a protein substance) content, resulting in stronger more dense bones. So strengthening one's muscles has the advantage of *increasing bone density and tensile strength* as well. The increased bone density affords one a stronger, more injury-resistant skeletal structure now, and later in life, when bone density decreases due to aging. Muscle resistance exercise is a powerful deterrent to osteoporosis, and its "side effects" (prevention of injury and preservation of joints, increased ability to use calories, and improved ability to efficiently use glucose) make it a very clear treatment of choice for preventing this debilitating condition.

Muscle Strength

Muscle strength is defined as the maximum amount of force a muscle (or muscle group, since muscles rarely work alone) can produce in a single all-out effort. We rarely need to apply such an all-out effort, but it is an important concept, because it defines the upper limit of our muscles' capacity for producing force.

The amount of force a muscle can produce is dependent on ready availability of the energy substrate or "raw material" muscles use (ATP—adenosine triphosphate), the enzymes necessary for its utilization, and the size of the muscle. The muscles of men and women have the same force production capacity per unit of cross-sectional area; women, however, typically have approximately two-thirds the muscle strength of men. That is because, though there is significant variation in muscle mass within each gender, most men have proportionately greater muscle mass than most women. This is due to the influence of the hormone testosterone; men have approximately 15 times the amount of this hormone as women do. Since one of testosterone's effects is to cause hypertrophy of muscle tissue, it follows that men will have greater muscle mass than women and will experience significantly greater increases in muscle mass as a result of conditioning than women.

The capacity of a muscle group to produce maximal force at a particular point in time is dependent on several factors. They are:

1. *Muscle size*: The greater the cross-sectional area of muscle tissue, the more muscle fibers there are to contract, the greater the force that can be produced. The amount of muscle tissue is determined by gender, heredity, nutritional status and state of conditioning.

2. *Coordination of nerve impulses to the muscles*: You recall from the last chapter that muscle is organized functionally into motor units. When we perform a particular movement, we "recruit" motor units; the more effectively we do this, the greater is the net force we produce. We know that early in a strength training program, one can progress fairly quickly in the amount of resistance they are using; part of that rapid progress is "learning" to effectively recruit motor units.

3. *Psychological inhibitions*: Our ability to produce muscle force is partially dependent on our allowing the muscle to contract as forcefully as it can. If we fear that muscle contraction will "hurt", we are unlikely to make the muscle work. We need to learn the feeling of effort that occurs when a muscle works against resistance, distinguishing it from the "pain" of injury. In doing so, we can over-ride some of those inhibitions. In times of excitement, competition or danger, those inhibitions are overridden by adrenal hormones, sometimes resulting in great feats of strength. Those unusual bursts of muscle force give a glimpse of the potential of human muscle, and of what may be achieved by systematically conditioning.

4. *Fatigue*: Local muscle fatigue, general physical fatigue, and psychological fatigue all interfere with muscle strength. One of the purposes of strength conditioning is to delay the onset of fatigue by increasing the force production capacity of the muscle.

Muscle Endurance

Muscle endurance is the ability of a muscle group to produce a less-than-maximum force repeatedly, or to maintain a contracted state for an extended period of time. This differs from CARDIORESPIRATORY ENDURANCE discussed in Chapter 5; this type of endurance is a function of skeletal muscle tissue itself. The endurance of skeletal muscle is based in the capacity of muscle cells to produce energy (in the form of ATP) both anaerobically and aerobically. The energy production process used to fuel a particular muscle endurance task is determined by how much force the effort requires. A task requiring little force is supported by aerobic ATP production; the greater the force needed, the more dependent it is on anaerobic energy production. The interplay of these quite different biochemical energy-producing mechanisms underlies all of our movement activities.

Muscle endurance is related to strength, but the relationship lies in the ATP-production process as well as in the muscle's force-production capacity. Suppose that two people, Bill and Bob are given the task of repeatedly lifting a 35 lb. weight. Bill's maximal strength in the muscle group used for lifting is 100 lbs. while Bob's is 50 lbs. Bill's muscle will only be working at 35% of its capacity (35/100) while Bob's will be working at 70% of capacity (35/50). Bob's muscle tissue will make ATP by the anaerobic series of reactions, resulting in lactic acid as a metabolic by-product, which causes fatigue. Bill's muscle tissue will produce most of the energy needed by aerobic processes, with very little lactic acid accumulation.

As we strengthen skeletal muscle, it improves not only in ability to produce force, but also in its ability to produce ATP aerobically. The more a muscle works aerobically, the less the amount of lactic acid produced; the less the lactic acid, the less we experience the combination of sensations we term "fatigue". When we do muscle conditioning, we are working to improve both strength and endurance.

Types of Exercise for Strength and Muscular Endurance

There are three major categories of exercises that can be used to increase muscle strength and endurance. They are based on the kind of resistance used to create a force for the muscle to work against or resist (thus the term "muscle resistance exercises").

ISOMETRIC exercise involves an unchanging and immovable resistance. The muscle contracts, but no movement occurs. One might push against a doorframe, or some other immovable object, or simple tighten a muscle group (like the muscles on the front of the thigh) without moving the leg. Research has shown that isometrics do increase strength, but only in the joint positions the exercises are done. We desire better muscle force production throughout a joint's range of motion as opposed to just one position, so for most of us, isometrics are not a good choice. One situation in which they are quite valuable, however, is in the immediate post-operative period following joint surgery, before one can actively move the joint. Isometric contraction of muscles will help to preserve muscle strength while the joint is more or less immobile to allow for healing.

ISOKINETIC exercise uses a device that holds constant the rate of speed with which an exercise movement is done. The amount of muscular force applied may be minimal or maximal, but the speed is controlled by hydraulic cylinders, or by electrical resistance. In theory, one can work a muscle group to its maximum capacity throughout the range of motion. These kinds of devices are most useful in testing the strength of specific muscle groups, or in rehabilitation work.

ISOTONIC exercise involves a muscle group contracting against a resistance to move that resistance through a range of motion. The muscle contracts, and movement occurs. Lifting a barbell is an example; if you grasp the bar with a palm-up grasp and flex your elbows bringing the bar to your chest, your elbow flexors shorten in what is called a CONCENTRIC CONTRACTION. When you gradually lower the bar, the muscle works, but lengthens, which is called an ECCENTRIC CONTRACTION.

If one uses free weights (barbells, dumbbells), the "effective resistance" against which you work is not the same throughout the range of the movement. If you hold a 10-pound dumbbell at your side and flex your elbow, you must exert more than 10 pounds of force to bring the weight to the middle of the range of motion, and less than 10 pounds to complete the movement arc. A muscle can exert its greatest force through the mid-portion of the joint's range of motion; it can exert its least force in either full extension or full contraction. Thus the 10-pound weight may cause the muscle to use 70% of its force production ability at the beginning and end of the effort, but only 50% of what it can do in the middle portion of the effort.

By using a system of cams, levers and pulleys, exercise devices like those produced by Nautilus or Cybex vary the amount of effective resistance the muscle works against; thus this equipment better matches what the muscle can do throughout the range of motion. The effective force produced by the muscle's contraction allows it to utilize close to the same percentage of its force production ability throughout the effort. Theoretically, the muscle is more efficiently trained if it must work at a higher percentage of its force-producing capacity throughout the range of movement.

Exercise using free weights is termed *constant resistance* isotonic exercise, because the amount of resistance is the same throughout the exercise. Use of exercise machines like those described above is called *variable resistance* isotonic exercise, because the machine is designed to vary the resistance throughout the range of motion of an exercise and thereby more closely match the force production ability of the muscle group throughout that effort. Both are effective in increasing/maintaining muscular strength, provided they are used in accord with the *principles of training* presented in this chapter.

For the average person whose goal for a muscle conditioning program is personal fitness, the variable resistance machines are ideal because they are safe, effective, and very user-friendly. The weight selection is such that even a very de-conditioned person can find a resistance they can handle to get started. The design of the machines allows one to concentrate on specific muscle groups; a workout in which several of the machines are used allows one to get a good workout in an efficient manner. Use of the variable resistance machines is safe, in that there is no danger of dropping a weight on one's foot. They are also adaptable to adults of most sizes and shapes.

For the serious athlete who is conditioning for competition, use of free weights may be the better mode of muscle resistance training. When using free weights, the individual must recruit muscle groups other than those being emphasized in order to control the weight, and stabilize the body while handling the weight. For a sport like football, for example, training with free weights is more like what is experienced in competition.

This text is being written primarily for the person whose purpose in strength training is improved personal health and fitness. For that reason, the type of training discussed will be the use of variable resistance exercise equipment.

Guidelines for Developing Muscular Strength and Endurance

1. **For a muscle group to become stronger, it must be made to overcome a resistance outside its present "comfort zone", and that resistance must be increased as the muscles become stronger.** That is known as the principle of "progressive overload". We suggest that you (through "trial and error") determine a

resistance at which you can do a specific exercise properly for 8-12 repetitions. For each repetition, you should count to two during the first phase of the effort, and count to four during the return to the starting position. Remember, the purpose is to work the muscle group, not to move the weight. We use the weight to create the experience for the muscle. Don't minimize or compromise the benefit by doing each repetition too fast. The muscle group should be fatigued; if 12 repetitions do not produce fatigue, you need to increase the weight. As a muscle group becomes stronger, you will need to increase the amount of resistance to produce fatigue.

2. **The workout should include exercises for all the major muscle groups.** In a series of 10–12 exercises, muscle groups of the arms, shoulders, trunk and legs should be worked. Our bodies are designed so that muscle groups work in pairs at each of the body's joints. The elbow and knee flexors are paired with groups that are extensors of those joints. Muscles along the spinal column extend the trunk; muscles of the abdominal wall flex the trunk, and so on through all the body's major joints. The workout should include exercises for all our major "pairs" of muscle groups.

3. **For purposes of personal fitness, a strength/endurance workout need include just one set of 8–12 repetitions of each exercise.** Formerly it was thought, and taught, that one had to do at least 3 sets of each exercise in a workout to achieve significant gains in muscle strength. Wilmore and Costill, for their textbook *Physiology of Sport and Exercise*, Third Edition (2004), reviewed studies that compared single sets to multiple sets with regard to strength gains achieved. They concluded that workouts consisting of a single set of several different exercises were just as effective as workouts including three sets of the same exercises for increasing muscle strength. Thus, it is possible to put together a strength workout consisting of exercises for all the major muscle groups that can be easily completed in an hour. That is really important as we strive to incorporate a personal exercise program into our busy lifestyles.

We emphasize that the exercise program we are talking about here is that of the busy college student or working professional who must find time to exercise in a daily schedule already crowded with the responsibilities and demands of work and study. Serious competitive athletes have muscle strength and endurance needs specific to their sport, and should follow the advice of their strength training coaches or personal trainers.

4. **Breathe properly when exercising.** When doing moderate to heavy muscular work, we tend to take a breath and hold it, tightening the muscles of the chest and abdomen. This is called a Valsalva maneuver; it results in a sharp rise in pressure within the chest cavity, and thus should be avoided because of the danger it presents to the cardiovascular system. Experts do not agree as to which part of the breathing cycle should occur during the muscle shortening part of the exercise, and which during the lengthening phase, but the essential thing is that your BREATH SHOULD NOT BE HELD during the exercise effort (Aaberg, p. 47).

5. **Plan to do your muscle strength/endurance workouts two or three days/week.** Strength-building exercises bring about a "remodeling" of skeletal muscle cells, which results in larger and stronger muscles. Muscles need 48–72 hours to make those changes, and be ready for the next workout. Research has shown that people working out for personal fitness two days/week achieve 75% of the strength gains made by those who workout three days/week (Westcott, p. 33). While three workouts a week is ideal, two will also bring significant strength gains.

6. **When you have achieved your strength goals (or have reached your strength potential for specific muscle groups) work on the endurance of those muscle groups.** Reduce the weight for the exercise, and do 1–3 sets of 10–15 repetitions.

Muscle Soreness

Most of us have experienced the muscle soreness that sets in a day or two after we have done activities to which our muscles are not accustomed. The clinical term for this is DELAYED ONSET MUSCLE SORENESS (D.O.M.S.). The causes of this are not completely understood, but there is agreement that it results from a combination of micro-trauma to the muscle cell membrane, leakage of intracellular enzymes and other substances into the extra-cellular space, and inflammation resulting from those processes (Wilmore and Costill, p. 102). We know that, even for athletes, starting a training program at a lower intensity and increasing gradually decreases soreness considerably. Also, most find that a short aerobic warm-up gets the muscles "ready" for a strength workout, and that post-workout stretching tends to lessen muscle soreness. The soreness will gradually lessen and disappear, and should not interfere with continuing your workout schedule.

Once in a while, a muscle that is working will contract in a painful "cramp". Exercise-induced muscle cramps that occur during a strength workout done by a healthy individual are neurologic phenomena. Muscle fatigue causes the muscle spindles (neuromuscular bundles that govern muscle contraction) to be "overactive," while similar structures (Golgi tendon organs) which cause relaxation of muscle, are suppressed. Stretching the affected muscle group will relieve the cramp.

Muscle cramps associated with heavy physical exertion, particularly in the heat, are different. They are caused by disturbances in fluid and electrolyte balance, and usually can be prevented by proper nutrition and fluid intake, both before and during the exertion, as well as conditioning prior to undertaking vigorous physical exertion.

"Aids" to Developing Muscle Strength

An appropriate training regimen will, without doubt, increase ones strength and muscle mass; the degree of visible muscular hypertrophy is dependent on gender and heredity. However, there is always the quest to become "bigger and stronger," particularly among athletes whose events are strength and power dependent. Hence, there is the pervasive search for something that will enhance training effects and "give them an edge."

Creatine monohydrate is one of the supplements widely used by strength/ power athletes. It is a normal constituent of muscle tissue, and is available commercially in various forms. It has been shown to increase muscle tissue synthesis, thus increasing mass. This tends to improve performance of trained athletes in high intensity, short duration events. Higher muscle creatine content causes less need for anaerobic glucose production, thus reducing lactic acid formation. This forestalls fatigue and facilitates the muscle's recovery from intense work.

Concerns have been raised about the long-term effects of creatine use on renal and liver function, hydration and electrolyte balance. There has been conjecture that significant increases in muscle cross-section would result in tendon damage. To date, no evidence has been found to warrant any of those concerns. Well-controlled studies of persons with creatine use for at least five years have shown no adverse effects.

Williams, *et al.*, after an extensive review of the literature, concluded that, although there is no evidence of harm, athletes who decide to use creatine should do so with the knowledge and advice of a qualified health professional. We would add that periodic monitoring of renal and liver function (by means of blood tests) would give an added measure of safety.

Another group of substances that have been used by athletes to increase muscle size and strength are the anabolic steroids. These function much like testosterone in their effect on skeletal muscle tissue, causing increased size and strength.

First used medically in the 1950's to treat individuals suffering from muscle wasting diseases, they quickly came to the attention of the athletic world. Since that time, use among athletes has continued and grown, in spite of testing and severe penalties to athletes found to have used them.

Anabolic steroids do cause harm to the body; liver damage, early-onset coronary artery disease, suppression of normal testosterone production and psychological changes have been documented. The non-medical use of this class of drugs is dangerous, unpredictable and contrary to the rules and spirit of sport. A practice considered unethical and hazardous by those not even concerned with honoring God can absolutely not be justified for a Believer.

Muscle Tone

Muscle tone is the firmness of muscle tissue, and is to a degree a reflection of its state of functioning. The better conditioned the muscle, the more firm it is when it is working. In females an increase in muscle tone may be the only observable result of muscle conditioning; a *measurable* result, of course is an increase in the muscle's ability to produce force. Females lack the hormonal stimulation needed to cause marked increases in muscle size, but make strength gains proportionately similar to those of males.

Maintaining Muscle Strength and Endurance

Strength and muscle endurance, once gained, are lost at a much slower rate than they were developed. Several studies have shown that as little as one resistance workout every two weeks will maintain strength gained through a strength conditioning program. That is, of course, assuming that the individual is leading a healthy, active lifestyle!

How Strong Do You Want to Be?

For most of us, the answer is probably that we would like our muscles to be strong enough to allow us to get our work done without undue tiredness, and strong enough to take part in chosen recreational/sport activities. Do you avoid taking textbooks to class because they get too heavy to carry by afternoon? Have you avoided recreational activities because you did not have the strength to do them at an enjoyable level? If you answer "yes," then you are not as strong as you'd like to be.

Technology has taken much of the "muscle-work" out of our every-day activities; it does not take much physical effort to do the work most of us do or are preparing to do. But, life is not all about work. God created us with a need for play, especially play that involves moving the body through space, or throwing balls, or hitting them with bats, racquets or clubs. To do those recreational activities at an enjoyable level takes a modicum of strength and muscle endurance. Most of us won't have that unless we plan for and carry out a regular program of conditioning; 45 minutes to an hour, 2–3 times/week is a very manageable time commitment, and will result in stronger muscles.

Those with specific neuromuscular limitations need to condition those muscles they can use in order to maximize mobility and well-being. If you need help with developing a muscular conditioning program to meet specific needs, talk with your instructor. They will help you or perhaps refer you to someone who can help you design the kind of program you need.

We have differing muscle conditioning goals, and differing capacities for muscle strength development. However, we share the over-arching goal of caring for and being good stewards of our physical bodies. As 1 Corinthians 6:19 and 20 remind us: "Or do you not know that your body is a temple of the Holy Spirit within you, whom you have from God? You are not your own, for you were bought with a price. So glorify God in your body."

Bibliography and Resources for Further Study

Aaberg, Everett. *Resistance Training Instruction*. eBook Human Kinetics, 1999.

ACSM, *ACSM's Health-Related Physical Fitness Assessment Manual*, 3rd Edition, Kluwer Lippincott Williams & Wilkins, 2010.

Antonio, Jose and Jeffrey Stout, *Sports Supplements*, Lippincott Williams & Wilkins, 2001.

Baechle, Thomas R. and Roger Earle, *Editors, Essentials of Strength Training and Conditioning*, 3rd Edition, Human Kinetics, 2008.

Corbin, Charles B., Gregory Welk, Ruth Lindsey, and William Corbin. *Concepts of Fitness and Wellness: A Comprehensive Lifestyle Approach*, 9th Edition, New York, NY: McGraw-Hill Higher Education, 2011.

Floyd, Patricia A and Janet E. Parke. *Walk Jog Run For Wellness Everyone*, 4th Edition, Winston-Salem, NC: Hunter Textbooks Inc., 2003.

Greenberg, Jerrold, George Dintiman, and Barbee Myers Oakes. *Physical Fitness and Wellness: Changing the Way You Look, Feel, and Perform*, 3rd Edition, Champaign, IL: Human Kinetics, 2004.

Heyward, Vivian H., *Advanced Fitness Assessment and Exercise Prescription*, 6th Ed., Human Kinetics, 2011.

Jackson, Allen, James Morrow Jr., David Hill, and Rod Dishman. *Physical Activity for Health and Fitness*, Updated Edition, Champaign, IL: Human Kinetics, 2004.

Kenney, W. Larry, JH Wilmore and DL Costill, *Physiology of Sport and Exercise*, 5th Edition, Human Kinetics, 2011.

McArdle, William, Frank Katch and Victor Katch, *Essentials of Exercise Physiology,* 4th Edition, Lippincott Williams & Wilkins, 2011.

McArdle, William, Frank Katch and Victor Katch, *Sports and Exercise Nutrition*, 3rd Ed. Lippincott Williams & Wilkins, 2009.

Sharkey, Brian J. *Fitness & Health*, 6th Edition, Champaign, IL: Human Kinetics, 2006.

Westcott, Wayne, *Building Strength & Stamina*, 2nd Edition, Human Kinetics, 2003.

Williams, MH, RB Kreider and JD Branch, *Creatine: The Power Supplement,* Human Kinetics, 1999.

Chapter 8

Flexibility: Stewardship of Our Joints and Connective Tissue

Essential Terms

Active Range of Motion Exercises

Ballistic Stretching Exercises

Flexibility

Passive Stretching Exercises

PNF Exercises

Static Stretching Exercises

Objectives

Upon completion of this chapter, students should be able to:

1. Define, explain, and effectively use the essential terms listed above.

2. Identify the factors affecting flexibility.

3. Explain flexibility and its role in our body care program.

4. Discuss the results of too little or too much flexibility in a given joint.

5. Present the various roles of flexibility exercises in our body care efforts.

6. Explain and utilize knowledge of how to improve and maintain flexibility using static, dynamic, and PNF exercises.

7. Implement a program to develop or maintain an optimally functioning back.

Flexibility is often forgotten as an essential component of good musculoskeletal fitness. Its importance is overlooked or underestimated by athletes and non-athletes alike. Doctor's offices, rehabilitation centers, athletic training rooms and sports medicine clinics across the nation are filled with individuals suffering the effects of poor flexibility or inadequate attention to proper or sufficient stretching. Those who have suffered the debilitating effects of too little or too much joint motion are well aware of the significance of healthy joints and muscles in optimal body functioning. As noted in the *Healthy People 2010: Objectives for Improving Health* (Public Health Service, p. 22–16), "Although flexibility may appear to be a minor component of physical fitness, the consequence of rigid joints affects all aspects of life, including walking, stooping, sitting, avoiding falls, and driving a vehicle. Lack of joint flexibility may adversely affect quality of life and will lead to eventual disability."

Flexibility Defined

Flexibility by definition is the quality of being easily bent, or pliant. As it is applied to the body, it technically refers to the functional range of motion about a joint. Although it is often used as though it were a general quality of the body, flexibility is a joint-specific capacity. Thus, having good flexibility in one joint does not mean there is good flexibility in all joints.

The phrase "range of motion" refers to the maximum ability to move the bones about the joint through an arc of a circle. For example, if your elbow can extend from 30 degrees at full flexion (angle between upper and lower arm) to 180 degrees (a straight line formed by upper and lower arm), the range of motion for your elbow is 150 degrees. If, however, you can only flex your elbow to 45 degrees and extend it to 170 degrees, your range of motion is only 125 degrees and your elbow is less flexible than in the first situation.

The total range of motion in a joint varies from joint to joint as well as from person to person. By design, the degrees of movement that can be experienced when abducting the shoulder joint are much greater than that which can be experienced when flexing the knee joint.

Factors Affecting Flexibility

1. **The bone structure**. There are six types of moveable joints in the body, each of which has a bony structure which partially or primarily determines the type and amount of motion that can occur there. (See Tables 6.1 and 6.2 and Figure 6.4.)

2. **Ligaments and joint capsule**. These soft tissue structures also play a significant role in determining the type and amount of motion that can occur at a joint. Their exact placement and natural strength are genetically determined, but their ongoing length and strength can be altered by exercise. The ligaments and joint capsules have two somewhat contradictory roles: they must provide both stability and mobility. They are the means by which the bones of the skeleton are held together, yet they must allow and support a vast array of movements and movement ranges at those connection sites or joints.

3. **Skin, fat and muscle tissue**. The range of motion available at a given joint may be limited by the amount of fat and/or muscle tissue in the converging body parts as well as by the skin covering the area.

4. **Condition of the muscle-tendon unit**. The amount of extensibility (ability to be lengthened) and elasticity (resilient stretch) in the muscle-tendon units which cross a joint affects the flexibility of the joint. If muscles are not stretched to their full potential length with some degree of regularity, they will lose their ability to be lengthened. As muscle and connective tissue ages, it loses its elasticity, resulting in stiffer, less fluid motion. A strong, appropriately conditioned and regularly stretched muscle-tendon unit will maintain extensibility and elasticity, while at the same time contributing significantly to joint stability. Conversely, a weak, deconditioned muscle-tendon unit, while providing no resistance to motion at the joint, also provides no stability for the joint. Especially as a muscle is conditioned

and its resting tone is improved, regular lengthening will help preserve both extensibility and elasticity, yet help maintain joint stability.

5. **Temperature**. Elastic and pliant tissue is more so at higher temperatures and less so at lower temperatures. Active (provided by the body itself) or passive (provided by some external source) warming of the tissues results in greater flexibility. This knowledge underscores the importance of warm-up in exercise efforts.

6. **Genetic differences**. Females tend to have greater ranges of motion at most joints than males. This may be due to joint structure, ligament thickness, and/or resting muscle tone.

7. **Integrity of joint surfaces and structures**. The amount of movement at a joint is significantly determined by the "health" of the joint surfaces and structures (refer to Chapter 6). Any deterioration in those due to disease (arthritis) or injury (stretched or torn ligaments, torn cartilage) results in painful, unpleasant motion and ultimately compromised movement at the joint or excess movement that contributes to joint instability which itself then causes destruction of the joint surfaces.

8. **Age differences**. It is generally agreed that as a person ages, flexibility in the major joint areas decreases. Typically, small children are very flexible, and that flexibility is maintained or increased until adolescence. At this point it tends to level off and then decrease through the rest of the lifespan. The major factors contributing to the loss of flexibility with age include, among other things, the following:

   a. An increased amount of calcium deposits
   b. An increased level of dehydration
   c. An increased number of adhesions and cross-links among the connective tissue fibers

Although it is common to see declines in flexibility and active range of motion in many seniors, there is evidence (Campanelli, 1996) that not all older individuals lose flexibility at the same rate and that declines in these areas are due in part to decreased physical activity (American Council on Exercise, *Exercise for Older Adults*, p. 11).

The Importance of Flexibility

While it is readily apparent that success in certain activities (e.g., gymnastics, cheerleading) requires high levels of flexibility in certain joints, efficient and pleasurable movement of any kind depends on an appropriate amount of flexibility in each joint. Essentially this means that optimal body condition requires keeping the joints functioning as they were designed to function with appropriate stability as well as mobility. Many musculoskeletal problems and injuries, especially among adults, are directly related to flexibility problems. Such problems as low back discomfort and even painful menstruation may be contributed to by poor flexibility in the torso.

Excessive looseness in a joint may be caused by injury (sprain, partial or complete dislocation), by genetics, or by lack of muscle tone. Joint instability gives an "uneasy" feeling about the use of the limb. This causes movement to be less comfortable, and it is then often avoided out of feelings of self-preservation. Joint instability can also hasten the development of secondary osteoarthritis, resulting in painful movement.

Flexibility exercises fulfill other roles in our body stewardship efforts. They should be used for warm-up and cool-down before and after the resistance exercises we do to develop muscle tissue condition. They should also be used before and after the various activities we are using to develop and maintain cardiorespiratory endurance.

Stretching also feels good, and assists muscles in relaxing when stress has caused them to assume a condition of constant "alertness" or tension. Muscle cramps (involuntary constant contraction in a muscle) are relieved by a slow, gradual stretch of the cramping muscle while a gentle pressure is applied to its surface. Stretching exercises can also be used to both prevent and relieve muscle soreness.

How to Improve Flexibility

There are several different types of stretching exercises that can be used to improve the range of motion in joints with limited flexibility. These are referred to as static stretching, passive stretching, and proprioceptive neuromuscular facilitation (PNF) stretching exercises, which involve alternating contractions and stretches.

Static Stretching

Static or slow, sustained stretching exercises are very effective in improving joint flexibility. They involve the slow, gradual lengthening of the muscle to the extreme end of the range of motion and then holding the end position for several seconds. While holding the end position, a conscious effort should be made to relax the involved muscle(s). The end position should be held for at least 10 to 30 seconds, and the exercise should be repeated at least 4 times. These exercises can and should be done daily. (See Sections at the end of this chapter for some recommended static stretching exercises. Figure 8.1 presents some stretching exercises that should be avoided.)

Sometimes the muscle group that must contract to stretch the opposing muscle group to its full length is not strong enough to do so effectively. For example, the hamstrings are usually incapable of providing adequate stretch for the quadriceps in the front of the upper leg. In these situations other body parts or another individual may need to assist in the gradual lengthening and holding of the end position. Such assistance must be provided carefully but can result in a very effective exercise routine.

Passive Stretching

Passive stretching is a stretching technique during which the person being stretched makes no contribution to the exercise. Instead, some type of outside agent is used to apply a force to move the joint through the range of motion. This outside agent may be another person or a specially designed machine. This type of stretching is particularly helpful when the agonist (the muscle primarily responsible for the movement) is too weak or unable to cause the movement. It also allows stretching beyond the individual's normal active range of motion. When some of the specialized equipment is used to apply the external force in rehabilitation, the direction, duration, and intensity of the motion can actually be measured to more specifically monitor performance progress.

Standing Straddle Floor Toe-Touch

- makes knees hyperextend
- increased pressure on lumbar spine
- stresses medial aspect of the knees

Straight-Leg Standing Toe-Touch

- makes knees hyperextend
- increased pressure on lumbar spine

Deep Knee Bend

- stretches lateral ligaments of the knees
- pinches and may damage knee cartilage

The Plough

- places pressure on the lumbar spine

The Hurdler

- pinches cartilage of the bent knee

Torso Twist

- increased pressure on the lumbar and thoracic spine
- stresses the medial and lateral ligaments of the knees

Figure 8.1 | Stretching exercises to be avoided.

When partners are used for passive stretching, care must be taken to apply the force correctly, especially with regard to amount and speed. Increased familiarity with the exercise and the person will assist with this concern.

Proprioceptive Neuromuscular Facilitation (PNF)

Proprioceptive Neuromuscular Facilitation (PNF) exercises were originally used by physical therapists in the care of individuals with various types of neuromuscular disease or paralysis. They have recently become more widely used as exercises to increase flexibility. While they have the disadvantage of requiring another person to assist, they are very effective in safely increasing range of motion.

There are several slightly different techniques that can be used in PNF exercises, but each involves some combination of alternately contracting and relaxing the involved muscles. A PNF exercise to increase the flexibility of the hamstrings will illustrate the technique. Chris lies on the floor, face up, with the right leg extended on the floor and the left leg (knee straight) flexed at the hip as far as possible (foot will be up toward ceiling). Partner Shawn holds Chris's left leg at the ankle and the knee (just on the body side of the knee). Chris then contracts the hamstring muscles and pushes against Shawn's hands for 6 seconds (maintaining a normal breathing pattern). Chris then relaxes the hamstrings, and Shawn pushes on the leg slightly, flexing the leg a little farther, and holds that position for 10–30 seconds. Chris then contracts the hamstrings again for 6 seconds, and the contract-stretch cycle is completed at least 3 times. Then the right leg is done. This same PNF technique can be used to stretch most of the muscles in the body.

Why Ballistic Stretching Is NOT Recommended

Another type of stretching exercise, ballistic stretching, has been used to improve flexibility, but is no longer recommended. Ballistic stretching involves "bobbing" or forceful jerking of the joint and associated muscles beyond the end point of its range of motion. While these exercises are able to cause increased flexibility, they are not recommended because there is a strong possibility of damage to the muscles and ligaments with this type of motion.

The bobbing or jerking motion that is typically part of this type of exercise tends to stimulate the "stretch reflex" in the muscle. Within the body of the muscle there are specialized sensory cells that are part of the body's internal awareness or "proprioceptive system." This specialized cell is sensitive to stretch, so when the muscle is stretched, this cell is stimulated and its response is to have the muscle cells in its area contract. Thus a quick stretching of a muscle causes the specialized cell to make the muscle contract. (NOTE: This can be easily seen when the doctor strikes the patellar tendon, causing the tendon to stretch the muscle. This in turn makes the muscle stretch, which causes the specialized cells to stimulate the muscle to contract, extending the knee.)

It can be understood, then, that the bobbing of ballistic stretching exercises actually can cause the muscle to **contract** when what you really want is for the muscle to relax so it can be stretched. It is easy to see how these two opposing forces can result in soreness and injury to the muscle-tendon unit. The forces involved in the jerking motion are also difficult to regulate; this motion may cause overstretching or tearing of the joint ligaments, resulting in joint instability.

Summary of How to Improve Flexibility

While PNF exercises have been shown to provide for the greatest improvement in range of motion when compared to the static or passive techniques, they are somewhat more complicated to do and in addition to requiring another person, may result in more muscle soreness. For convenience and effectiveness, static stretches represent an excellent choice for most. Research suggests that holding the stretch for 10 to 30 seconds at the point of mild discomfort enhances flexibility without significantly greater benefit from holding it longer (Pollock, p. 985). While there is not conclusive evidence available regarding the optimal number of repetitions, one study found that the greatest increase in range of motion occurred in the first four repetitions with minimal gains after that (Taylor et al., 1990). Thus it is recommended that your flexibility program implement the following:

1. Start with an active "warm-up" activity like walking and comfortable stretching to warm and slightly stretch the tissues that will be involved in the flexibility exercises you will be doing.

2. Identify specific stretching exercises using either static, passive, or PNF activities that involve the front and back of the legs, the hips, the trunk, the shoulder girdle, and any particular areas of the body that are "problem" areas for you. Resources listed at the end of this chapter and marked with an asterisk (*) have drawings, pictures, and descriptions of exercises you can use in addition to the ones included at the end of this chapter.

3. Static stretches should be held for 10 to 30 seconds; PNF techniques should include a 6-second contraction followed by a 10 to 30-second assisted stretch.

4. At least four repetitions per muscle group should be completed for a minimum of 2 to 3 days per week; they can be done daily, however.

5. Flexibility exercises should be performed in a slow, controlled manner with a gradual progression to greater ranges of motion until an optimal level is achieved.

After achieving desired levels of flexibility in given joints, movements should be incorporated into life activities and/or your exercise program that utilize these newly acquired or re-acquired ranges of motion at the various joints. These recommendations are based on the American College of Sports Medicine's Position Stand on "The Recommended Quantity and Quality of Exercise for Developing and Maintaining Cardiorespiratory and Muscular Fitness, and Flexibility in Healthy Adults" (Pollock, pp. 984/5) which were also incorporated into the latest edition of ACSM's *Guidelines for Testing and Exercise Prescription* (Franklin, p. 158).

Maintaining Flexibility

Flexibility is a very dynamic component of our body's functioning ability. At very young ages, it is a natural component of the body's structure in the healthy child. Vigorous activity maintained through the adolescent years tends to preserve or improve those flexibility levels. But with aging (adolescence and beyond) and/or inactivity, flexibility at the major joints often begins to diminish.

What is encouraging, however, is the knowledge that appropriate exercises that move joints through their full range of motion can increase flexibility by as much as 20% to 50% in men and women at all ages (McArdle, et al., p. 559). Both static and passive stretching as well as PNF exercises can be used to maintain flexibility as well as to improve it. Another type of exercise that can be used to maintain flexibility is that type known as active range of motion (ROM) exercise.

Active Range of Motion Exercises

These exercises involve the active (self-initiated, self-powered) movement of the joint and involved muscles gradually through the entire range of motion, allowing momentum to assist only slightly in the exercise. All of the various types of movements for which the joint is designed should be used in the maintenance program. Such exercises as wrist circles, arm circles, trunk circles, and arm swings are all examples of active ROM exercises that can be used to maintain current flexibility levels. Active ROM exercises should also be used for the transition portions (warm-up and cool-down) of the muscle resistance and cardiorespiratory activity exercise efforts. Maintenance of flexibility requires that stretching and range of motion activities be done at least 2–3 days per week, since flexibility improvements are very temporary.

A Specific Consideration—Low Back Problems

At some time in their lives, 60–80% of all individuals experience low back pain, and for up to 5% of the population, the condition is disabling. The direct cost of medical care and the indirect costs of absenteeism from work are in the billions of dollars. After headaches, low back pain is the second most common ailment in the United States and is topped only by colds and flu in time lost from work. Next to arthritis, it is the most frequently reported disability. Males and females appear to be affected equally with most cases occurring between the ages of 25 and 60 years (Plowman, p. 107, 109; Nieman, p. 158).

While there are likely many different causes of low back pain, lack of adequate musculoskeletal strength, endurance, and flexibility plays a key role. Several studies support the fact that individuals who have suffered low back pain have weaker, more fatigable, and less flexible muscles in the trunk region than those who have not had low back pain (Plowman, p. 107). Occupational risk factors include heavy lifting; lifting with bending and twisting motions; pushing and pulling; slipping, tripping, or falling; and long periods of sitting or driving. Individual risk factors include obesity, smoking, poor posture, psychological stress and anxiety, minimal physical activity level, and reduced degree of muscular strength and joint flexibility (Nieman, p. 160).

Guidelines for a Healthy Back

For most individuals, developing and/or maintaining an optimally functioning back involves three things:

1. **Learning and using positions and activities that are "back-friendly" and avoiding positions and activities that place inappropriate demands on the back's supporting structures (muscles, ligaments, discs, and vertebrae)—living "back-smart."**

This includes sitting correctly (see Figure 8.2) as well as maintaining good posture while standing. Good posture helps insure proper alignment of the vertebrae and decreases the likelihood of back problems. Sitting causes the greatest stress on the discs between the vertebrae and thus should be done properly. Careful attention must also be given to the appropriate use of backpacks and book bags with regard to amount of weight, balance of weight, and duration of use. Learning and implementing proper lifting, pushing, and pulling techniques will help promote your back health and enable you to live "back-smart." These include some of the following:

Relieve strain by sitting well forward and flatten your back by tightening your abdominals. Cross your knees

This is the correct way to sit while driving. Stay close to the pedals. Use a seatbelt and a backrest.

Having the knees higher than the hips relieves sway-back. Use of a footrest will accomplish this.

Avoid TV slump! Sitting this way strains the neck and shoulders. It also weakens muscles of the abdomen and lower back.

Figure 8.2 | How to sit correctly.

a. Keep the back relatively straight and bend at the hips and knees when lifting anything. Use the strength of the legs to provide the power and stability, not the back.

b. Keep objects being lifted or carried as close to the body as possible.

c. Do not try to lift or carry objects (or weights!) that are too heavy. Any shift of the weight will cause excessive strain and injury to the spinal structures and musculature.

d. Never bend from the waist only; bend the hips and knees.

e. Always face any object (or child!) you are going to lift.

f. For correct standing posture, a line dropped from the ear will go through the tip of the shoulder, middle of the hip, back of kneecap, and front of anklebone. Take a picture and check it, or stand by a full length mirror and have a friend check using the edge of the mirror as a guide (Hoeger, p. 177).

2. **Developing a comprehensive God-honoring body care program that avoids the individual risk factors listed above and effectively manages any occupational risks that must be encountered.**

As you reflect on your responsibilities and their potential "cost" on your back health, you are provided with added incentive for maintaining a consistent, effective body care program. The debilitating effects of back pain or injury can adversely affect most of life's activities and interfere significantly with accomplishing one's responsibilities. Implementing or continuing a lifestyle that honors God by honoring your body clearly has implications for promoting back health as is seen by the individual risk factors that have been identified that contribute to back problems. Each of us must evaluate our vocational responsibilities in light of back health and develop the necessary skills and techniques to minimize our risk. Students, nurses, computer technicians, engineers, musicians, and physical educators all, for example, have particular risks with regard to back health associated with their "professions."

3. **Including in the body care program exercises that develop a healthy balance of flexibility, strength, and endurance in five major anatomical areas and abilities.**

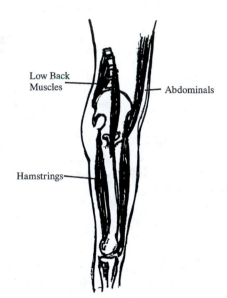

Figure 8.3 | Musculature important for healthy lower back.

The health of the lower back is dependent on the appropriate levels of flexibility, strength, and endurance of the musculature and connective tissue structures in and around the spine, pelvis, and lower abdominal areas. See Figure 8.3 to see how the musculature of the low back, the abdominals, and the hamstrings are all interrelated in keeping the pelvis in correct position. It is recommended (Plowman, p. 108) that for the development and maintenance of a healthy low back, particular emphasis be given to

a. low back lumbar flexibility (use single or double knee to chest stretch),
b. hamstring flexibility (use modified hurdler's hamstring stretch),
c. hip flexor flexibility (use bench hip flexor stretch),
d. strength and endurance of the forward and lateral abdominal muscles (use pelvic tilt and/or curl down), and
e. strength and endurance of the back extensor muscles (use bend over).

For the stretches, move into the stretch positions slowly and hold for 10–30 seconds; repeat at least 4 times. For the pelvic tilt, hold the contracted position for 10–15 seconds (keep breathing, however) and repeat 5–25 times. For the curl downs and bend overs, repeat the controlled movement 5–25 times, focusing on only using the intended muscles to accomplish the movement.

Exercises for a Healthy Back

Following are brief descriptions and diagrams of the exercises that should be used to help develop and maintain a healthy low back. These exercises should be used daily to stretch the lower back and hamstring muscles and strengthen the abdominal and back extensor muscles. (NOTE: They may also be used to reduce the discomfort in painful menstruation.)

A. Single Knee to Chest Stretch

Lie on your back flat on the floor with both knees bent almost half-way and feet flat on the floor. Reach behind one knee and gradually pull it toward your chest as far as possible. Keep your head and shoulders on the floor, and hold the end stretch position for 10–30 seconds, breathing regularly. Switch legs and repeat the exercise, eventually doing each leg at least 4 times.

B. Double Knee to Chest Stretch

Same starting position as "A." Reach behind both knees and gradually pull both legs toward your chest as you bring your head and shoulders up to meet them. Hold the end stretch position for 10–30 seconds, breathing regularly. Return to starting position for 10–15 seconds and then repeat the exercise at least 4 times.

C. Modified Hurdler's Hamstring Stretch

Sit on the floor with one leg straight and the other flexed so that the sole of the foot is against the inside of the straight leg as close to the hip as possible. Slide your hands along the straight leg toward the ankle, bending as far as possible at the waist, but continuing to look at the toes of the extended leg. Attempt to touch your trunk to your extended leg. Alternate legs.

D. Bench Hip Flexor Stretch

Lie on a bench, table, or bed so that your buttocks are on the edge. Pull one knee up to your chest and lower the other leg toward the floor (you don't have to touch the floor). Be sure to hold your spine in a neutral (straight) position (don't arch). Keep your lowered leg slightly bent for less stretch; straighten it for more stretch. Then switch sides. The lower leg is the one that is being stretched.

E. Pelvic Tilt

Same starting position as "A," except that knees should be bent slightly more than half-way. Tilt the pelvis by contracting the abdominal muscles and flattening the lower back against the floor, raising the lower buttocks area slightly off the floor. Hold this position for at least 10 seconds, maintaining normal breathing. Relax and then repeat the exercise up to 25 times. This same exercise can be performed against a wall with the legs bent only about a third of the way (hips must be higher than knees).

F. Curl Down

Assume a bent-leg sit-up position in the "up" position, (legs bent close to half-way), arms wrapped behind knees. Gradually loosen arms and while keeping head and shoulders up, try to force the waistline toward the floor. Go about a third of the way back; hold for 10 seconds (maintain normal breathing) and return to starting position. (Use hands if necessary.) Rest for 10 to 15 seconds, and repeat up to 10 times.

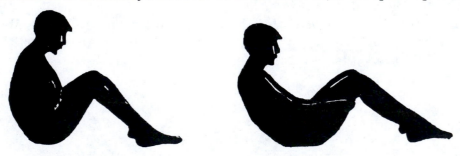

G. Bend Over

Sit on hard, stable chair, arms folded loosely in the lap. With folded arms leading, let the body drop slowly until head is between knees (arms in front of shins). Pull body back up into a sitting position while tightening abdominal muscles. Relax for 10 seconds and repeat up to 10 times. For each of these exercises, the stretch position should be held for 10–30 seconds and repeated at least 4 times daily. Be sure to continue normal breathing throughout the exercise.

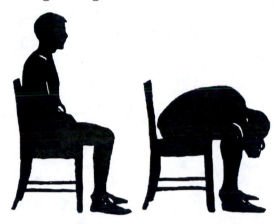

Static Stretching Exercises for General Conditioning

For each of these exercises, the stretch position should be held for 10-30 seconds and repeated at least 4 times daily. **Be sure to continue normal breathing throughout the exercise.**

A. Lower Leg (Gastrocnemius) Stretch

Stand at arms length from a wall with your feet shoulder width apart. Place your palms against the wall at shoulder height and lean forward, bending your elbows and keeping your feet flat on the floor. This may be done one leg at a time for better balance or a more extreme stretch. To do this, step forward and bend one leg while keeping the other leg straight and the heel flat on the floor.

B. Quadriceps Stretch

Stand upright with your hands against a wall or stable support. Rest the top of one foot on a chair or low stand behind you. Flex the knee of the standing leg to stretch the front of the leg with the foot on the stool. Change leg positions to stretch the other quadriceps.

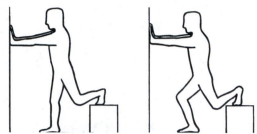

C. Modified Hurdler's Hamstring Stretch

See Exercise "C" under "Exercises for a Healthy Back."

D. Lower Back Stretch

See Exercises "A" and "B" under "Exercises for a Healthy Back."

E. Lateral Trunk Twist

Sit upright in a chair and turn to the right, placing your hands on the back of the chair. Staying seated and with your feet flat on the floor, try to pull your left side around as far as possible and hold. Repeat to other side.

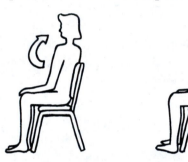

F. Lateral Trunk Stretch

Stand upright with feet shoulder width apart, knees slightly bent, hands interlocking and arms stretched straight overhead. Slowly lower your arms, head, and upper torso sideways as far as possible and hold. Repeat to other side. (Balance is more easily maintained if hips shift in the opposite direction of the arms.)

Summary

Flexibility is an essential component of a healthy, fit body. It is a quality that is specific to each joint and thus requires joint-specific evaluation and conditioning. While it is a characteristic that appears to be affected negatively by the aging process, it is able to be positively affected by a carefully planned God-honoring body care program that incorporates regular, varied activities. Those activities need to involve the various joints in healthy, full range of motion movement at controlled speeds. Particular attention needs to be given to any joints affected by injury or disease, and efforts need to be made throughout life to practice good body alignment especially during sitting and standing. Using the full range of motion in muscle resistance exercises will assist in efforts to maintain optimal joint function.

Bibliography and Resources for Further Study

(Note: Resources that describe and/or portray specific flexibility exercises you can utilize in your body care program are marked with an asterisk*.)

*Allerheiligen, William B. "Stretching and Warm-up" in Baechle, Thomas R. (Ed.), *National Strength and Conditioning Association's Essentials of Strength Training and Conditioning*, Champaign, IL: Human Kinetics, 1994, Chapter 19.

Alter, Michael J. *Science of Flexibility*, 2nd Edition, Champaign, IL: Human Kinetics Pub., 1996.

*Alter, Michael J. *Sports Stretch*, 2nd Edition, Champaign, IL: Human Kinetics Pub., 1997.

*American Council on Exercise. *Exercise for Older Adults*. San Diego, CA: American Council on Exercise Publication, 1998.

American Council on Exercise. *Personal Trainer Manual*, 2nd Edition, San Diego, CA: American Council on Exercise Publication, 1996.

*American College of Sports Medicine. *ACSM Fitness Book*. 2nd Edition, Champaign, IL: Human Kinetics, 1998.

Campanelli, L. C. "Mobility changes in older adults: Implications for practitioners." *Journal of Aging and Physical Activity*, 4(2), 1996, pp. 105–118.

*Editors of Fitness Magazine with Karen Anderson. *Fitness Stretching: Mind, Body, Spirit for Women,* New York NY: Three Rivers Press, 2000.

Franklin, Barry A. (Ed.) ACSM's *Guidelines for Exercise Testing and Prescription*, 6th Edition, Philadelphia, PA: Lippincott Williams & Wilkins, 2000.

*Fredette, Denise M. "Exercise Recommendations for Flexibility and Range of Motion," In ACSM's *Resource Manual for Guidelines for Exercise Testing and Prescription*, 3rd Edition, Baltimore, MD: Williams & Wilkins, 1998, Chapter 54.

Hoeger, Werner and Sharon Hoeger. *Principles and Labs for Physical Fitness*. Englewood, CO: Morton Publishing Company, 1997.

*Kuritzky, Louis with Jacqueline White. "Extend Yourself for Low-Back Pain Relief," *The Physician and Sportsmedicine*, 25(1), January 1997, pp. 65–66.

Kuritzky, Louis with Jacqueline White. "Low-Back Pain," *The Physician and Sportsmedicine*, 25(1), January 1997, pp. 56–64.

Malmivaara, Antti et al. "The Treatment of Acute Low Back Pain-Bed Rest, Exercises, or Ordinary Activity?" *New England Journal of Medicine*, 332(6), 1995, pp. 351–355.

McArdle, William D, Frank I. Katch, Victor L. Katch. *Essentials of Exercise Physiology*, 2nd Edition, Philadelphia, PA: Lippincott Williams & Wilkins, 2000.

*McGill, Stuart M. "Low Back Exercises: Prescription for the Healthy Back and When Recovering from Injury," in ACSM's *Resource Manual for Guidelines for Exercise Testing and Prescription*, 3rd Edition, Baltimore, MD: Williams & Wilkins, 1998, Chapter 13.

Nieman, David C. *Exercise Testing and Prescription*, 5th Edition, Mountain View, CA: Mayfield Publishing Co., 2003.

*Plowman, Sharon. "Physical Fitness and Healthy Low Back Function," in Corbin, C. B. and Pangrazi, R. (ed.) *Towards a Better Understanding of Physical Fitness and Activity*. Scottsdale, AZ: Holcomb-Hathaway, 1999, Chapter 13.

Pollock, Michael L, G. Gaesser, J. Butcher, J. Despres et al. "The Recommended Quantity and Quality of Exercise for Developing and Maintaining Cardiorespiratory and Muscular Fitness, and Flexibility in Healthy Adults," *Medicine & Science in Sports & Exercise*, 30(6), 1998, pp. 975–991.

Protas, Elizabeth J. "Flexibility and Range of Motion." In ACSM's *Resource Manual for Guidelines for Exercise Testing and Prescription*, 3rd Edition, Baltimore, MD: Williams & Wilkins, 1998, Chapter 44.

Public Health Service, U.S. Department of Health and Human Services. *Healthy People 2010, Vols. I and II*, 2nd Edition. Stock No. 017-001-00547-9. Pittsburgh, PA: U.S. Government Printing Office, Superintendent of Documents, 2001. (Also at www.healthypeople.gov.)

Sammann, Patricia. *YMCA Healthy Back Book*. Champaign, IL: Human Kinetics, 1994.

Chapter 9

Stress and the Steward

Essential Terms

Autonomic nervous system

Cortisol

Distress

Endorphins

Epinephrine

Eustress

General adaptation response

Hypothalamus

Norepinephrine

Parasympathetic nervous system

Pituitary

Stress

Stress response

Stressor

Sympathetic nervous system

Objectives

Upon completion of this chapter, students should be able to:

1. Explain the meaning of each of the terms above.

2. Explain the basic physiology of the stress response.

3. List accurately the physical and emotional manifestations of the stress response.

4. List signs and symptoms of prolonged stress.

5. Identify stressors in his/her own life at this time and begin to identify the degree of response they cause.

6. Identify ways in which one can minimize self-caused stressors.

7. Suggest ways he/she may be able to cope with unavoidable stressors.

8. Identify ways he/she has found to be helpful in moderating the stress response.

How many times in the last few days have you heard someone say "I'm SO stressed by....!" If you are typical, probably several times. Some have referred to this era as "the age of stress and anxiety." We know that a great many medical problems are exacerbated by life stresses; some are even brought about by events or situations in our lives that provoke what physiologists term the "stress response." Burn-out is an occupational hazard in some types of work; we read of the large numbers of military personnel who suffer from "post-traumatic stress disorder" following deployment.

Just what is this entity we call stress? Why is it so prominent now? How does it affect us? Are all its effects harmful, or does it have a positive side? As Christians, are we as vulnerable to stress as anyone else? What can we do about stress and its effects? These are some of the questions we'll address in this chapter.

What Is Stress?

We often use the word stress to refer to events or situations that make us uncomfortable, or perhaps feel threatened. Actually, stress is a combination of physiological responses that our bodies make in response to any situation or event that the brain interprets as one requiring action. It is a host of internal responses to external events or situations. The events or situations that bring about stress responses are stressors.

It's important to understand the difference between the terms. If we understand that stress consists of internal responses to external stressors, we're more aware that we can indeed exert some control over those responses. Otherwise, we may think of ourselves as victims of stressors, and absolve ourselves of responsibility for any effects they may have on us. To be sure, many stressors are outside our control, but we can learn some ways to modify how we respond to them.

God built stress responses into us for a variety of reasons. At least one reason is that humans face physical challenges and dangers of various kinds. As we'll learn, some of the physiological adjustments of the stress response help us gear up to overcome or flee from physical threats. Those can protect us from injury, or even save our lives. He also knew we would get into situations that, though perhaps not physically threatening, would evoke fear, anxiety, anger, or sadness; our physiological responses to those stressors can have either positive or negative effects on us. Those are some of the responses we need to learn to modify.

Are Stressors and Stress Responses Always Negative?

No, not at all. When we compete in a game, run a race, or take an exam for which we are well prepared, most of us experience some changes in the way we feel. An athlete usually feels excitement and exhilaration; those factors can actually enhance physical capabilities. When taking an exam, or making a presentation, we may feel anxious, but a heightened alertness as well. Those feelings are stress responses, and can be helpful to us.

Hans Selye, one of the world's foremost authorities on stress and stressors, termed those feelings of excitement and exhilaration "**eustress**" or joyful stress. He contrasted those with negative feelings like fear, and anxiety that interferes with performance, he called those "**distress**". (Selye, 14) Both bring about disturbances of our emotional and physical homeostasis, or balance. However, joyful stress is positive in that it can enhance an athlete's performance, enable a speaker to make a great presentation, and help a prepared student to score well on an important exam. Distress, on the other hand, can impair performance. If prolonged, it causes fatigue and varying levels of emotional and physical dysfunction. It can affect the quality of our work or play, and detract from our joy in living. It can actually make us ill.

There is a fine line, though, between eustress and distress. If winning the contest becomes all-important to an athlete, the joy of effort and exhilaration of competition may become anxiety and fear of not performing well. The student to whom grades become more important than understanding what's being studied may experience anxiety and fear at exam time. Challenges of any sort provoke in us a stress response; whether it is eustress or distress depends on how we view the challenge, and whether the stressor in question is episodic, or prolonged.

Examples of acute stress most experience at one time or another include such things as having to give a presentation in public when we don't enjoy public speaking or going to our car to drive home, only to find one of the tires flat. These events provoke feelings of frustration, anxiety, or perhaps anger, but those are time-limited. Examples of chronic stress include such things as having a job you don't like; living with a chronic disease or disability; or having a large debt that will take years to pay off. The feelings of discontent or frustration these evoke typically are less intense, but continue over time.

People vary in their capacities to experience both eustress and distress. Some thrive in a competitive setting; whether it is athletic, academic, or work-related, these people are at their best when meeting a challenge. Others find such situations tense and uncomfortable, perhaps even threatening.

What is a positive stress for one may be negative for another. One of the things we need to learn about ourselves is how much challenge we can handle. How much do we need to be motivated to do our best before becoming so tense that we can't perform up to our level of ability? Some need to be pushed by challenge to achieve our potential; these people thrive in a fast-paced, highly competitive environment. They enjoy the challenge of decision-making, and are spurred-on rather than snowed under by time pressures.

For others, that type of situation is a negative stressor. They do their best work in low key situations, with less time pressure, and little, if any, aura of competition. In the right kind of job, they do excellent work, but it's important that they receive appropriate career guidance. For them, a high pressure job could be disaster.

Just as it is important that we learn about the aptitudes the Lord has given us (and the ones He's NOT given us), it is important that we learn our stressor-tolerance. If we are attentive to the various challenges life presents, and how they make us feel, we discover this about ourselves. The college years help us learn these things about ourselves.

Stress in Today's World

The world in which we live is considerably different from the one in which our parents and grandparents lived during their young adult years. We are in the second decade of a new century; technology has dramatically changed nearly every aspect of our lives in some way. To your grandparents, a "text" was a book and a phone sat on a hall table or hung on the wall and did not take pictures or provide games. Lap-tops were literally that...people's laps on which children or pets might sit. Most work in your grandparents' day required physical energy, but jobs were readily available both to folks with special skills and education and those without. Their focus was, for the most part, local; their family, community, and nation, rather than worldwide. Though they experienced change at a greater rate than had prior generations, it was not as rapid as we experience today.

Technology has altered teaching/learning methods and opportunities, placed tremendous volumes of information literally at our fingertips, enabled us to communicate worldwide, and changed the way we work both in our jobs and at home.

Technology has enriched our lives and facilitated productivity in many ways, but it has had its negative effects as well.

We have access to real time reports of natural disasters, acts of terrorism, and political unrest anywhere in the world. We are aware of our country's current economic and social problems to a greater degree than most people were 20-30 years ago. Many report feeling overwhelmed by situations and problems beyond their control, and concern for their futures as well as that of our nation.

Twenty-first century technology has dramatically changed the kinds of work people in our country do. The technology that has made life easier has also resulted in many of the jobs formerly done by people to be more efficiently accomplished by computer-controlled robots. That, together with some manufacturing being out-sourced to overseas plants and the change in job-skills now needed for many kinds of work has resulted in unemployment or under-employment for many. Loss of income and the lifestyle adjustments that have resulted from these changes in the employment picture have become major stressors for many.

Those who are engaged in business or the professions, though they may not have the economic stresses, do find themselves working longer hours than their predecessors and having less leisure time. They constantly must update skills and adapt to new ways of doing their jobs. Their work often requires relocation to parts of the country far from the support of family and friends; they are less likely to know their neighbors or feel a sense of belonging to the community in which they live.

Change and the rate at which it occurs is identified by every psychologist as a powerful stressor. Today, we live in an age of rapid change. We cannot turn back the clock, or isolate ourselves in any practical way from change and its potential to cause us to experience distress. What we must do, as good stewards of our bodies, is to find ways of either modifying the stressors in our lives or the ways we respond to them.

How Prevalent Is Stress?

Stress today is pervasive. Kristine Fish, in her book *Stress Management for Healthy Living* cites a study by the American Psychological Association which found the following:

- 73% of adults surveyed reported experiencing anxiety and depression, which they attribute to stressors they experience

- 77% reported having physical symptoms in stressful situations

- 1/3 of the group surveyed felt themselves to be experiencing extreme stress

- 48% said that they experience more stress now than they did five years ago

- 1/3 of the group said that they have difficulty managing both work and family responsibilities, which is very stressful for them

- one in four reported having had relationships to friends or family members damaged because of stress (Fish, 48-49)

Out-of-school adults aren't the only ones feeling the effects of stress. A 2009 poll of college students found that:

- 58% report anxiety or worry about their grades

- 78% say that their class grades have an impact on how they feel physically

- More than a third of college freshmen admit to feeling overwhelmed much of the time

- Students report they feel greater stress over academics than they do over financial concerns

- 85% of students report feeling stress symptoms on a daily basis (Fish, 50)

What do college students find stressful? Of course that depends on the person, but a review of surveys asking about college stressors (Hansen, Stalk and Dickman, Wright) show a common trend. The greatest source of stress among college students is academic, followed by financial concerns and social relationships.

College student stress appears more prevalent in the freshman and senior years. Freshmen come into a totally new physical and social setting, new and more challenging academic expectations, and more freedom over how they use their time than most have ever had. They are away from whatever household rules Mom and Dad had about eating, sleeping, and getting homework assignments done. Most college classes meet two or three times a week, giving the illusion of more free time, and providing more "forgetting" opportunities than most students have had in their previous educational experiences. In most college settings, there are more than enough opportunities for involvement in student organizations and other campus activities to fill up out-of-class time. And, yes, there are still all of the social network and other screen-time distractions even more readily available.

It's easy to understand why many freshman students report feeling overwhelmed. They quickly become aware of the importance of time-management and task prioritization; if they acquire those skills, they will likely go on to complete their degrees. As seniors, students begin to anticipate life beyond college, whether it is further education, work, marriage, or all of the above! Anxieties over admission to graduate or professional school, getting a job in their field, and/or beginning a marriage are major stressors and for most, there will be a change of venue. Added to those concerns for many is the daunting burden of college debt they must begin repaying.

Individuals already in the work force, whether they completed college or not, report significant stress. A 2009 nationwide survey of American workers reported:

- More workers felt tense and stressed during their workday than they did in 2007, and they reported a lower degree of job-satisfaction in 2009 than in 2007

- 52% of workers said that they are more affected by work stressors than by home or family stressors

- More than 30% of workers said they are always or often under stress at work

- 54% are concerned about health problems brought about, or exacerbated by work stress

- 45% identified lack of job security as a major cause of stress (Fish, 52-53)

Stress affects children as well. The American Psychological Association conducts an annual "Stress in America" survey; one portion of the poll compared responses of children and adolescents (ages 8-17) regarding stress they experience with parents' perceptions of their children.

Essentially, the study showed that parents do not fully realize how stressed their children are.

- 30% of teens and 42% of pre-teens say they get headaches, while only 13% of parents think their children have headaches

- 39% of teens and 49% of pre-teens report difficulty sleeping; only 13% of parents believe their children have sleeping difficulties

- 14% of teens said they worry "a lot", and 28% said they worry a "great deal"; only 2-5% of parents perceive their children as worrying "a lot" or "a great deal" (Fish, 51)

It is obvious that stress is very much a part of American life. It is common to people of all ages, all occupations and all income levels. It can be motivating and energizing, or fatiguing and depressing. It is our responsibility to have some understanding of its physiological effects, and develop some healthful ways of coping with those.

Physiology of the Stress Response

God has provided us with a rapid response mechanism that prepares us to meet sudden real or perceived threats. This is known as the "generalized alarm response." When an event or situation occurs which constitutes a potential threat, it is appraised at either a subconscious or conscious level. It is filtered through our store of information and experience in order to evaluate the nature and seriousness of the threat. This usually goes on without our being consciously aware of the process.

At the same time, the HYPOTHALAMUS stimulates both the PITUITARY gland and the sympathetic (accelerating) portion of the autonomic nervous system. The pituitary releases a substance called ACTH (adrenocorticotrophic hormone) which in turn stimulates the adrenal glands. The adrenal glands respond by discharging "stress" hormones into the blood (primarily CORTISOL, EPINEPHRINE, and NOREPINEPHRINE.) In lay terms, one or more of these is often referred to as "adrenalin." These hormones, together with the sympathetic nervous system stimulation, act on target organs to produce a heightened state of physical/emotional readiness to act. This readiness state has often been termed the "flight or fight" response.

Physiological adjustments include increases in blood pressure, heart rate, respiratory rate, blood sugar, and blood lipids. Blood flow to skeletal muscle increases, as does muscle tension; air passages in the respiratory tract dilate, and the skin's sweat glands are activated. These, and other less observable changes, prepare one to leap out of the way of an oncoming car or run away from the large, angry dog encountered while jogging.

Interestingly, the generalized alarm reaction occurs also in situations that we find exciting, challenging, angering, frightening, or frustrating. So, when we are waiting for the game to begin or for our turn to give a speech, we sense our heart pounding, our muscles tensing, and our palms sweating.

When the situation is one that can be met with physical exertion (as in avoiding danger or in an athletic contest), or is one that is over in a fairly short time (as in giving a three-minute speech and sitting down), stress hormone levels quickly drop, and the physiological manifestations of the alarm reaction return to normal. This is not the case when physical confrontation with a stressor is impossible or inappropriate, or when the stressful situation is prolonged. Our bodies respond to these situations with a second level stress response; this has been termed the GENERAL ADAPTATION RESPONSE.

General Adaptation Response

This is the term that Hans Selye, one of the pioneer stress researchers, applied to the ways in which the body responds to stressors that are chronic, or prolonged. We may be in situations where it seems we have too much to do in too little time, or we may work under a supervisor who is very demanding, doesn't treat us fairly, or with whom we simply have a personality clash. We may have financial burdens that seem insurmountable. These are common stressors, and yes, they do happen to Christians as well!

In these types of situations, though there is nothing to physically "fight,", or nothing from which we can take "flight,", our endocrine and nervous systems initially respond as though there is. That is the initial, or "alarm stage" of the General Adaptation Response.

As the stressful conditions continue, the rapid heart rate, elevated blood pressure and other manifestations of the alarm response drop lower, but still above normal, resting levels. They remain at those somewhat elevated levels for extended periods of time.

The reason those parameters remain elevated is that the amount of cortisol in the blood is sustained at a high-normal level, not high enough to be recognized as "abnormal" on a screening laboratory test, but high enough to affect target organs. This is the "resistance" or "adaptation" stage of the General Adaptation Response.

We have varying degrees of tolerance for this "hyperstress" resulting from too much cortisol stimulation for too long a time. Unless one changes either the situation that is stressful or the way it is being managed, fatigue and exhaustion will set in. This is the third, or "exhaustion" stage of the General Adaptation Response, and the point at which it becomes a serious threat to health.

Signs of stress overload may be mental or emotional as well as physical. Examples are heightened irritability, nervous or inappropriate laughter, inattentiveness to tasks, paranoia or depression.

When these kinds of signs are apparent, we must act to protect ourselves from physiological damage. Cortisol elevations over time cause several potentially life-threatening problems. These include:

a. Hypertension, which increases the work of the heart.

b. Alterations in liver function, leading to elevated cholesterol and atherosclerosis.

c. Changes in the endothelium (lining) of blood vessels, resulting in scarring and weakening of the vessels.

d. Deposition of intra-abdominal fat, which predisposes to diabetes and heart disease. (Malarkey, Peeke, and Snyderman)

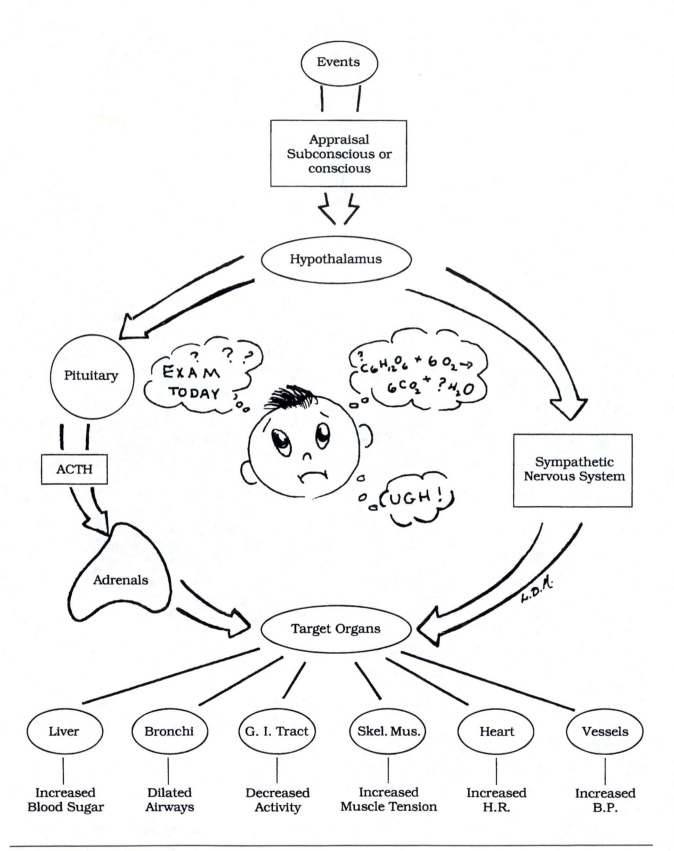

Figure 9.1 | Physiology of the stress response.

Some typical signs and symptoms of prolonged stress are:

Fatigue not attributable to physical exertion, and not relieved by a normal amount of rest and sleep

Frequent, persistent headaches

Frequent, recurring gastrointestinal symptoms (nausea, vomiting, diarrhea, pain)

Frequent colds or other minor infections

Frequent or persistent skin rashes

Rapid, pounding pulse, even at rest

Moodiness, impatience, irritability

Difficulty concentrating on a task

Marked appetite change—either increase or decrease

Change in sleep patterns

Nervous tics (small facial muscle twitches, usually around the eyes)

Depression in the absence of an obvious cause

This list of signs and symptoms is not all-inclusive, but does include the most commonly experienced warnings of over-stress. Experiencing these singly or in some combination without an obvious cause should prompt us to examine our lives and identify stressors.

Stress Resistance

Some people seem to be able to cope with stress more effectively than others. These are the athletes who "come through" when the game is on the line, and the paramedics and other professionals who are able to do their jobs well under the most demanding circumstances. This has long been a topic of research interest for psychologists: determining characteristics common to those who seem more "stress-resistant."

Resilience to stress is not gender-specific, nor does it seem related to level of education. Studies have shown that people who handle stress well, and who are less likely to develop stress-related health problems, share specific characteristics. They tend to have an optimistic view of situations that confront them, and to focus on how problems might be solved rather than on the consequences of not solving them.

They also tend to have good personal health habits, such as getting regular exercise, eating well, and getting adequate rest. They are individuals who tend to form strong friendships, and maintain ties with family, so they have an emotional support system in place.

A number of psychologists who have studied stress-resistance extensively have described what they term the "hardy" personality. This is a personality characterized by the "three C's": control, commitment, and challenge. (Kobasa, Allred, Funk, et al.)

Control: Faced with a stressful circumstance, the "hardy" individual doesn't consider himself/herself to be helpless; although realizing they can't fully control situations and events, they continue to perceive themselves as having resources and options that may influence and improve their situation. Faced with more work than time to do it, the hardy personality is more likely to organize/prioritize tasks, and set about checking them off one-at-a-time, rather than being overwhelmed by them. They concentrate on finding solutions to problems as opposed to worrying about their possible consequences.

Commitment: Those with "hardy" personalities are involved with people, and form strong, lasting friendships; they have a strong sense of loyalty to family, as well as to institutions of which they are a part. They value others, and perceive themselves as being valued by others.

Challenge: The "hardy" personality is likely to consider the demands of a difficult situation as an opportunity rather than as an obstacle. Confronted with a stressful work-situation, he/she tries to find ways to do the job more efficiently, lessening work pressure.

Are these ways of coping innate? We tend to believe them to be learned behaviors. If parents or others we're close to approach stressors in this fashion, we are likely to do the same. We think that, to a large degree, how we deal with life's stressors is a matter of choice, as well as faith in God's sovereignty over all situations.

The Apostle Paul spent a lot of time in prisons; rather than viewing himself a helpless victim, he exercised the options he had. He found a way to minister to converts by way of his letters; who knows how many hours of deep conversation with his guards, and with what ultimate results in their lives. Paul exercised control over those things he could control; he was thoroughly committed to his LORD, his friends, and his many converts. He made a choice to find opportunity in the obstacles he faced. He is a great example of a hardy, stress-resistant personality.

Recognize Stressors in Your Life

If we are to cope with our stress, we need to identify those things that are stressful, and our responses to them. You may feel anxious, or down, or be irritable, and don't know why. Those are vague sensations that are often occasioned by things that happen during our day. The next time you feel that way, think back to what has occurred in your day. Were you not prepared for a quiz in one of your classes? Or did you get back an exam on which you thought you'd done better than the grade you received? Or perhaps you had a disagreement with one of your friends?

Sometimes our stress response takes the form of physical sensation, like tight muscles in our neck, or mild headache, or fatigue. Other times, our response may be more emotional, i.e., we may be irritated or angry, or feel anxious, or depressed.

If we can identify the causes of our stress responses, then we can see how we might either eliminate the stressor, or modify its intensity. If we can't do that, we may be able to modify how it affects us. But, before we can do anything about stressors, we have to recognize them. Everyone, regardless of gender, age, or any other demographic you can name is susceptible to the effects of stress. The stressors may differ, but the effects are very similar.

Table 9.1	How Many Stressors Are Part of Your Life?

The inventory below is an opportunity for you to identify how many stressors are a part of your life. If your total score is 35 or higher, you have a significant number of stressors, and should seek some assistance in developing ways to cope with them. For each item, note the number that best represents the typical situation in your life.

Use the following scale: 1—Never, 2—Rarely, 3—Sometimes, 4—Often, 5—Most of the time

1.	I work/study long hours.	1	2	3	4	5
2.	My parents/faculty don't notice or realize how hard I work.	1	2	3	4	5
3.	It takes all of my energy to get through the day.	1	2	3	4	5
4.	I have family problems (health, finances, disagreements).	1	2	3	4	5
5.	I am personally having financial problems.	1	2	3	4	5
6.	I am having serious academic problems.	1	2	3	4	5
7.	My home/apartment/room is typically a mess.	1	2	3	4	5
8.	I don't really have time for fun.	1	2	3	4	5
9.	I have difficulty making friends.	1	2	3	4	5
10.	I am on a diet.	1	2	3	4	5
11.	I have trouble keeping a friendship or relationship very long.	1	2	3	4	5

Total Score _____

NOTE: This inventory is adapted from "Work vs. Play: A Nation in Search of Balance" and several other similar stressor inventories.

Table 9.2   Exploring How Stress May Affect Your Health

This is an adaptation of the Holmes and Rahe's Stress Scale. In 1967, psychiatrists Thomas Holmes and Richard Rahe studied whether or not stress contributes to illness. They surveyed more than 5,000 medical patients and asked whether they had experienced any of 43 life events in the previous two years. Each event, called a Life Change Unit (LCU), had a different "weight" for stress. The more events the patient added up, the higher the score. The higher the score, and the larger the weight of each event, the more likely the patient was to become ill. The scale has been adapted to include several more student-oriented types of experiences. Check all that apply and total. Below is a total score interpretation guide to use.

	Event	Point value	Your point value
1	Death of spouse	100	
2	Divorce	73	
3	Marital separation of parents	65	
4	Jail term	63	
5	Death of close family member	63	
6	Personal injury or illness	53	
7	Marriage	50	
8	Fired at work or suspended from school	47	
9	Marital reconciliation	45	
10	Engagement or break-up of engagement	45	
11	Change in health of family member	44	
12	Unplanned or undesired pregnancy	40	
13	Sex difficulties	39	
14	Gain of new family member	39	
15	Business readjustment	39	
16	Change in financial state	38	
17	Death of close friend	37	
18	Change to a different line of work	36	
19	Increase in number of arguments with close friend	35	
20	A large mortgage or loan	31	
21	Foreclosure of mortgage or loan	30	
22	Change in responsibilities at work or school	29	
23	Sibling leaving home	29	

24	Trouble with roommate	29	
25	Outstanding personal achievement	28	
26	Parent begins or stops work	26	
27	Begin or end school/college	26	
28	Change in living conditions	25	
29	Revision of personal habits	24	
30	Trouble with boss, coach or professor	23	
31	Change in school or work hours or conditions	20	
32	Change in residence	20	
33	Change in course load	20	
34	Change in recreation	19	
35	Change in church activities	19	
36	Change in social activities	18	
37	A moderate loan or mortgage	17	
38	Change in sleeping habits	16	
39	Change in number of family get-togethers	15	
40	Change in eating habits	15	
41	Vacation	13	
42	Christmas	12	
43	Minor violations of the law	11	
	YOUR TOTAL		

Score Interpretation

300+	You have a high or very high risk of becoming ill in the near future due to stress.
150–299	You have a moderate to high chance of becoming ill in the near future due to stress.
<150	You have only a low to moderate chance of becoming ill in the near future due to stress.

NOTE: The higher your score, the more intentional you must be in developing and implementing effective stress management behaviors. These should include such things as seeking professional assistance (counselor, pastor, psychologist, psychiatrist), utilizing healthy levels of physical activity, rest, and appropriate nutrition, in addition to the obvious intense continuation and cultivation of your spiritual disciplines. It is the fool who attempts to handle the stressors of life without the Source of Life.

Reprinted from *Journal of Psychosomatic Research*, Vol 11, Issue 2, Thomas H. Holmes and Richard H. Rahe, "The Social Readjustment Rating Scale, pp 213-218, Copyright 1967, with permission from Elsevier.

Table 9.3 How Stress Resistant Are You?

This series of statements is designed to help you see how "resistant" you are to stress. Keep in mind this instrument is NOT diagnostic and is given for your own use only. Identify the number that indicates how true this statement is of you typically.

Statement	Never True	Rarely True	Sometimes True	Often True
1. I enjoy going to work or school on most days.	1	2	3	4
2. I get nervous if I have to make a lot of decisions.	4	3	2	1
3. I feel confident about and look forward to my future.	1	2	3	4
4. I hesitate to get too involved in personal relationships.	4	3	2	1
5. I am confident that my college experience will be beneficial.	1	2	3	4
6. I believe I can make a positive difference in the world.	1	2	3	4
7. One can work hard and do all the right things and have fate prevent your success.	4	3	2	1
8. Being successful in life is more often a matter of circumstances and breaks than of effort.	4	3	2	1
9. I put a lot of pressure on myself to please other people.	4	3	2	1
10. It is hard for me to adjust to change in my plans or schedule.	4	3	2	1
11. It is hard for me to put aside feelings of hurt or anger, even after the causative situation has been resolved.	4	3	2	1
12. I look forward to new challenges.	1	2	3	4
TOTALS				
GRAND TOTALS				

SCALE: 40–48 = High Resistance to Stress,
   30–39 = Moderate Resistance to Stress, <30 = Low Resistance to Stress

Adapted from Corbin, Lindsey, and Welk, Concepts of Physical Fitness, 10th ed. Boston: McGraw-Hill, 2000.

What Can We Do about Stress?

As Christians are we somehow "insulated" from stress and its negative effects? Of course not! God does not shelter His children from life's challenges, demands, or annoyances. In fact, sometimes He uses stressful events and situations to motivate and strengthen us, or to teach us lessons He wants us to learn. Scripture gives us numerous accounts from the lives of the patriarchs, prophets, and apostles who faced stressors far greater than most of us experience.

We are not immune to life's stressors, nor should we expect to be. How can one manage them to keep stress responses at a level that will not be harmful? There are entire books written in answer to this question; our purpose in this brief chapter is to give some simple, useful suggestions.

Attend to the Needs of Your Spiritual Life

God does not shield us from stressors, but our strength and ability to cope come from Him. Following are some specific ways we can care for our spiritual well-being.

1. *Be sure about your salvation.* If you have any doubts, get them resolved. Don't play the role, saying and doing the right things. In time, such pretending becomes a tremendous stressor, and the ultimate cost is life itself, both physical and spiritual.

2. *Establish and maintain a regular time for reading and reflecting on the Word and for prayer.* Think on the awesome greatness of our God, and wonder at His mindfulness of us and our needs. Read Psalm 8:3–9 and Matthew 6:25–34 and let these truths penetrate your current concerns and anxieties. Remember that while God expects us to exercise diligence and prudence in managing our lives, He is firmly and forever in control.

3. *Don't misapply Phil. 4:13.* We can't do **all things,** but rather those things God would have us to do. Jesus himself did not heal everyone, feed everyone, or disciple everyone. During His time on earth in human form, He was not every where at once, but traveled from place to place at a normal pace. We need to be sensitive and attentive to those things He calls us to, but not try to do **all.**

4. *Don't allow unconfessed sin to persist in your life.* Regardless of how many "layers" of rationalization and/or denial we apply, our subconscious knows we are doing (or have done) something wrong in God's sight. This knowledge, even though it may be sub-conscious is a nagging, persistent stressor.

Learn to Avoid Self-Caused Stressors

Many of the stressful situations we experience grow out of our own actions. Some ways to avoid self-caused stressors include the following:

1. *Don't procrastinate.* The exam that is two weeks in the future, or the paper due at the end of the term will become stressors, if you put off preparing for the exam, or starting the paper. Develop a specific plan for exam prep, and for working on term projects, and <u>follow it!</u> Don't kid yourself that "you do better work under pressure;" time pressure is a negative stressor, and we <u>don't</u> do our best work when up against deadlines.

2. *Do not allow small problems to grow into big ones before doing anything about them.* Problems ignored do not go away, they escalate. This is strikingly true in academics, where concepts build one upon another. When there is something you don't understand, see your instructor, your advisor, or someone who can clear up your uncertainties. Don't wait until you are lost in a class and facing an exam before getting help.

3. *Don't over-commit your time, regardless of how worthy the activity.* There are literally scores of student organizations and ministries in which a student may become involved. All are wonderful and fun, but all take time and energy. Choose only those you can manage with your class schedule; it is very easy to find yourself "majoring" in extra-curricular activities. If you play on an intercollegiate athletic team, you need to be especially careful about committing to other activities.

4. *Set a limit on the amount of time you spend on social media (Facebook, MySpace, etc.), texting, and chatting on your cell phone. Also, don't try to study or do assignments while you're using electronic communication devices.* A study of >2500 college students found that, on average, they spent 3 hours texting, an hour-and-a-half on Facebook, an hour on email, and another hour in cell conversations. That's more time than most students spend in class.

   Many attempt to study or do homework while engaged with electronic media; when asked about it, they say they are "skilled at multi-tasking." Researchers Junco and Cotten did a study of the relationship between multitasking (using Facebook, texting, etc.) while doing homework and college GPA. Analysis showed a negative relationship between the amounts of time spent multitasking with Facebook and texting and the student's GPA. Though some can assimilate/memorize isolated facts while doing something else, most college classes require more than that. Students must be able to relate and apply factual information rather than simply recall it. So...set a sensible limit, and stick to it; don't fall into the "I can multitask successfully" delusion.

5. *Establish a routine for your daily life.* Many of the small but nagging stressors we experience can be traced to a level of disorganization in our lives. On first leaving home, we may enjoy our freedom from the daily patterns structured by parents. Freedom is less attractive when we get up 20 minutes late, find we don't have a clean shirt or blouse (because we forgot to do the laundry), and can't find the assignment that is due today. Establishing times for going to bed and getting up, doing laundry on a regularly scheduled day or evening, and putting books, keys, I.D. cards, assignments and similar essentials in the same place all the time seem "ho-hum," but

don't underestimate their importance. Regularity in these simple but essential tasks brings order to daily living, and eliminates many unnecessary stressors.

6. *Don't demand perfection of yourself.* As Christians, we sometimes heap guilt on ourselves when we make mistakes, do poorly on exams, or fail to reach specific goals we have established. Guilt is a powerful stressor, and is largely counter-productive unless our response to it is to make a positive change. Our Creator knows we are not perfect. When we fall short in some endeavor, we must assess it and keep it in proper perspective. Then we must determine what we should do differently the next time. This is not meant to be an excuse for poor study or work habits; it is meant to encourage you to move beyond mistakes or failures and to learn to grow from them.

7. *When possible, avoid making a large number of significant life changes in a short period of time.* Stress-related research has revealed change as a significant stressor for most people. The person who graduates from college in early June, gets married two or three weeks later, and in July moves to a new location to start a new job and establish a home is likely to experience a significant stress response. Scheduling events that occur at our discretion so that they are not so close in time to those things we do not control will lessen the stressfulness inherent in life changes.

8. *Don't yield to the temptation of worry.* We can magnify relatively insignificant concerns into major stressors by dwelling on them, mentally constructing a "worst case scenario," and expecting the worst to happen. Our stress-response can be triggered by imagined situations; the response and its effect on us is real even though the stressor is not. It has been said: "Worry does not rob tomorrow of its sorrow, but does rob today of its strength."

9. *Deal appropriately with anger.* Anger is an emotion which all of us experience. Anger may be righteous or unrighteous, but regardless of its basis and/or legitimacy, it must be resolved. Unresolved anger is a devastating stressor. Ephesians 4:26, 27 directs us to "Be angry and do not sin: do not let the sun go down on your wrath, nor give place to the devil." Even if anger is for good cause, before the day ends, we must forgive those whose actions angered us or hurt us. This does not mean that constructive attempts to resolve issues should not be made or that restitution need not be made. What it does mean is that you must forgive (or ask forgiveness in the case of unrighteous anger) in order to be freed from the gnawing stressfulness of smoldering anger and resentment. Once that is achieved the path has been cleared for constructive solutions.

10. *Learn to live in the present, not yesterday nor tomorrow.* Often we exhaust ourselves dwelling on yesterday's mistakes or misfortunes and worrying about tomorrow's potential problems. Christ told His followers "Therefore, do not worry about tomorrow, for tomorrow will worry about itself. Each day has enough trouble of its own" (Matthew 6:34). God gives us grace for just one day at a time; live to the utmost the day you are in. When tomorrow arrives, we'll find God's grace has preceded us.

11. *Don't allow bitterness against people or situations to take root in your life.* Minirth, Meier, et al., identify bitterness as a primary cause of burnout (Minirth, Meier, et al., pp. 47–56). Bitterness gives one a negative mind-set, and makes it nearly impossible to see the positive side of less-than-optimal circumstances. It is an angry, hostile attitude that causes one to seethe inside much of the time. Often this grows out of feeling victimized by adverse situations or the unfair actions of others. Everyone will encounter adversity; don't make those negative experiences the focal point of your life. Instead,

periodically enumerate all the positive things in your life; remind yourself daily of all the "big and small ways that God 'daily loads us with benefits' (Psalms 68:19)" (Minirth, Meier, et al., p. 53).

Find Ways to Modify Your Physiological Stress Response

You can't stop the biochemical changes that occur, but you can minimize them. Some ways of doing this may include the following.

1. *When possible, work off the stress response with physical exertion.* Vigorous physical exertion, when it can be done immediately allows the stress response to run its natural physiological course, normalizing hormone levels and target organ responses. It may also induce ENDORPHIN release in the brain, producing a sense of well-being and relaxation.

2. *When circumstances do not allow opportunity for physical exertion, find a quiet place where you can relax and take several deep breaths.* This will help to normalize the stress response.

3. *Get thirty minutes of aerobic exercise at least five times each week.* People who do this tend not to experience the marked increase in heart rate and blood pressure observed in non-exercisers.

4. *Allow yourself the luxury of some unscheduled time at least two or three times each week.* Go for a walk, read something other than a textbook, listen to music—do something that allows you to relax and unwind.

5. *Manage your time so that you can get at least 8 hours of sleep on a regular basis.* Doing so takes some planning and good time-management, but it can be done. Shakespeare wrote "sleep that knits up the raveled sleeve of care"…The bard knew what he was talking about. While we're asleep, the brain processes the day's experiences, and prunes and strengthens neural connections. Guyton likens sleep to the "re-zeroing" of analog computers after a long period of use. He reasons that, just as devices can drift from their base-lines during long use, over-used neurons in the brain during long periods of wakefulness could become "out of balance." Sleep appears to restore that balance. We know that sleep deprivation impairs concentration, and cause irritability, anxiety, and depression.

   On average, college students report sleeping less than 7 hours/night; the sleep need of college-age people is at least 8 hours/night. While it tends to be "part of the college experience" to have some late nights here and there, those should be few and far-between. Having adequate study time and getting enough sleep is a matter of discipline and time-management. Being well-rested helps you to cope better with whatever stressors the day may bring.

6. *Learn to laugh. Look for the humorous side of stressful situations, and let yourself laugh.* Hearty laughter relaxes tense muscles, causes deep breathing, and triggers a relaxation response. Obviously, some of life's difficult situations really don't have a "funny" side. When you find yourself mired in one of those for several days, take an hour out to read a humorous article or book, or watch a TV comedy.

7. *Develop a "support system" of friends.* By this we mean one or two persons with whom you can share your feelings about the stressors in your life. There is often relief in simply giving voice to your frustrations and fears, with the confidence that your listeners are "on your side." In turn, you can fulfill the same role for them, and derive the satisfaction of giving as well as receiving support.

8. *Build "margins" into your life in terms of your physical and emotional energy, your time, and your financial/material resources.* These are "cushions" that we establish to keep ourselves from becoming overextended, or over-stressed. If we don't give ourselves such margins, overstress is inevitable. (Swenson)

Remember that stress, in a physiological sense, arises from our internal responses to external events. We can exert some control over that response, particularly when it comes to life's minor annoyances. Delays, trouble finding a parking place, or spilling coffee on your favorite shirt or blouse or paper you're about to submit are the kinds of things that are inevitable and invariably occur at the most inconvenient times. Those things happen; but, we can decide how much we allow them to upset us.

Summary

We will be confronted, tried, challenged, frightened and frustrated by life's stressors. They are part of the human condition. Our built-in stress response is protective, but if improperly controlled, can be destructive. We have been given the spiritual, intellectual, and physical resources to cope with stressors and manage our responses to them. Exercise stewardship and...

> *"...do not be anxious about anything, but in everything by prayer and supplication with thanksgiving let your requests be made known to God. And the peace of God, which surpasses all understanding, will guard your hearts and your minds in Christ Jesus."*

(Philippians 4:6,7)

Bibliography and Resources for Further Study

Allred, K.D. and T.W. Smith. "The Hardy Personality: Cognitive and Physiological Responses to Evaluative Threat." *Journal of Personality and Social Psychology*, 56:1989, 257-266.

Ballard, Stanley, "Saints and Stress," *Torch*, Vol. 7, 1984, pp. 4–5.

Barefoot, John, Svend Larsen, et al., "Hostility, Incidence of Acute Myocardial Infarction, and Mortality in a Sample of Older Danish Men and Women," *American Journal of Epidemiology*, Vol. 142, No. 5, 1995, pp. 477–484.

Berger, B.G., "Coping With Stress: The Effectiveness of Exercise," *Quest*, Feb. 1994, pp. 100–118.

Diehl, Pamela S. "Hitting the Haystack," *Torch*, Vol. 7, 1984, pp. 10–11.

Dolph, Charles D. "Reducing Stress," *Torch*, Vol. 7, 1984, pp. 8–9.

Editors, "Work vs. Play: A Nation in Search of Balance," *Hippocrates*, Oct. 1994.

Fish, Kristine. *Stress Management for a Healthy Life*. Dubuque, IA: Kendall-Hunt Publishing, 2010.

Franks, B. D., "What Is Stress?" *Quest*, Feb. 1994, pp. 1–7.

Funk, S.C. "Hardiness: A Review of Theory and Research." *Health Psychology* 11:1992, 335-345.

Greenberg, Jerrold S. *Comprehensive Stress Management*. Dubuque, IA: Wm. C. Brown Company, 1983.

Guyton, Arthur C. *Textbook of Medical Physiology*. Philadelphia: W.B. Saunders, 1986, 373-374.

Hansen, Randall S. *"Top College Stessors That Affect Academic Performance."* www.mycollege successstory.com.

Junco, Reynol and Shelia Cotton. "The Relationship Between Multitasking and Academic Performance." *Computers & Education* (59) 2012, 505-514.

Kobasa, S.C. "Stressful Life Events, Personality, and Health: An Inquiry into Hardiness." *Journal of Personality and Social Psychology,* 37:1979, 1-11.

Kobasa, S.C., S.R. Maddi, and S. Kahn. "Hardiness and Health: A Prospective Study." *Journal of Personality and Social Psychology*, 42: 1982, 168-177.

Malarkey, William, Pamela Peeke, Nancy Snyderman, et al., *ABC News Special: Stress Hurts*, March 9, 2001.

Marieb, Elaine N. and Katja Hoehn. Human Anatomy and Physiology. Boston: Benjamin Cummings, 2010, 456.

Markell, Jan and Jane Winn, *Overcoming Stress*, Wheaton, IL: Victor Books, 1982.

Marx, Martin, Thomas Garrity, and Frank Bowers, "The Influence of Recent Life Experience on the Health of College Freshmen," *Journal of Psychosomatic Research*, Vol. 19, 1975, pp. 87–98.

Minirth, Frank, Don Hawkins, Paul Meier and Richard Flournoy, *How to Beat Burnout*, Chicago, IL: Moody Press, 1986.

National Association for Physical Education in Higher Education, "Physical Activity and Stress" *Quest*, Oct. 1994.

Rice, Phillip L. *Stress and Health – Principles and Practice for Coping and Wellness*. Belmont, CA: Brookes-Cole Publishing, 1987.

Siegman, Aron, "Cardiovascular Consequences of Expressing, Experiencing, and Repressing Anger," *Journal of Behavioral Medicine*, Vol. 16, No. 6, 1993, pp. 539–569.

Selye, Hans, *Stress Without Distress*, New York: J.B. Lippincott, 1974.

Sherman, C., "Stress: How to Help Patients Cope," *The Physician and Sportsmedicine*, July 1994, pp. 66–71.

Stalk, Irene M, and Carol Dickman. "Self-Reported Stressors of College Freshmen." Presented at Mid-South Education Research Association, Louisville, KY, 1988.

Swenson, Richard A. *The Overload Syndrome – Learning to Live Within Your Limits*. Colorado Springs, CO: Navpress,, 1998.

Swenson, Richard *A., Margin: Restoring Emotional, Physical, Financial and Time Reserves to Overloaded Lives*, Colorado Springs: Navpress, 1992.

Swenson, Richard A. *In Search of Balance – Keys to a Stable Life*. Colorado Springs, CO: Navpress, 2010.

Tubesing, Donald A. *Kicking Your Stress Habits – A Do-It-Yourself Guide for Coping with Stress*. Duluth, MN: Whole Person Inc., 1981.

Wright, J.J. "Reported Personal Stress Sources and Adjustment of Entering Freshmen." *Journal of Counseling Psychology* 14: 1964, 371-373.

Chapter 10

Stewardship through Sound Nutrition

Essential Terms

Amino Acids	*Macronutrient*
Anabolism	*Metabolism*
Antioxidant	*Micronutrients*
Calorie	*Net Carb*
Caloric Density	*Nutrient Density*
Catabolism	*Omega-3 Fatty Acid*
Complete Protein	*Ovolactovegetarian*
Essential Amino Acids	*Polyunsaturated Fat*
Free Radical	*Protein*
Gluconeogenesis	*Saturated Fat*
Glycemic Index	*Trans Fatty Acids*
Lactovegetarian	*Unsaturated Fats*
Lipoproteins	*Vegan*

Objectives

Upon completion of this chapter, students should be able to:

1. Define and correctly use the terms listed above.

2. Discuss scriptural directives that relate to our attitudes about and uses of food.

3. Name the macronutrients, and explain their primary roles in the body's metabolism.

4. Have a general understanding of how the body uses the micronutrients: vitamins and minerals.

5. Compare personal eating patterns to recommended guidelines.

6. Explain why extremes in eating behaviors are not part of a godly body care program.

7. Differentiate between more and less healthful food choices, based on nutrient density.

8. Be familiar with the current U.S. Dietary Goals and Guidelines.

9. Knowledgeably discuss the use of nutritional supplements.

10. Make use of the nutrition information found on labels of commercially prepared foods.

11. Recognize common myths and misperceptions about foods and diet.

Food: A Believer's Perspective

The great Creator-Designer of our physical bodies structured them to "run on" and be maintained by a regular, daily intake of food and water. He "stocked" our world with a great variety and abundance of plant and animal foods for our sustenance and enjoyment. He gave us our senses of taste, smell, and sight, in part, to enhance our enjoyment of foods. The abundance of the food supply is obvious in a country like ours; however, the potential for the earth to bring forth crops of grain, vegetables and fruits is present even in those countries where people are hungry. This book is about our responsibility for stewardship of the body. However, God did give to humans the job of wisely managing His earth. Famine exists where man has been foolish in cutting forests and causing soil erosion, or failing to properly manage water supplies. Given an opportunity, God's wonderful earth will "come back" after fires, floods, volcanic eruptions and all manner of natural disasters. Man's folly and greed are the primary impediments to an abundant food supply.

It is evident from scripture that Christ partook of food, and He considered eating important enough that on at least two occasions, He performed miracles so that great crowds of people who came to hear Him could be fed (Matthew 14:14–21, 15:30–38). Our Heavenly Father has given us great freedom of choice in food selection, and has allowed us to develop technologies that have enhanced the production, preservation, preparation and distribution of foods.

We have freedom to satisfy our individual preferences in food choice; we don't all have to like spinach or broccoli. We can choose to eat meat or not, and to have our ethnic and regional tastes in foods. We have a responsibility, as good stewards, to use foods in ways that promote well-being. Eating or not eating must not enslave us (Matthew 6:25; 1 Corinthians 6:12). It may be an area in which Christian liberty, at times, must yield to brotherly love (Romans 14:15, 20, 21; 1 Corinthians 8:13). How we structure our eating habits is a part of the God-honoring lifestyle (1 Corinthians 10:31).

A great many factors converge to shape our food preferences. Childhood experiences, parental influences, cultural/ethnic heritage, geography, economics and time constraints all have some part in forming the eating patterns we have now. We seldom really examine something so basic and "taken for granted" as eating. Since food choices and amounts are central to the body's energy supply and tissue maintenance, we should periodically "check up" on our eating habits.

To be good stewards of our bodies, we need to relate to and use foods in healthy ways. While it's appropriate to enjoy eating, and it is certainly part of most social occasions, our lives shouldn't revolve around it. Food choices and quantities need to be characterized by discipline, moderation and wisdom. *Discipline* is the exercise of self-control, and the use of principles to guide our actions. We discipline ourselves as to the amounts and kinds of foods we eat. We do so based on what we know about what's good for the body.

Moderation is the avoidance of extremes, and aiming for balance in choices and behaviors. This principle guides us away from excesses or deficiencies in amounts and kinds of foods. It counsels against excluding some food types and over-consuming other types. Neither prolonged fasts nor "fad" diets, for example, are part of the God-honoring lifestyle.

Wisdom is judicious, appropriate application of knowledge. Nutritionists have given us a great volume of knowledge about foods and how the body uses them. As stewards of our body's well-being, we have the responsibility to use what we know to "tweak" our food likes and dislikes so that our diet will provide what the body needs for optimal function.

What Foods Do for the Body

Foods are sources of energy and are the raw materials from which the numerous substances essential to cell function are synthesized. They provide the materials needed for the growth, repair and replacement of tissues. The complex combination of processes by which foods are broken down and used in the body is termed *metabolism*. The processing of foods to their ultimate end products of energy and tissue constituents is *catabolism*. Synthesis of body tissues, energy stores and numerous biochemical substances from foods is *anabolism*.

Foods are made up of *nutrients*, or substances that provide matter necessary to life. Four of those, namely carbohydrates, proteins, fats and water are termed *macronutrients*; more than 95% of the foods we consume are made up of these in varying combinations. No less necessary to life processes, but needed in much smaller amounts are the *micronutrients* vitamins and minerals. Although these contain no energy, they are essential to the numerous chemical reactions always occurring in body cells.

Most of the plant and animal foods we eat consist of nutrients in combination. Whole wheat bread for example, is made up of carbohydrate, protein, a little fat and a little water; it also contains vitamins and minerals. A slice of roast beef is protein and fat, with vitamins and minerals; a broiled chicken breast is nearly all protein, with vitamins and minerals. A health-promoting diet is one that includes nutrients in appropriate proportions and meets the individual's energy needs.

The energy content of foods is expressed in units called calories, which are units of heat energy. The number of calories that a person needs depends on several factors, including age, gender and activity level. A male between the ages of 19 and 30 who is moderately active needs about 2600–2800 calories/day to maintain his present body weight. A moderately active female in the same age range requires 2000–2200 calories/day.

The energy available from carbohydrates and proteins is four calories per gram; a gram of fat provides 9 calories. Foods that are higher in fat content are said to have high *caloric density* because they contain more than twice the calorie content of an equivalent amount of carbohydrate or protein. A handful of potato chips has as many calories as a medium-sized apple; the potato chips have a higher caloric density than the apple.

We've all heard recommendations to follow a "balanced diet." Although we've all heard the term, there are many notions as to exactly what it means. One of the charges given to our government's Department of Agriculture is promoting the nutritional health of Americans. The department, together with the Department of Health and Human Services, issues dietary guidelines designed to improve the wellbeing of citizens. They also make available a host of helpful material in print, and over the internet.

These materials are updated, and "re-packaged" to make them more user-friendly every five years. The current guidelines are *Dietary Guidelines for Americans–2010*. The 2010 version of the guidelines summarizes recommendations for nutritional health as:

1. Balance calorie intake with activity level.

2. Balance intake of carbohydrates, proteins, and fats for optimal function.

The Guidelines include helpful information on food types to increase in one's diet, which types to decrease, and gives suggestions for developing healthy eating patterns. The entire document can be viewed or downloaded from http://www.health.gov/dietaryguidelines/dga2010/DietaryGuidelines2010.pdf.

Helps for implementing healthy food choices are attractively packaged in the new, user-friendly www.choosemyplate.gov tool, which replaces "My Pyramid." Readers are urged to go to the site and explore the options and information it provides.

Table 10.1	Estimated Daily Calorie Needs by Gender, Age, and Activity Level		
Gender	Age	Activity Level		
		Sedentary	Moderate	Active
Female	14–18	1800	2000	2400
	19–30	1800–2000	2000–2200	2400
	31–50	1800	2000	2400
	51 and older	1600	1800	2000–2200
Male	14–18	2000–2400	2400–2800	2800–3200
	19–30	2400–2600	2600–2800	3000
	31–50	2200–2400	2400–2600	2800–3000
	51 and older	2000–2200	2200–2400	2400–2800

(Adapted from Dietary Guidelines for Healthy Americans-2010, 14)

Note that calorie need at each activity level declines with age. That is because one's metabolic rate, the rate at which energy is used, declines gradually as one ages. That, together with the change in daily activity level that is usual for adults once they leave school, accounts for the gradual weight gain most adults experience.

Nutrient Balance

For optimal health, one's energy intake needs to not only be appropriate for activity level, but also sufficient to contain the macronutrients carbohydrates, proteins, and fats in the proper proportion for the body to function well.

Table 10.2	Recommended Nutrient Percentages and Amounts for a 2200 Daily Calorie Requirement	
Nutrient	Percentage of total calories	Amount in Grams
Carbohydrate	45–65%	248–358
Protein	10–35%	85–193
Total Fat	20–35%	49–86
Saturated Fats	<10%	5 to 9

Adapted from Dietary Guidelines for Healthy Americans-2010, 16 and 76

Nutrients

Carbohydrates

These are the starches and sugars found in plant foods like grains, vegetables and fruits. They are the body's preferred energy source because they can be digested and converted to energy most efficiently. Their chemical make-up is simple: atoms of carbon, hydrogen and oxygen arranged in various configurations; the process by which plants do this is exquisitely complex and bears witness to the wisdom of the Creator.

Plants, with their green pigment chlorophyll, are able to use the sun's energy to combine carbon dioxide from the air with water drawn from the ground to form high energy molecules known as sugars, as well as larger molecules called starches. As a by-product of the process, free oxygen is released into the atmosphere, replenishing our air supply. The miracle that is photosynthesis will feed the earth's population if man will care properly for soil and water. God has allowed us to learn how to develop plants suited to various soil and climate types; it's our responsibility to be faithful stewards of the earth and of the knowledge we've acquired.

Carbohydrate foods or "carbs" are those made from grain, like breads, cereals and pasta. They are the starchy vegetables like potatoes, corn and peas; they are fruits and fruit juices. They are also sugars and syrups made from sugar cane, sugar beets, sweet corn plants and maple sap. These foods, and the things made from them, differ in the ease and speed with which the body can break them down and begin to use or store the calories provided.

Carbohydrate foods can be divided into two groups: "simple" carbohydrate that the body digests and absorbs quickly, and "complex" those which contain sugars, starches and fiber which require longer digestion times. Simple carbohydrate foods are those that have sugar or syrups as their primary ingredient, perhaps followed closely by refined flour. Examples are candies, cookies, cakes, soft drinks, etc.

Complex carbohydrates are grains, vegetables and fruits. They are made up of long-chain sugar and starch molecules, which take longer for digestion and absorption. The glucose derived from them is absorbed into the blood gradually over a period of several hours. The complex carbohydrates are grains like corn, oats, wheat and barley; vegetables like potatoes, lima beans, carrots and peas; fruits like apples, bananas, strawberries and pears. Complex carbohydrate foods are *nutrient dense* because in addition to energy, they provide vitamins, minerals and fiber. Plant fiber is not broken down by the digestive enzymes and provides no nutritive value, but by adding bulk to the material passing through the digestive tract, the work of the colon is facilitated.

We now know that not all complex carbohydrate foods are created equal in terms of the blood glucose response their ingestion produces. A measure known as the *glycemic index* was devised as an indicator of a food's ability to raise blood glucose in a short period of time. This grew out of what we've learned about non-insulin-dependent diabetes, which is on the increase among both adults and adolescents.

We had traditionally thought of diabetes as a condition in which the body does not produce enough insulin. We have learned that people with non-insulin-dependent diabetes actually have become insulin-resistant. This comes about due to repeated insulin surges, in response to over-consumption of high glycemic index carbohydrates. Over a period of time, insulin-resistance develops and cells are unable to use the glucose for energy. Blood glucose then remains elevated, setting in motion the process of damage to the body's organs.

Choosing carbohydrates with moderate or low glycemic indices avoids the frequency of insulin peaks, and lessens the likelihood of becoming insulin-resistant. This may help prevent the onset of non-insulin-dependent diabetes. In those with a familial predisposition to this type of diabetes, avoiding high glycemic index foods may delay the onset of the condition, as well as lessen its severity.

Table 10.3	Examples of High, Medium and Low Glycemic Index (G.I.) Foods	
High G.I.	Medium G.I.	Low G.I.
White potatoes, baked/boiled	Spaghetti, macaroni	Apples, peaches
Waffles, pancakes	Oatmeal	Tomatoes
White bread, rolls	Corn	Raw carrots
Honey, corn syrups	Peas	Dried beans
White or brown rice	Sweet potatoes	Milk
Most dry cereals	Watermelon	Grapefruit
Bananas	Oranges	Yogurt
Raisins	Whole wheat bread	Soy products

Note: There is considerable variation among references as to these groupings; the listing here represents a consensus of many sources.

For most of us, the relevance of a food's glycemic index is simply that when we eat a meal primarily made up of those foods, we will be hungry again sooner than if our meal includes mostly carbohydrate foods of medium or low glycemic index. The sweet pastry or donut for breakfast is a primary reason for the mid-morning hunger many experience. If we have a genetic predisposition toward diabetes, eating foods with high glycemic indices on a regular basis will cause increased insulin release, and foster insulin-resistance.

In his book *Eat, Drink and Be Healthy*, Harvard nutritionist Walter Willett stresses the importance of obtaining most of our carbohydrate intake from whole grains, non-starchy vegetables and fruits. His position is, now that we know all carbohydrates are not equal in terms of their effect on blood glucose, we should choose foods accordingly. This means we should choose foods like pasta, white rice, potatoes and most dry cereals on an occasional, rather than a frequent, basis (Willett, pp. 16–26).

Carbohydrate foods are the foundation of a healthful diet: over half of our daily energy intake should be made up of these. Of that amount, at least three-fourths should be in the form of vegetables, whole grains and fruits. These provide not only energy, but other nutrients as well; you're getting more nutritional value for the number of calories you're taking in. Simple sugar foods, like soft drinks, candies and cookies should be occasional treats; they give energy, but very little in the way of additional nutrients for the calories consumed.

Carbohydrates and Body Function

The main role of carbohydrates is to provide the energy needed for muscular work and for basic life processes. There are some additional functions that this nutrient performs; knowing about these helps one understand the importance of well-chosen carbohydrates to health, and the folly of any diet that excludes or severely limits their consumption.

The body stores carbohydrates in the form of *glycogen* in the liver and in skeletal muscles. This is the energy source one draws on to do demanding physical work over an extended period of time, such as running a marathon or competing in a long-distance bicycle race. Endurance athletes follow specific regimens of diet and exercise so that they come to their event with maximal stores of glycogen. Even so, those stores are depleted by a two-hour strenuous workout (McArdle, Katch & Katch, p. 214). This underscores the need for adequate intake of carbohydrate foods on a daily basis.

Our red blood cells can use only glucose, which, as we've seen, is most easily and efficiently obtained from carbohydrates. Our central nervous system runs primarily on energy from glucose; if our carbohydrate intake is too low, we become irritable and tired, and may have difficulty concentrating.

In order to keep nerve cells functioning, the body will activate a metabolic pathway called *gluconeogenesis* which converts protein to glucose. Protein used in this way is lost from its normal use for tissue growth and repair. An adequate daily carbohydrate intake "spares" protein for its normal uses (McArdle, Katch, Katch, *Sports and Exercise Nutrition*).

There is no substitute for carbohydrate; it is an essential nutrient. The absolute minimum amount needed in order to spare proteins being burned for energy is 100 grams for an average-sized adult. Three to four times that much is recommended for optimal function (Sizer and Whitney, p. 114).

This food group has been misunderstood by many, and has been cast in the "villain's role" with regard to unhealthful weight gain. Just about any type of food consumed in excessive quantities can add pounds. You should now have a better understanding of carbohydrates and their contribution to a healthy diet.

Proteins

Protein is a nutrient made up of carbon, hydrogen, nitrogen and oxygen atoms arranged in a variety of structures. Like the carbohydrates, proteins consist of many simpler molecules linked together; these subunits are called *amino acids*. Protein contains 4 calories of energy per gram, the same as carbohydrates.

There are 20 different amino acids that are needed by the body; of these, eight must be obtained "already made" from foods. These are the *essential* amino acids; the others can be synthesized in the body from available nutrient materials. Foods that contain the essential amino acids in sufficient amounts are called "complete proteins."

Examples of complete protein foods are eggs, meats and poultry, fish, and dairy products. Note that those are all of animal origin. Vegetable protein sources like dried beans, soy products, grains and nuts lack some of the essential amino acids, and so are not "complete" by themselves. Of the plant protein foods, soy products are the most-nearly complete in their amino acid make-up.

The typical American diet is high in complete proteins; the exceptions are those who choose to be vegetarians. The vegetarian eating-style can be a healthful one, but the individual needs to learn to combine foods in such a way that they "complement" one another. That is, the essential amino acids lacking in one food are present in another eaten at the same meal, or at least on the same day. Examples of complementary protein combinations are macaroni and cheese, peanut butter on whole-grain bread, baked beans and whole-grain bread, and red beans with rice.

Those who choose to be complete vegetarians or "vegans" don't use eggs or milk, but get all their protein from plant sources. These folk must be particularly attentive to combining foods so that they get adequate amounts of essential amino acids. They also should take supplements containing vitamin B-12, calcium and phosphorus. Vitamin B-12 is found only in foods of animal origin; calcium and phosphorus are not contained in significant amounts in plant foods.

From the standpoint of optimal nutrition, it probably is wiser for those who would rather not eat meats or fish to include eggs and dairy products in their diets. That way, they will get sufficient quantities of essential amino acids, vitamin B-12, calcium and phosphorus without necessitating the killing of animals for food.

Proteins and Body Function

The body's primary use of protein is as the "raw material" from which muscle and connective tissue is made and repaired. Smaller amounts are used in a host of ways, including:

1. Making hemoglobin, antibodies, hormones, neurotransmitters and enzymes

2. Maintenance of the body's water balance

3. Maintenance of the body's acid-base balance

4. Production of factors essential to blood's clotting process

At rest or during light-to-moderate activity the body does not use protein as an energy source, provided that the diet includes adequate carbohydrate foods. If the carbohydrate intake is very low or the exercise effort is strenuous and prolonged, the body withdraws the amino acid alanine from skeletal muscle. The alanine is converted to glucose in the liver by a series of biochemical processes known as the glucose-alanine cycle. In prolonged strenuous exercise, like for example a triathlon, the catabolism of skeletal muscle may provide as much as 10–15% of the needed energy, because body carbohydrate stores have been exhausted (McArdle, Katch and Katch, p. 36).

So, although protein can and is at times used for energy, that is not its preferred use. If skeletal muscle is catabolized, or broken down for energy, over an extended time because carbohydrate is not available, muscle wasting and weakness is the result. You have seen pictures of starvation victims whose limbs seem to have nearly no muscle at all; that's because it was literally consumed to provide energy to maintain life.

The Body's Protein Requirement

About 18–21% of our total calorie intake ideally should be in the form of proteins; most Americans consume considerably more than that. The recommendation for sedentary adults is 0.8 grams of protein per kilogram of body weight. For a person weighing 70 kg. (154 lbs.), that amounts to just 56 grams of protein/day. Active people and athletes benefit from a higher protein intake, ranging from 1.2–1.8 grams/kilogram of body weight (Williams, 7th Ed. p. 221). That would change the protein need of the 70 kg. person to 84–126 grams/day.

Increasing protein intake to those levels doesn't require the use of special foods or supplements; we are blessed with an abundance of protein foods. Most people, without thinking about it, consume about 100 grams of protein daily. We need to be a bit cautious in choosing protein foods, in that many of our "favorites" (meats, cheeses, eggs) come with considerable fat content, so we need to be aware of total calorie intake as well.

Table 10.4 presents the protein content of some often-consumed foods. This shows how easy it is to consume adequate protein from normal foods.

Table 10.4 Protein Content of Commonly Consumed Foods	
Milk, 2%, one 8-ounce glass	8 grams
Eggs, 2 scrambled	12 grams
Roast beef, 3 ounces	25 grams
1/2 cup navy beans, cooked	7 grams
Macaroni and cheese, 1/2 cup	9 grams
Roasted chicken, 6 ounces	43 grams
Peanut butter, 1 tbsp.	4 grams
Whole wheat bread, 2 slices	6 grams
Cheddar cheese, 1 ounce	7 grams
Tofu, 1/2 cup	10 grams
Peanuts, 1 ounce	7.5 grams

Note that the brief listing of foods above are from both animal and plant sources. Most Americans eat a diet containing both animal and plant protein foods, with the majority coming from meats, eggs and dairy products. Because of the amount of fat that "comes with" those foods, they have a high calorie value. If we were to get at least a third of our protein intake from non-animal sources like dried beans, lentils, soy-based foods and nuts, we could more easily stay within an appropriate total calorie range.

Fats

Fats, more properly called lipids, are the most concentrated energy nutrients. Each gram of fat contains 9 calories. Fats, like carbohydrates, are made from carbon, hydrogen and oxygen atoms; they differ in the way the atoms are arranged, the way they are bonded together, and the ratio of hydrogen to oxygen atoms.

Nutritionists refer to fats as "saturated," "monounsaturated" or "polyunsaturated," depending on the structure of the molecule. When the bonds between carbon atoms are all single, each carbon's remaining two bonds is attached to a hydrogen atom. The molecule holds the maximum possible number of hydrogen atoms, and is said to be "saturated." When the molecule contains one double bond, there are two fewer hydrogen atoms, so the fat is "monounsaturated." When there are two or more double bonds, the lipid is "polyunsaturated."

Food sources of saturated fats are mainly of animal origin: beef, pork, lamb, egg yolks and dairy fats like butter and cream. Among the fats derived from plants, coconut oil and palm oil are saturated. Other vegetable oils, like corn oil, olive oil, peanut oil and others, are unsaturated. Unsaturated fats are liquid, or very soft, at room temperature; saturated fats are solids at room temperature.

From a health standpoint, the molecular structure of fat molecules is significant because of what happens in the body. Saturated fats, once digested and absorbed into the blood have a tendency, over time to form plaques on the walls of arteries, narrowing the vessel and reducing its ability to deliver blood to tissues in the area of the narrowing. This is the process known as *atherosclerosis*; we know that there is an association between this condition and high blood lipid levels. Atherosclerosis significantly increases risk of heart attack, stroke and other vascular disease. There are genetic as well as dietary factors involved in the development of atherosclerosis; these are further confounded by lifestyle factors like lack of exercise and cigarette smoking.

As mentioned, unsaturated fats are liquid, or nearly so, at room temperature; a corn-oil margarine starts out as a thick oil. However, most of us prefer what we spread on our toast to be somewhat firm and to look like the butter for which it's substituting. Manufacturers give us this by altering the lipid molecules, partially hydrogenating them, in effect making a saturated fat from what naturally was an unsaturated one. In addition to satisfying consumers, manufacturers find that partially-hydrogenated vegetable oils have a longer shelf-life than unsaturated oils.

In the hydrogenation process, the positioning of hydrogen atoms is also altered; the position change makes the molecule a "*trans fatty acid*" or trans fat. We've discovered that these artificially-created fats, even though they begin as vegetable oils, behave in the body just like saturated fats; that is, they form fatty plaques in blood vessels.

Like most body processes, lipid-metabolism is very complex, and so far we've mentioned only the fats we obtain from the foods we eat. Most of those are chemically called "simple" fats, or triglycerides. Two other lipid molecules, found in foods and also manufactured in the body, are the phospholipids and cholesterol. Phospholipids, because of their chemical structure, are able to regulate the passage of materials across cell membranes; we synthesize most of the phospholipids we need. Cholesterol is a fat with quite a different molecular structure; we obtain it from animal fats, egg yolks and shellfish, but we also manufacture it in the liver. Cholesterol is essential to the formation of many of the body's hormones; the problem is that some of us, due to hereditary makeup, manufacture too much.

We have learned that a high level of cholesterol in the blood is also a risk factor for heart disease, just as are high levels of triglycerides (derived directly from the diet). We've learned also that cholesterol is transported in the blood by "carrier" molecules, known as lipoproteins. These are combinations of fat and protein, as their name suggests, and are synthesized in the liver. Two of these are of special interest: high density lipoprotein (HDL) and low density lipoprotein (LDL). It seems that HDL is the "good guy" of the two, since it binds excess cholesterol in the blood, and carries it away from arterial walls, returning it to the liver where it is chemically broken down. In this way it tends to have a protective effect against atherosclerotic plaque formation.

Low density lipoproteins (LDL) behave in the opposite way. They transport cholesterol into body cells, and have a particular affinity for arterial walls. They are the "bad guys" in that they are instrumental in the atherosclerotic process. Elevated LDL is associated with increased heart disease risk; elevated HDL is associated with a low risk.

In the last forty-five years we've learned a great deal about the lipoproteins, dietary lipids, cholesterol and how these interact with an individual's genetic make-up and lifestyle. We know that HDL levels can be increased by physical exercise, and that by minimizing the saturated and trans fats in our diet we can lower LDL levels. God has also allowed scientists to synthesize medications that will alter the amounts of cholesterol we produce.

Role of Fats in the Body

Although most American diets are a bit high in total fat content, fats should not be thought of as "the enemy" of sound nutrition and a healthy diet. Fats are vital to human nutrition, and besides that, they are largely responsible for the satisfaction we derive from the taste and texture of foods. It's fat that makes biscuits fluffy, steaks juicy, ice cream smooth and pie crusts flaky. Fat is responsible for a "satisfied" feeling we have following a good meal.

Physiologically, fats perform many essential roles, among them the following:

1. Fat is a concentrated energy source, providing 9 calories/gram; under certain conditions, like moderate-intensity exercise, the body uses fat to fuel the work it is doing.

2. Fat that is not needed for immediate use is stored in adipose cells; storage fat is an energy reserve, as well as an insulation and protection for body organs. Obviously, if the amount of storage fat is excessive, it becomes a hindrance.

3. Fats are essential to the body's ability to absorb and use vitamins A, D, E, and K.

4. Fats are essential to maintenance of cell membranes throughout the body.

5. There are two "essential" fatty acids, linoleic and alpha-linoleic acid. These can't be synthesized in the body, but are obtained from nuts, fish, vegetable oils and soy products. They both are necessary to the formation of substances that regulate many complex bodily processes, like blood clotting and inflammatory responses.

6. Fats are the chemical bases for numerous body substances, like hormones.

Nutritionists have been recommending that we reduce the amount of fat we consume for at least two decades; amazingly, we have actually done so! In 1965, the average American got 45% of his calories from fats; in 1995 that had fallen to 34% (Thompson and Manore, p. 172). However, before we pat ourselves on the back, we must acknowledge two facts. First, we are consuming more total calories; and second, of the fats in our diet, a high proportion is either saturated fat or trans-fat. Worthwhile goals to work toward are to keep total fat consumption to not >35% of total calories, to minimize our use of saturated fats, and to avoid trans-fats as much as possible.

A difficulty we have in food selection is that so much fat is "hidden." A seemingly "lean" piece of beef or pork contains considerable fat. Commercially baked breads and pastries are made with hydrogenated shortenings; the fats are "invisible" once the food is prepared. Crackers and other snack foods are very high in fat, even though they don't appear so. A great many of the fats contained in these common foods are of the "trans" variety. We must become discerning consumers, read the labels of commercially prepared foods, and learn the meanings of "low fat," "reduced fat, and "fat free."

A serving of regular Oreo cookies (3) has 160 calories, 23 grams of carbohydrate and 7 grams of fat. Reduced fat Oreos (serving of 3) has 130 calories, 25 grams of carbohydrate and 3.5 grams of fat. Regular fig newtons have 210 calories in a serving of 3, 30 grams of carbohydrate and 4.5 grams of fat; fat free newtons contain 204 calories/3 cookies, and 27 grams of carbohydrate. What we must be aware of is that the "reduced fat" or "fat-free" designation doesn't always mean significantly fewer calories.

For a product to be labeled "reduced fat" it must contain 25% less fat than the regular version of the same product. To be "low fat," it must contain no more than 3 grams of fat/serving; to carry the label "fat free" a product must contain less than 0.5 grams of fat/serving. One must also pay attention to serving sizes as well.

Here are some suggestions that may help us make healthier choices when it comes to the fats in our diet.

1. Read labels carefully. Manufacturers may proudly tell you their product is made with "all vegetable" shortening, but the fine print may tell you that it contains coconut or palm oil, which are both saturated fats. When corn, canola or peanut oils are used, be alert for the word "hydrogenated," which makes a saturated fat of an originally unsaturated one; it typically also makes it a trans-fat.

2. Limit red meats to two or three times/week, and trim off all the visible fat possible. Buy leaner, less expensive cuts of beef, and cook it longer; it will taste good, and total fat content will be lower. Reduce your serving size of meat to the size of a deck of playing cards.

3. Remove skin and visible fat from chicken or turkey before cooking it.

4. If you like fish, have it once/week; remember that crispy breading, although delicious, defeats the effort to reduce fat intake. At earlier writings, we recommended eating more fish; knowing now that ocean fish like swordfish and mackerel may have high levels of contaminants we advise less. When you buy canned tuna (considered safe from contaminants), buy the kind packed in water rather than oil. Experiment with herbs and fruit juices to enhance flavor.

5. Processed meats like cold cuts and hot dogs contain a lot of fat, although you can't see it. Don't eat them often. In addition to their high fat content, they have a lot of salt and preservatives.

6. Reduce your dairy fat intake by using 2% milk, by using white cheeses like mozzarella (it is made from skim milk), and by substituting frozen yogurt for ice cream often. Plain yogurt can be used as a sour cream substitute in salad dressings and vegetable dips. In earlier writings, we advised the use of vegetable oil margarine instead of butter; now, with what we know about how fats are changed by the hydrogenation process, butter doesn't seem such a bad choice. Of course, moderation in the amounts used is important.

7. Be disciplined in the amounts of high-fat snacks you eat. If you buy potato chips, look for the baked ones; they are lower in fat and salt. Nuts are a better snack choice, but remember that although they contain vitamins and minerals, and "good" fat, they are high in calories, so be moderate in amounts.

8. Baked goods like doughnuts, croissants and Danish rolls taste so good because they are very high in fats. Have them as occasional treats.

9. The relationship of egg consumption to blood cholesterol levels hasn't been resolved; however, most of us should limit our "eggs as eggs" consumption to four/week or less. We get the equivalent of another three or four eggs in baked goods, ice cream, salad dressings and other prepared foods.

10. Be aware that a number of foods now are available in which various man-made substances are used to give foods the flavor and texture previously derived from fats. These substances, made from such materials as egg whites, oat fiber, or vegetable fiber are used in salad dressings, frozen desserts, cheeses and many other foods. They reduce the total calorie intake and eliminate saturated fat. These fat substitutes have trade names like "Simplesse," "Oatrim" and "Beta-trim"; watch for them on labels.

Vitamins

Vitamins are organic compounds present in small amounts in all plant and animal foods. They contain no calories, but are essential to the body's numerous complex chemical processes. They function primarily as co-enzymes in regulating processes by which carbohydrates, proteins and fats are converted to energy, and in the maintenance of nerve tissue and the synthesis of blood cells. Most of the vitamins are water-soluble; that means that the body depends on receiving a new supply daily, as any surplus will not accumulate, but will be excreted in the urine. The few vitamins that are fat-soluble, vitamins A, D, E, and K, are bound to body fats, so deficiency is rare. Two of that group, vitamin D and vitamin K are made by the body as well as obtained from foods. Getting too much of the water soluble vitamins (developing toxicity) doesn't happen, because excesses are eliminated; however, we need to be careful about using supplements of the fat soluble vitamins, since they can accumulate in the body.

The water soluble vitamins include a group known as the "B-complex" and vitamin C. The B-complex group includes: thiamin, riboflavin, niacin, folacin, biotin, pantothenic acid, vitamin B-12 and vitamin B-6. The functions of the B-complex vitamins include energy production, red blood cell synthesis, and the synthesis and maintenance of nerve tissue.

If one eats a diet that includes whole grains, meats, milk, eggs and green vegetables, he will have all the B-complex vitamins needed for health. Vitamin B-12 is present only in animal foods, so the total vegetarian (no meats, milk or eggs) will need to take a B-12 supplement to avoid deficiency.

Vitamin C (ascorbic acid) has several vital functions. It is essential to the formation of a tough protein called collagen, that is part of all the body's connective tissues; it is essential to wound healing and to the resilience of ligaments and tendons. Vitamin C enhances the body's ability to absorb iron from foods, and enhances our immune response; there is no proof, however, that large amounts of vitamin C will keep us from getting colds. Good food sources of vitamin C include all citrus fruits, tomatoes, melons, sweet peppers, broccoli and cauliflower.

Vitamin C and vitamin E have an important protective role in the body's chemistry; they act as *anti-oxidants*. Metabolism, the production of energy from the foods we consume, is an oxidative chemical process. In oxidation, atoms lose electrons; most immediately gain or share an electron with another atom, and so are chemically stable; there are always some atoms, however, with an un-paired electron in its outermost energy level. Those atoms are unstable and are called free radicals.

Although they are the result of normal and necessary metabolic processes, free radicals can do serious damage to cell membranes, disrupting normal cell function. Free radical damage is thought to be linked to heart disease, arthritis, Alzheimer's disease and Parkinson's disease as well as cancer. Anti-oxidants like vitamins C and E donate electrons to free radicals, stabilizing them and preventing cell damage. Beta-carotene, a substance found in yellow vegetables and fruits is also an important antioxidant.

Vitamin E is found in wheat germ, vegetable oils, nuts, seeds and avocados. It is also plentiful in soy products, broccoli and peanuts.

Vitamins A, D, and K are the others in the fat-soluble group. Vitamin A has a vital role in maintaining the tissues essential to vision. In parts of the world where the diet is poor in milk, eggs and a variety of green and yellow vegetables, vitamin A deficiency is a significant cause of blindness. Most of the vitamin D we need is synthesized in the body, provided we're exposed to adequate sunlight. Vitamin K also is made by bacteria in the intestinal tract; it is essential to the normal clotting of blood. Food sources include green leafy vegetables and pork.

There is little evidence that today's food supply is depleted of its vitamin content. We are blessed to live in a nation whose agricultural output is abundant, varied and wholesome. The herbicides and pesticides that farmers use to maximize yield/acre are not harmful to humans. There is no proof that crops grown organically (without use of fertilizers, herbicides, pesticides) are more healthful or nutritious; they are significantly more expensive!

Elapsed time between the field and the table is the chief threat to vitamin content; the fresher a food is the better. Typically, with today's transportation, that time is short and nutrient loss is not great enough to be significant. How foods, particularly vegetables, are prepared is significant to nutrient content; cooking in water does destroy some of the vitamin content. The most nutrient-preserving way to prepare vegetables is to steam them just to the desired degree of tenderness. If vegetables must be boiled, save the water to use in soups.

We aren't quite as confident about the nutrients we get from consumption of meats and poultry. The government does a pretty good job of regulating processing plants, but is less effective in regulating how livestock intended for meat are fed. Cattle and poultry feed typically contains antibiotics and various growth enhancers to increase yield; questions about how these affect humans have yet to be fully answered. If affordable, meats produced without use of chemicals may be an appropriate option.

Meats are more susceptible to rapid chemical deterioration, so they need to be refrigerated properly, and frozen or cooked within a short time. All should be cooked until thoroughly done, to assure that any bacteria have been destroyed.

Minerals

Minerals are inorganic substances, that, like vitamins have no caloric value, but which are essential to the body's functions. Some, like calcium and phosphorus, are essential to formation and maintenance of structures like bones and teeth. Others, like sodium, potassium and magnesium are essential to bioelectric processes like muscle contraction and nerve impulse conduction. Some, like iron and iodine are needed only in tiny amounts, but are nonetheless absolutely essential to oxygen transport and regulation of metabolism. Trace minerals like cobalt, chromium, selenium, copper, fluoride, sulfur, zinc and manganese are involved in body chemistry in a host of different ways, and are present in most foods, so deficiency is unlikely. Two minerals, calcium and iron, are singled out for comment because they are the ones for which food sources alone may not be adequate.

Calcium

Calcium is a major constituent of bones and teeth. It is also significant in nerve transmission, muscle contraction, regulation of acid-base balance and blood clotting. The majority of our body's calcium (99%) is crystallized around collagen in our bones; this combination gives bones the qualities of hardness and resilience that make them so durable.

Dairy products are the most concentrated food sources of calcium, and usually are consumed in sufficient amounts through adolescence. While many adults either get out of the habit of drinking milk, or develop a degree of intolerance, plenty of calcium can be gotten from foods like yogurt and low-fat cheeses. Other good food sources are vegetables like broccoli, cauliflower, cabbage and brussels sprouts. Many commercially prepared foods offer "calcium fortified" versions; examples are dry cereals, orange juice and breads.

As people age, the calcium content of the bones lessens; this is partially due to poor dietary intake, changes in hormone levels, decreased physical exercise, and aging factors that are not yet understood. The result is that there is a loss of bone's calcium content, leaving bones brittle. This condition is called *osteoporosis*. Deformity of the vertebrae cause one to become shorter, and stooped; fractures of bones result from trauma that, at an earlier time in the person's life, may have produced only a bruise. Hip fractures are the most common cause of surgical procedures and prolonged disability among the elderly.

Both men and women experience loss of bone mass after age 35. The loss is more pronounced in women, and accelerates significantly at menopause. This process can be slowed by increasing calcium intake to 1000 mg./day at age 40; since even a good diet typically only provides about 500 mg. of calcium, taking a supplement is appropriate. Intake should be increased to 1200–1500 mg./day for post-menopausal women. Regular weight bearing exercise like walking also contributes to maintaining bone mass. Although some people are genetically predisposed to osteoporosis, life-long attention to bone health by means of proper diet and regular exercise can significantly lessen its impact on the individual.

Iron

Iron is a trace mineral; very little is needed, but iron deficiency is the world's most common nutrient deficiency. Iron is the critical component of hemoglobin, the substance in red blood cells that binds to oxygen and transports it to body tissues. When a person is deficient in iron, his red blood cells contain less hemoglobin, and so oxygen transport is compromised. The individual begins to tire easily, and perhaps feel "light-headed" on standing up; this is because tissues are not receiving the oxygen they need to function normally. This condition is *iron deficiency* anemia, and is the most common dietary deficiency around the world.

Men need about 8 mg. of iron daily, and most readily obtain it from their diets. About six milligrams of iron is absorbed for each 1000 calories consumed in a mixed diet; most men consume at least 2000 calories/day, so their iron need tends to be met easily. Pre-menopausal women require 18 mg. daily; the requirement drops to 8 mg./day after menopause; monthly menstrual blood loss is the reason for young women's higher iron need. Iron is lost from the body, so is not available for re-processing into new red blood cells; over time, deficiency develops. Even with a 2000 calorie/day diet, women will only absorb about 12 mg. of iron, not enough to meet the need. This should be remedied by taking a one/day vitamin with iron.

Endurance athletes and other very active people may also incur iron loss. Intense exercise, particularly distance running is associated with red blood cell rupture; the hemoglobin, with its iron content is then excreted by the kidney. Sweat is another route for iron loss; losses are tiny, on the order of 0.2 mg. per liter of water lost, but it's not unusual for an athlete to lose 2 liters of sweat in an intense workout. Given that total body iron stores are very small, over time these seemingly insignificant losses could become significant (Williams, p. 311).

Dietary iron occurs in two forms: *heme iron* and *non-heme iron*. Heme iron is found only in meats; beef is the richest source, followed by chicken, turkey and fish. This form of iron is more readily absorbed by the body. Non-heme iron is found in whole grain cereals and breads, vegetables like broccoli and peas, legumes like cooked dried beans, and dried fruits like apricots, prunes and raisins. Combining small amounts of meat with beans, rice, or vegetables enhances the body's absorption of iron from the plant foods. Adding a food rich in vitamin C also increases iron absorption, so chili with beans and spaghetti with tomato and meat sauce not only tastes good, but is good nutrition. Likewise, having an orange at breakfast will help the body absorb the iron in your whole-grain toast.

Water

Water is a nutrient, even though it contains no calories or vitamins. Mineral content differs with locality, but is not nutritionally significant. It is present in all foods, and is absolutely essential to body chemistry. Approximately 60% of the human body is water; it is part of all body tissues, and is involved in processes varying from muscle contraction to temperature regulation.

We need about two liters of water daily. This increases if one exercises heavily, causing profuse sweating. If water losses aren't replaced, normal processes are impaired. The most critical of these is temperature regulation. Since thirst is not a reliable indicator of hydration status, it's important that when people work or exercise in the heat, that they also take in small amounts of water frequently. Research has shown that solutions containing sugar and electrolytes are not better than plain water unless the exercise is intense enough and long enough to deplete energy stores. A glucose-electrolyte solution might be helpful in vigorous exercise continuing two or more hours; otherwise, plain cool water is quite adequate.

Questions and Controversies in Nutrition

There are many of these, and only a few will be addressed here. Others that relate more specifically to weight management will be addressed in a later chapter.

I see a lot of foods with terms like "net carbs," or "impact carbs" on their labels. What do these terms mean?

The weight-loss industry has succeeded in making a significant proportion of the population very "carbohydrate conscious"; not surprisingly, food manufacturers are appealing to this in their labeling. At this time there are no rules governing use of these terms, as there are for "low fat," "low sodium," etc., so it's difficult to determine exactly what a given label means. The "impact" or "net" carb claims are rooted in the fact that carbohydrate foods effect blood sugar levels at different rates, i.e. they differ in glycemic index, as explained earlier in the chapter. All carbohydrates that the body absorbs contribute calories to the body's fuel supply; one group called "sugar alcohols" have been used as sweetening agents for years in foods intended for use by diabetics, because their calorie content is a bit lower (about 3 calories/gram) than typical carbohydrate, and because they don't cause sharp increases in blood glucose levels. Compounds like xylitol and sorbitol are examples. Also, in the United States, the fiber content of a food is included with carbohydrates for labeling purposes. So, if an energy bar contains 30 grams of carbohydrate, and 27 grams come from sugar alcohols and 1 gram from fiber, the label proclaims "only 2 grams of impact carbs." *Consumers should also look at the total calorie content!*

Calories consumed compared to calories burned remains the most important factor to those concerned with managing body weight.

Some recommend that all adults take a daily multiple vitamin supplement? Isn't it better just to eat a healthy diet?

If we all would actually eat all the vegetables and fruits that we should, a supplement wouldn't be necessary. However, only a small proportion of Americans come even close to an appropriate and varied intake of fruits and vegetables;

French fries with ketchup really don't count as two servings of vegetables. Unless we really do include lots of vegetables on a regular basis, a daily vitamin supplement is a good idea.

Should that vitamin supplement come from a "health food" store?

Your vitamin supplement should be the most inexpensive commercially made vitamin pill you can find; vitamins are organic chemical compounds. Whether they are synthesized in a laboratory or derived from food sources doesn't make a difference.

Farmers use all sorts of chemical fertilizers and pesticides; fruit trees are sprayed with chemicals to prevent blight and pests. Are foods grown this way really safe?

Fertilizers put back into the soil elements that growing crops take out, so are really essential to renewing the fields, and preserving their fertility. Most pesticides are now synthetic analogs of substances plants produce to protect themselves from pests and disease; these are called biopesticides, and act to suppress rather than eradicate the pest or disease population. (Thompson and Manore, p. 522-523) They have minimal environmental impact, and are not toxic. The bottom line is: we want/need an abundant, wholesome and affordable food supply; judicious use of modern agrichemicals enables that.

For years, nutritionists and health providers have told us to eat more fish; now we hear some is not safe to eat because of the mercury it contains. What should we do?

Mercury is a naturally occurring element, and has always been present in ocean and freshwater fish; now, however, due to manufacturing processes that release mercury into the environment, its concentration in water and aquatic life has significantly increased over time. Ocean fish like swordfish, shark and mackerel, and shellfish tend to accumulate mercury, which of course is passed on to those who eat them. The current recommendation is that eating these foods once/week is safe (Thompson and Manore, p. 522).

What are all those hard-to-pronounce ingredients listed in the fine print on food labels? Can all those chemicals in foods be safe?

The tongue-twisting names belong to substances added to foods to make them look more attractive, taste better and resist spoilage longer. If they're in foods processed and packaged in the U.S., they are on the "generally recognized as safe" (GRAS) list maintained by our FDA. These are flavorings, coloring agents, emulsifiers, stabilizers, desiccants and humectants that keep salad dressings from separating, give ice creams attractive color and taste, make it possible for items like marshmallows to remain soft and pliable for months, and for bread to remain mold-free for an extended time. The fearsome listing of chemical additives is not a cause for concern; a few have allergies to specific agents, usually food colorings, and can avoid them by carefully reading labels.

Are foods that have been irradiated (treated with radiation) safe to eat?

Irradiating foods with x-ray or gamma ray beams is used to rid foods of bacteria or fungi that would cause spoilage; the rays leave no residue in the foods, and don't alter the appearance or texture of the foods themselves. The taste of dairy foods is significantly affected, so they are not preserved in this fashion. The process was developed by the National Aeronautics and Space Administration (NASA) to preserve foods used on long space flights. Foods that have been irradiated must carry a symbol on their labels; irradiation has been shown to be a safe way to preserve foods for an extended period of time.

Are genetically modified food crops really safe?

Since the 1990's, many of the food crops grown in the United States and around the world have been genetically modified in various ways. Since the earliest days of agricultural research, scientists have crossed different plant varieties to produce hybrids that have higher yields, better taste, or other desirable characteristics. That's why we can enjoy seedless grapes, navel oranges, and dozens of apple varieties. Genetic plant modification, though, goes further.

Molecular biologists have learned how to isolate the gene responsible for a specific trait, like drought-resistance from one plant species to another. They can also do this with genes from non-plant organisms. For example, a bacterium, *Bacillus thuringiensis*, produces a protein lethal to the corn borer, a common menace to the corn crop. Corn modified in this way literally produces its own pesticide, eliminating or greatly reducing the need for chemical pesticides. Soybeans have been modified to be tolerant of herbicides used to control weeds, thereby reducing the amount of chemicals needed. Genes have been spliced into a number of food crops to make them resistant to fungal disease. Agricultural geneticists are working to produce grains, vegetable, and fruit plants that are better able to withstand environmental conditions like drought or frost.

In the United States, many of our processed foods, like breakfast cereals, grain-based snack foods, and vegetable oils are made from genetically modified (GM) crops. In Europe, genetic modification of food crops has become a "cause" of activist groups, charging that "agribusinesses" in the pursuit of profit have been allowed to make potentially harmful alterations to food crops. In some countries, food products containing GM plant material must carry special labeling, while some have enacted a ban on growing GM crops. There are some vocal groups in the United States that are opposed to the use of gene technology in agriculture. It's doubtful that it will be banned here, but some form of labeling will likely be required.

The concerns cited by these groups are: hazards to human health; unintended harm to other species; possible gene-transfer to non-targeted species, perhaps resulting in herbicide resistant "super-weeds."

With regard to human health, in studies done during the 15-20 years humans have consumed GM food products, no harmful effects have been documented. Researchers do exercise due diligence; one company abandoned a plan to incorporate a gene from Brazil nuts into soybeans, because of the numbers of people allergic to nuts.

At this time, our suggestions are: if you've been enjoying your corn-flakes and crunchy snacks without incident, relax. If you are an individual with multiple food allergies, eat oatmeal, and grow your own popcorn...but don't use vegetable oil when you pop it. Be cautious and thoughtful in evaluating claims of activists.

Bibliography and Resources for Further Study

Beaser, Richard and Staff of Joslin Diabetes Center. *Joslin's Diabetes Deskbook-A Guide for Primary Care Providers*. 2nd ed Lippincott: Williams & Wilkins, 2010.

Boyle, Marie and Sara Long. *Personal Nutrition*. Thomson-Wadsworth, 2010.

Brown, Judith. *Nutrition Now*. 5th ed., Thomson – Wadsworth, 2008.

Hayes, Jennifer. "What to Tell Patients About Eating Fish." *The Clinical Advisor*. Feb. 2005, 35-43.

Nestle, Marion. *Safe Food: The Politics of Food Safety-Updated and Expanded*. University of California Press, 2010.

Perry, Patricia H. *Made for Paradise—God's Original Plan for Healthy Eating, Physical Activity and Rest*. New Hope Publishers, 2007.

Rubin, Jordan and David Remedios. *The Great Physician's Rx for Health & Wellness*. Nelson Books, 2005.

Russell, Rex. *What the Bible Says About Healthy Living*. Regal Publishing, 1996.

Sizor, Frances and Ellie Whitney. *Nutrition Concepts and Controversies*. 12th ed. Thomson-Wadsworth, 2010.

Thompson, Janice and Melinda Manore. *Nutrition: An Applied Approach*. 3rd ed. Pearson-Benjamin-Cummings, 2011.

U.S. Department of Health and Human Services; U.S. Department of Agriculture, *Dietary Guidelines for Americans: Healthy People 2020*, U.S. Government, 2010.

Wildman, Robert and Barry Miller. *Sports and Fitness Nutrition*. Thomson-Wadsworth, 2004.

Willett, Walter C. and P.J. Skerrett. *Eat, Drink and Be Healthy: Harvard Medical School Guide to Healthy Eating*. Free Press, 2005.

Whitman, Deborah. "Genetically Modified Foods: Harmful or Helpful?" *CSA Discovery Guides*. Accessed March 31, 2012: www.csa.com/discoveryguides.

World Health Organization. "20 Questions on Genetically Modified Foods." *WHO Food Safety*. Accessed April 1, 2012: www.who.int/foodsafety/publications/biotech.

Chapter 11

Good Stewardship through Wise Weight Management

Essential Terms

Adipocytes

Adipose Tissue

Anorexia Nervosa

Body Composition

Body Mass Index

Bulimia

Ectomorph

Lean Body Mass

Mesomorph

Obesity

Set Point Theory

Objectives

Upon completion of this chapter, students should be able to:

1. Define and correctly use the terms listed above.

2. Describe various ways of assessing and describing one's nutritional status.

3. Understand the importance of lean body mass to well-being.

4. Discuss various factors that determine one's body type.

5. Identify those factors that affect nutritional status, and differentiate those we can control and those we can't.

6. Identify health risks associated with the eating disorders anorexia and bulimia.

7. Distinguish among and discuss sound and unsound approaches to weight management.

In this chapter, we will consider body image, body weight, body composition and how those factors interact to affect well-being. We will consider how we might be "good stewards" of our body's energy reserves, managing them so they might support overall health. We will likely introduce some ideas that are not typical of a "health and wellness" publication. Our goal is to inject some "wisdom" and "moderation" into our national concern for the health implications of one's being overweight.

God gives us our unique set of "variations on the basic human model"; just as He gives us differing skin tones, eye colors, and hair texture, so He endows us with a body type that is "us." Some of us are tall and slender (ectomorphs); others are stocky, with thick, bulky muscles (mesomorphs); still others are small-boned and "plump"; a few are truly "petite" . . . and there are infinite gradations along the continuum that underlies these body types. We believe it is incumbent upon us to accept and become comfortable with the bodies we have, caring for them in ways that promote optimal function, rather than trying to conform to a "model" that the culture has labeled "desirable," or "healthy."

America's "Weight Problem"

There is no doubt that Americans today, on average, are both taller and heavier than they were 25 years ago. An hour of people-watching at a shopping mall convinces one of that. If you have ever tried to sit comfortably in the seats of an old sports stadium, you realize those seats were constructed for people smaller than most fans today.

Americans today are not only "broader" and heavier, but taller as well. Fifty years ago, an inch or so above 6 feet was considered "tall" for a man; it was fairly unusual for women to be taller than 5'8"; today, those heights are common. Certainly our athletes at all levels, both male and female, are physically "bigger" than those of an earlier day. The question is, "How significant a health concern is that?"

In 2003, Dr. Julie Geberling, then Director of the Centers for Disease Control, declared the increasing body weight of Americans to be an "epidemic" and that its health impact would be greater than that of the influenza epidemic of the early 1900's. Health and Human Services has declared that fully two-thirds of American adults are overweight, and that one-half of that number are clinically obese. HHS further estimates that overweight and obesity account for about 300,000 deaths in the United States annually. There are, however, some who view those statistics with skepticism. As is often the case, truth lies somewhere between the extremes.

The difficulty lies with the method used to identify "overweight" and "obese." Body mass index (BMI) is a computation based on an individual's height and weight only. It reflects only body mass in proportion to height. Body composition, that is, the proportion of the body weight that is lean muscle, compared to fat tissue is not reflected at all. The values classified as "overweight" or "obese" are arbitrary. Body Mass Index values of 19-24 are classified as healthy, values of 25-29 are classified as overweight, and values that are 30 and above are classified as obese. A very athletic person who is 5'2" tall and weighs 138 lbs. is classified as overweight, for example, and numerous very fit athletes fall into the obese category.

There are methods for calculating body composition which give a more accurate estimate of an individual's nutritional status; the problem is that they are more time consuming, and require expertise and special equipment in their application. The BMI is quick, convenient, and requires no instrumentation beyond a scale and means of measuring height. For the average non-athlete, it may give a fairly accurate estimate of nutritional status; its shortcoming is that it overestimates body fatness in the person with greater muscle mass, and underestimates it in those with less lean muscle tissue. Total reliance on the BMI as the "gold standard" for classifying individuals as overweight or obese is the primary reason for our belief that there is an epidemic of obesity in America.

What Should Be Our "Real" Concern?

Are we suggesting that we shouldn't be concerned about overweight and obesity as health risks? Of course not, but we do wish to take a more balanced view than has been presented by those who style it as one of the greatest health risks of our day. We think that over-reliance on the BMI for identifying overweight and obesity has been a bit misleading. A large number of epidemiological studies found little or no relationship between BMI and morbidity/mortality. A huge study which followed the health of >110,000 nurses over 16 years found that the comparative mortality rates of those with BMI's of 19-24 were practically identical to those with BMI's of 25-32, categorized as overweight or obese.

Similarly, a 1999 study showed that persons with BMI's of 20 have the same risk for premature death as those with BMI's of 30 and higher. Paul Campos, in his book *The Obesity Myth,* cites numerous examples like these in which overweight is termed the "cause" for most of the chronic ills from which adults suffer, like hypertension, heart disease, arthritis, cancer, and diabetes. So, while we should be concerned about the numbers of persons who carry too much body fat, it is important that we look at other factors that are part of Americans' lives, and not simply body mass.

There are numerous studies showing that levels of physical activity are better predictors of morbidity/mortality than body weight, or indices derived from it. The Cooper Institute for Aerobic Research in Dallas, Texas has tracked several health parameters, together with body mass assessments and activity levels of more than 70.000 people over a period of at least 25 years. The data show that active people classified as overweight or obese, based on BMI, have no greater incidence of cardiovascular, or any other disease, than sedentary people in the "ideal" BMI category. The Institute did a series of studies on persons classified as obese by both BMI and fat percent criteria. The subjects in that group, who engaged in moderate physical activity three or more days/week had half the mortality rate of sedentary people classified as having "ideal" body mass.

Are we not concerned about the "super-sizing" of many Americans? Yes, but we need to be concerned particularly about the nutritional status and the observable over-fatness of our children and teenagers. We need to be concerned about their consumption of sugary drinks, cereals, snacks, and fast foods. We should have a major concern about the lack of vigorous physical activity that is characteristic of so many. Unfortunately, physical education requirements have been dropped or greatly reduced in many states, so even that twice-a-week involvement in exercise has disappeared. Some mistakenly reasoned that school and community-based sports programs would fill that physical activity void; that has been true only for those interested in and skilled at the various sports. It is true that we have some very fit, athletic boys and girls among our school age population; sadly, there are many more who are not.

Most adult Americans are engaged in work that requires little physical exertion. Labor-saving technology has enhanced productivity, but has also removed from our day the physical work that helped us to maintain a healthful body weight, and stronger muscles. Today, most of us have to be intentional about including physical activity in our daily lives; it will not just happen in the course of a normal day.

Healthcare providers, educators, community leaders, and parents need to focus on encouraging people of all ages to not only make better food choices, but to become more active. A sedentary lifestyle is a major contributing factor underlying conditions like diabetes and cardiovascular disease. Americans of all ages need places to walk, run, or bike safely. Children need places where they can simply play ball or other games without having to be organized into teams and leagues. The organized activities have their place, but they should not supplant spontaneous, kid-directed play. Parents need to set strict limits on the amount of time their children spend watching TV or movies, and playing electronic games. Likewise, they need to limit time spent on internet social media.

The bottom line is that Americans of all ages need to spend more discretionary time in being physically active, rather than sitting. We need to make sensible food choices, both in content and amounts. If we do those things, all of us will not be slender; we will have the body types our genetics dictate. But we will likely feel better, will reduce our risk of metabolic and cardiovascular disease, and will be better stewards of the bodies God has given us.

Ways of Assessing Nutritional Status

Body Type

Some of us are tall and thin, with long, slim arms and legs. They have what is termed an "ectomorphic" body type. On the basis of body mass index alone, they will likely be classified in the "desirable" range; but they must not be complacent. Their lean body mass may be low in relation to their fat percentage, so while not having a "weight" problem, they have the same risk for cardiovascular disease as any other sedentary group.

Some are stocky, with thick muscular limbs; these are the "mesomorphs." They will likely never be considered thin, at least while in good health. They most likely will have body mass indices in the overweight or obese categories, though their fat percentage may be quite low.

Some, by virtue of their genetic make-up, have a smaller skeletal structure, and are somewhat plump in appearance. They are termed "endomorphs." They tend to have a higher percentage of body fat, regardless of body weight. Regular exercise, including both aerobic activity and resistance exercise, is critical for them, as they are at risk for becoming overweight or obese.

Regardless of the body type you have, regular exercise that challenges both your skeletal muscles and your cardiorespiratory system is essential to optimal well-being. To a great extent, we must learn to be comfortable with the body type we have; we can make only small changes in our physique type. We can make significant improvement in function by making exercise part of our daily routine.

Body Mass Index

Although it has significant limitations when used as a single measure of nutritional status, it is appropriate that you know how BMI is calculated.

$$BMI = \frac{Body\ weight\ in\ pounds \times 705}{Height\ in\ inches^2}$$

You can also go to internet sites like www.myplate.gov and find a BMI calculator; plug in your height and weight, and it will determine your BMI instantly. Many other internet sites provide BMI calculators as well.

Waist Circumference, Waist-to-Hip Ratio, and Waist-to-Height Ratio

Studies of relationships between nutritional status and health problems such as hypertension, heart disease, and diabetes have shown distribution of body fat a better predictor of health risk than body weight relative to height. A large volume of research has shown that fat around one's midsection, i.e. "belly fat", has different implications for health than subcutaneous fat. There is a strong association between abdominal obesity and elevated blood lipid levels, as well as hyperinsulinemia (which leads to insulin resistance), which increases risk for both type II diabetes and cardiovascular disease. Thus, we should have particular concern for those who carry their body weight around their waist, regardless of their BMI classification.

The "culprit" leading to excessive insulin production and increased blood lipids is visceral fat. That is, fat deposited around the liver and other abdominal organs. A study by Nguyen-Duy et al. in 2003 found visceral fat to be a significant factor in dyslipidemia. (Nguyen-Duy et al., E1065) Dyslipidemia, or high levels of fat in the blood, is known to be a strong risk factor to the development of both cardiovascular disease and diabetes.

A number of researchers have measured visceral fat using magnetic resonance imaging; although obviously the most accurate noninvasive method, it's not practical outside well-equipped medical research centers. Waist-to-hip ratio and waist circumference have been used to estimate visceral fat. Wajchenberg, in a study published in *Endocrine Reviews* found waist circumference to be more closely correlated with visceral adiposity than waist-to-hip ratio in both men and women. (Wajchenberg, 729)

Waist circumference is measured by putting a tape measure around the waist, half-way between the last rib you can feel and the top of the hip bone. For adults, circumferences greater than 35 inches for women, or 40 inches for men, carry increased risk for type II diabetes, hyperlipidemia, hypertension, and other cardiovascular disease. This holds true regardless of BMI classification.

Waist-to-hip ratio is a quick, easy to obtain measure that reflects how ones central body mass is distributed. Epidemiologists refer to an "apple-shaped" distribution, and a "pear-shaped" distribution of central body mass. Those whose body mass is centered around the waist (apple-shaped) have greater risk for diabetes and cardiovascular disease than those whose mass is concentrated around their hips and thighs.

To obtain the ratio, measure the waist circumference at the level of the umbilicus, and the hip circumference at their widest point. Divide the waist circumference by the hip circumference, and refer to Table 11.1 for an estimate of health risk.

Table 11.1	General Waist-to-Hip Ratio Standards	
Female	Male	Health Risk
0.80 or Below	0.95 or below	Low Risk
0.81 to 0.85	0.96 to 1.0	Moderate Risk
0.85+	1.0+	High Risk

SOURCES: USDA, ACSM, NIH

A number of researchers have looked at the waist-to-height ratio as another convenient means of estimating central body fat distribution. In a paper which collated findings of numerous such studies, Oxford University researchers Ashwell and Browning found that the preponderance of evidence supported 0.5 as a suitable "boundary value" for waist-to-height ratio. (Ashwell and Browning, 74) That is, WHt ratios > 0.5 were associated with increased risk for cardiovascular and metabolic disease.

So it seems that any of these easy to obtain measures might give a credible estimate of central fat distribution, a factor known to be associated with increased risk for cardiovascular and metabolic disease.

Body Composition Estimates

The purpose of these procedures is to estimate how one's body mass is proportioned between lean and non-lean tissue. There are a number of ways these estimates can be made, two of which will be described here. The major uses of a body composition estimate are for tracking the effects of an exercise program on relative muscle mass and adipose (fat) tissue, and for establishing an appropriate goal body weight when it's desirable to decrease body mass.

A very quick and easy body composition assessment can be made using a hand-held bio-electric impedance device. Your instructor will show you how the device is used, and make it available to those who wish to obtain estimates of lean body mass in this way. The device, when you hold it in both hands and press the "start" button passes a small, painless electric current through your body. The amount of resistance the current encounters from your body tissue is used to estimate tissue density; that, together with your height, weight, gender and age (which you program into the device) is processed to give you an estimate of percent body fat. Lean body percentage is obtained by subtracting the obtained value from 100; to convert percentages to pounds, multiply your body weight by the decimal form of the percentage. (A person whose weight is 150 lbs. with an estimated 22% body fat would have 78% lean body mass; 150 × .78 = 117 lbs. lean wt; 150 × .22 = 33 lbs. fat weight.)

Other means of estimating body composition include underwater weighing, the measurement of skinfold thickness at specified body sites, and an assessment based on air displacement using a device called the "BodPod." Determination of body density by means of underwater weighing has been for a long time the "gold standard" against which all other methods are compared. Although facility dependent, time consuming, and not particularly pleasant for the subject, it continues to be the most accepted method for determining body density, and deriving from that estimates of lean and fat body mass.

Technology like the dual energy x-ray absorptiometry (DEXA) scanner and magnetic resonance imaging (MRI) may eventually replace underwater weighing as the most accurate tools for estimating body composition. However, the equipment required is quite expensive, and typically found in imaging centers focused on medical diagnostic procedures rather than research on body composition.

Researchers in exercise science seeking to find a less cumbersome means of estimating body density, and body fat percentage, found that measuring the thickness of skin folds at specific sites could give an estimate that correlated reasonably well with estimates obtained by underwater weighing. They reasoned that much of the body's fat is found in the subcutaneous tissue just under the skin. Many combinations of skin folds were evaluated against underwater weighing. The combination of a measure taken at the tip of the scapula, and over the triceps muscle, midway down the dominant upper arm seem best for both genders.

If you would like to estimate your percent body fat by this method, ask an instructor for assistance. Once you have obtained the skin fold measures, you can use the following formulae to estimate fat percent.

For women, ages 17-26

    A. Triceps skin fold, in millimeters   B. Subscapular skin fold in millimeters

%Body Fat = 0.55(A) + 0.31(B) + 6.13

For men, ages 17-26

%Body Fat = 0.43(A) + 0.58(B) + 1.47

From: McArdle, Katch and Katch, 394

Once you have an estimate of body fat %, subtracting that amount from 100 gives you your % lean body mass. You can compare that to the values in Table 11.2 that follows to see where you stand, and decide whether you want to make any changes.

Table 11.2	Evaluation of Lean Body Mass	
	Men (17–26)	Women (17–26)
Optimal lean mass for athletes	90–94%	82–86%
Optimal for active non-athletes	86–89%	77–81%
OK, but could be improved with exercise	81–85%	71–76%
A bit low; need a work-out regimen	<80%	<70%

Making Use of Your Lean Body Mass Calculation

The value of having a lean body mass estimate is that it can be used to establish a reasonable body weight goal for those who would like to make a change in their body composition. When that is desirable, it is adipose tissue weight that one wants to decrease, rather than simply absolute weight.

Suppose that a young man who weighs 220 lbs. finds that his %body fat is 22; his %lean therefore is 78. His present lean body mass is 220 × .78, or 171.6 lbs. He looks at the chart, and decides he would like to try increasing his exercise and modify his eating habits a bit to increase his %lean body weight to 85. To see what his body weight goal would be, he uses the following equation.

$$\text{Weight Goal} = \frac{\text{Present Lean Body Weight (lbs.)}}{\text{\% Lean Body Weight Desired*}}$$

*Decimal form

$$\text{Weight Goal} = \frac{171.6 \text{ lbs.}}{.85}$$

Weight Goal =   201.88 or approximately 202 lbs.

A Caution Regarding Skin Fold Measurement in Calculating Fat Percentage

Accurate skin fold measurements are difficult, even for those experienced in the technique; also, accurate measures are easier to obtain on leaner subjects. The calipers used to take the measurements must be accurate; the plastic calipers found in many fitness facilities and health clubs are not particularly accurate.

If you have access to someone skilled in doing skin fold measures, and who has accurate instruments with which to do it, this is a pretty accurate means of determining body composition. If you don't, and are most interested in assessing nutritional status as it relates to cardiovascular and metabolic disease risk, we suggest you use a simple waist circumference measurement.

Energy Balance

The young man in our example wants to make a change in his body's lean-to-fat ratio. He has determined that he wants to lose about 18 pounds, and that most of those should be in the form of adipose tissue. Now how does he do that? To begin with, he needs some understanding of the body's energy conservation system.

God designed our bodies for survival under varying and often stressful circumstances. Examples of such circumstances are illness, times of prolonged physical exertion, and times when food might not be available. He also built into us some cushioning protection for our vital organs; all of us have a layer of adipose (fat) tissue surrounding and protecting our abdominal organs. Much of our stored energy is in the adipose tissue just under the skin, the "subcutaneous" fat. This is the reserve we draw upon in times of illness, stress, prolonged exertion or food deprivation.

When we take in more calories than are needed for immediate metabolic needs, we convert that energy to fat molecules and store it in fat cells or "adipocytes." We all conserve energy in this way, but rates and degrees of this process vary from person-to-person. Factors like gender, age, genetic heritage, ethnicity, endocrine status, food intake, and activity level are determiners. Some of these variables are immutable, some we must accept, and some we can modify by making lifestyle changes. Accumulated research suggests that about 25–30% of our fat storage is due to our individual biochemistry; the other 70–75% is rooted in lifestyle factors.

A great deal of on-going research focuses on biochemical determinants of our energy-storage processes. Several theories have grown from observing groups of people; one is known as the "set point theory." This is the idea that the rate at which we burn calories (metabolism) is "programmed" to maintain our body weight within a defined and fairly narrow range. For example, people may lose weight by intent or due to illness; in a few months, most will return to near their original body weights. They will return to their "set-point," that distribution of lean and fat tissue mass that is unique to them. Can the set-point be adjusted? Apparently it can be, within limits. Daily exercise over time (both aerobic and strength training) will increase muscle mass and energy use; studies suggest that metabolic rate can be raised by a small amount. Such changes are likely to be quite small; stocky people are unlikely to become extremely thin, and the long-limbed slender folks aren't likely to become stocky.

While there is a lot of interesting research into the genetics and biochemistry of weight gain and loss, what most of us need to focus on are our everyday life patterns. We can choose to include more activity in our daily lives; we can do things like walk to the library rather than riding, parking farther from the door of the grocery store rather than looking for the closest spot, and planning a 30-minute walk or strength workout into our busy day. We can take a look at our food selections, so that we don't consume a lot of "empty" calories (like soda-pop) or potato chips. We can try to plan our schedules so that we limit our "fast food" meals to 1–2 per week, rather than daily. With the help of aids like www.healthypeople.gov we can work toward balancing the food energy we take in with the energy we use in work and recreational activity.

Changing body weight and particularly changing the energy stored in subcutaneous fat stores is basically a matter of creating a calorie deficit. That is, over time, we must expend more energy than we take in. A one-pound weight change is the equivalent of a 3500 calorie deficit or excess. Energy balance is simply the relationship between the energy derived from the food we eat, and the energy we use or burn. When energy intake equals energy expenditure, weight remains stable; if intake is greater than expenditure, the excess is stored in our fat cells. Taking in less and expending more results in energy being withdrawn from adipose cells and used to fuel the activity being done.

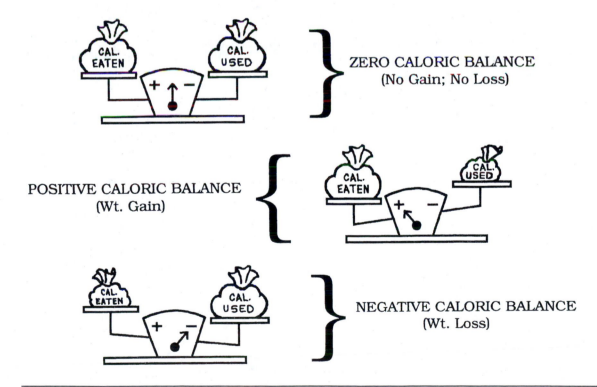

Figure 11.1 | Caloric energy balance

Determining Energy Requirements

Our energy requirement has three components: 60–70% of the calories we need are consumed in maintaining our basic life functions. Processes like circulation, respiration, maintenance of body temperature, synthesis and repair of cells and tissues and nervous system activity use energy. The number of calories expended in those processes is termed basal or resting metabolism.

Age, gender, body size, muscle mass and thyroid function are primary determinants of one's resting energy requirement. An estimate of this value can be made using the equations below.

Table 11.3	Estimating Resting Energy Requirement
Males	
Age (In years)	
10–17	(17.5 × body wt. in kilograms) + 651
18–29	(15.3 × body wt. in kilograms) + 679
30–60	(11.6 × body wt. in kilograms) + 879
>60	(13.5 × body wt. in kilograms) + 487
Females	
Age (In years)	
10–17	(12.2 × body wt. in kilograms) + 746
18–29	(14.7 × body wt. in kilograms) + 496
30–60	(8.7 × body wt. in kilograms) + 829
>60	(10.5 × body wt. in kilograms) + 596

Adapted from: Williams, Nutrition for Health, Fitness & Sport, 7th Edition. p. 95.

Example: A girl weighs 121 pounds; dividing by 2.2 converts her weight to kilograms: 55. She is 19 years old. Her resting energy requirement = (14.7 × 55) + 496, or 1304.5 cals.

The second component of our energy requirement is the energy we need for the physical activities that are part of our day; for most of us, that is between 20 and 30% of the total requirement. There are several ways to estimate our "above resting" energy expenditure. One way is to refer to resources which give information about energy amounts expended in various types of exercise. Moderately intense activity requires from 3.5 to 7 calories/minute for a person weighing 70 kg. (154 lbs.) Those who weigh less will be at 3.5 and those who weigh more will be closer to 7. Vigorous activity requires 8–10 calories/minute, depending on body size. You can use this as a guide in determining your energy expenditure in activity.

There are also several internet sites you can use to track "energy consumed – energy burned;" one of the best is www.choosemyplate.gov, which offers a wealth of nutritional information. If you go to the site and select "SuperTracker," you can track your calorie intake and calories used in physical activity. The site offers a wealth of resources, and is easy to use. Another site that will give you estimates of your energy consumption based on gender, body size and age is http://nutrition-data.self.com/tools/calories-burned. We encourage you to become acquainted with both and use them in your body stewardship program.

The final component of our total energy requirement is a value called the "thermic effect of food." This is the energy the body uses in processing the foods we eat; it is a small amount, about 5–10% of a meal's calorie content. A 500 calorie meal will need 25–50 calories to fuel the digestion of the meal; a meal high in protein and/or complex carbohydrate requires relatively more energy to process than does a high fat meal.

Adding these together gives us an idea of how we need to balance our food choices and amounts with the exercise we get. The best approach to making changes is to adjust both energy intake and energy expenditure by modest amounts. Large decreases in our food intake are unpleasant and short-lived; large increases in energy expenditure are unrealistic and unlikely to be continued for more than a few days. The key to maintaining a healthy body mass is keeping the balance or, if losing some of your energy stores is a desirable and health-promoting thing to do, reducing intake by 250 calories/day, and adding 250 calories-worth of exercise to your day. Do that for a week, and you've lost a pound of energy stored as fat.

General Suggestions for Healthy Weight Management

1. Make changes gradually, and don't be discouraged by your body's slow response; the "calories in-calories burned" equation always works, but not quickly!

2. Eat a variety of the foods you enjoy, but make your portions smaller; we've become accustomed to "super sizing." Don't eat in a hurry; give your appetite control center in the hypothalamus time to signal when you've had enough.

3. Your energy intake shouldn't go below 1200 calories for women or below 1800 calories for men. Energy intakes less than that result in a "downward adjustment" of metabolic rate, and make us tired. Also, it's difficult to get sufficient vitamins and minerals (particularly iron) in fewer calories.

4. Keep caloric density in mind as you choose foods; those that contain lots of fat and refined sugar pack a large number of calories into a small amount. Potato chips and cheesecake are two examples.

5. When you anticipate having a large meal for a special occasion, plan some time into your day for 400–500 calories-worth of exercise a few hours before the meal. You can then go into the meal knowing that you have "extra" calories accounted for, and are free to enjoy the occasion without guilt feelings.

6. When it comes to weight management, physical activity of moderate intensity is better than very vigorous exercise. Moderately intense exercise promotes drawing on subcutaneous fat stores; highly intense exercise will draw upon muscle glycogen stores, which will only hasten fatigue.

7. Plan to distribute your food intake so that about 75% of your calories are eaten by mid-afternoon, leaving just 25% for the evening meal and evening snacking. This way, most calories are consumed during the part of the day when they are more likely to be burned in activity.

8. Eat at least three meals per day. Distributing your food intake provides the body with an "even" energy supply, prevents hunger, and makes you less likely to overeat at the next meal. When schedule and responsibilities allow, "grazing" (eating small amounts frequently during the day) is a good approach to eating.

9. Studying, watching TV, listening to music or just talking with friends usually is accompanied by snacking. It is inevitable, so prepare for it by having available foods that are relatively low in calories but high in bulk. Examples are popcorn, raw vegetables and raw fruit.

10. Don't be fooled by the promises of the latest "fad" diets or weight loss aids. There is no magic, regardless of the claims made for a plan or product. There are minimal controls over such products and their advertising, so you can't assume that, because a product is advertised in the media, it is safe and effective.

11. Similarly, don't be fooled by the short-term weight loss promised by the "No-or-Low-Carbohydrate" diets. The reality is that the body needs carbohydrates for energy. What we need to do is choose carbohydrates wisely, limiting or avoiding those that offer <u>only</u> calories, such as soda pop, candy, cookies, etc. Whole grains, fruits, and dairy products are sources of both energy and important nutrients. Nutrient-dense carbohydrates should make up 50-60% of your total daily food intake.

12. While with persistence anyone can make some healthful changes in body composition, there is no guarantee of the "ideal" body. If you have inherited heavy thighs, you can trim them and firm the muscles, but proportionately they still will be "heavy." Accept your body; live in it rejoicing that you are exercising stewardship in your care of it. God has made it, and it is good!

Table 11.4	My Relationship with Food		

Some basic principles of good body stewardship and our relationship with food are to eat only when you're truly hungry, eat slowly and stop when you are full, and choose foods that are good for you. Sound good??? But you're right…it's not easy. The following questionnaire gives you the opportunity to reflect on your relationship with food. How many of the following are <u>true</u> of you?

My life would be better if I were thinner, so I often feel guilty when I eat.	True		False
I often eat when I'm stressed, depressed, anxious, or angry.	True		False
I tend to overeat on social occasions.	True		False
I often keep eating even when I am full or no longer hungry.	True		False
I've tried numerous diets.	True		False
I can't resist desserts, and will often eat those rather than more nutritional food.	True		False
I am a very "picky" eater, not always for the most nutritious reasons.	True		False
I eat fairly well when I eat with my friends, but tend to over-eat when alone.	True		False
I typically "super-size" fast food orders because they are better bargains.	True		False
I think about food several times between one meal and the next	True		False
I rarely eat breakfast, and eat more of my calories from supper until I go to bed.	True		False
There are very few vegetables that I like.	True		False
I often feel guilty after I eat.	True		False
I often reward myself with food after I finish a project or when I need encouragement.	True		False

Total number of statements that are "True" for you: _____

Evaluation:

If 4 or less are true of you: You have a fairly healthy relationship with food, but must acknowledge that any of the "true" answers are in areas that can benefit from being addressed.

If 5 or more are true of you: You likely need to give some thought to your food choices and the place of food in your life. Now that you're a more "independent" consumer, use your freedom wisely and well.

Gaining Lean Body Mass

When the goal is to concentrate specifically on adding to one's lean body tissue, adjustments are made in the amount of energy taken in, and the type of exercise done. This kind of change is often sought by athletes in strength/power events as well as by persons recovering from significant illness, or a time of malnourishment.

To add muscle, it's necessary to increase food intake by 800-1000 calories/day, maintaining the balance of carbohydrate, protein and fat as described in chapter 10. A vigorous progressive-resistance regimen of exercise is the other essential. The use of special food supplements is not necessary to increasing muscle mass.

The use of anabolic steroids for this purpose is absolutely not appropriate. These are synthetic compounds that simulate the physiological effects of testosterone on body tissues. Prolonged use has been implicated in heart and liver disorders, mood swings and psychological dysfunction, as well as suppression of endogenous testosterone production in males. In females, steroid use is associated with the development of male-pattern facial hair, coarsening of the skin, as well as liver dysfunction. Use of these substances is banned by all major athletic governing bodies, and is dangerous to users.

Although it is possible to add to your lean body mass, remember that the degree to which it can be changed is limited by heredity. Some will have thicker, more defined musculature; others will continue to have smaller, more "wiry" physiques. Accept and rejoice in the body that God has given you.

Overemphasis on Thinness: Eating Disorders

Thus far, our discussion of body composition management has focused on the need of many to reduce body fat content, and the desire of some to increase lean tissue mass. Our society is to a degree "obsessed" with being thin; not only is it considered by most to be attractive, it is considered more healthful, as well.

Up to a point, that is true; however, we have to remember that some adipose tissue in the body is essential. Anatomists have identified adipose tissue they call "brown fat" which is stored mostly in the upper back, the back of the neck, and around internal organs. In this tissue the process of heat production or "thermogenesis" takes place.

The chapter would be incomplete without mention of the very destructive eating behaviors ANOREXIA NERVOSA and BULIMIA. One of the motivations for developing these problems is an obsession with thinness that can cause an individual to develop bizarre eating behaviors. However, a compulsion to be thin may be only a part of the pattern for an anorexic or bulimic person.

Anorexia nervosa is a physical and psychological disorder characterized by self-imposed starvation, often coupled with compulsive and excessive physical exercise. As the anorexic sees the pounds melt away, the compulsive behaviors typically intensify, producing a self-destructive downward spiral. If this spiral effect is not interrupted, biochemical imbalances develop which in turn produce cardiac irregularities and other life-threatening abnormalities.

Typically, the anorexic is a female teenager or young adult. There are some male anorexics, but they are in the minority. No doubt this is because thinness is not necessarily perceived as a requisite of physical attractiveness for males. In addition to an obsession with being thin, anorexic individuals may have a desperate desire to exert control over at least one aspect of their lives. They find one of the few things they can totally self-determine is their eating and exercising patterns, and rigidly doing so becomes an obsession. They may not have much self-esteem, and not eating and over-exercising may be the only way they believe they can alter their physical selves. For some, perhaps the rigid starvation/exercise regimen represents a form of self-punishment for imagined shortcomings.

Anorexia is a life threatening disorder. The anorexic needs both physical and psychological treatment to recover. Below are some typical signs of anorexia. If you detect these in a friend, roommate, family member or yourself, please seek help. The best place to start is with a health care professional who can give immediate treatment as needed, and make necessary referrals. If you don't know where to go for help, talk with your instructor.

Signs of Anorexia Nervosa

1. Frequent verbal reference to being "fat" or needing to lose weight made by a person who obviously has no need to lose.

2. Finding ways to consistently miss meals, and to avoid actually eating with others.

3. Spending an unusual amount of time in very vigorous exercise like running.

4. An obviously emaciated physical appearance.

5. Cessation of menstrual periods.

6. Chronic fatigue and lack of endurance.

7. Unusually low resistance to infections.

8. Slow healing of injuries.

9. Episodes of dizziness or fainting.

10. Episodes of irregular or very slow pulse.

The other dominant eating disorder, BULIMIA, can be equally dangerous, but differs in the specific behaviors involved. Bulimia is characterized by a pattern of binge eating and purging. The person typically eats large quantities of food, then attempts to remove it from the digestive system before it can be absorbed. This is accomplished by self-induced vomiting and/or use of laxatives.

There seems to be a wider range of intensity and persistence of the compulsive behaviors associated with bulimia as compared to anorexia. Many young people, again more often female, "dabble" in bulimic behaviors. To some extent we believe it has become somewhat of an "in" behavior on college campuses. Among some athletes, "making weight" or minimizing weight to enhance performance has been so emphasized that induced vomiting and laxative abuse have become all too common. For some, alternate binging and purging are manifestations of deep-seated emotional problems similar to those of the anorexic.

The bulimic person very often maintains a fairly normal body weight and physical appearance; however, there can be serious and damaging physiological effects. Repeated vomiting causes irritation of the esophagus and pharynx, and can result in bleeding and permanent scarring. Repeated exposure to the strongly acid stomach secretions damages teeth and gums. Similarly, laxative abuse irritates the tissues of the lower digestive tract, and can cause dehydration and electrolyte imbalances, which, in turn, can trigger life-threatening cardiac irregularities.

Below are some behaviors that can be signals of bulimia. If these are observed frequently, do all you can to get professional help for the individual. If you recognize one or more of these in yourself, seek help!

Signs of Bulimia

1. Indications that the person often eats large amounts of high-calorie foods, usually secretly. Indications of this include such things as foods hidden in unlikely places, or finding large numbers of wrappers or empty packages in desk drawers, closets, or other unusual places.

2. Purchase of unusual amounts of laxatives, and/or syrup of ipecac (a substance used to induce vomiting), or finding significant quantities of such items in medicine cabinets, drawers, etc.

3. A pattern of rushing to the bathroom immediately after eating.

4. Signs of frequent vomiting, including persistent sore throat, hoarseness, stained teeth, and bad breath.

Neither an anorexic nor a bulimic pattern is consistent with sound stewardship of the body. The Christian is not immune to these disorders, and needs to stay alert lest he or she develop the kinds of compulsive behaviors we've described. We suggest the following guides.

1. Remember the One who has created your body, and honor Him in your care of it. Most Christians readily identify chemical abuses as destructive and wrong. Recognize that anorexic and bulimic behaviors are just as destructive, but inflict their damage in different ways.

2. Remember that moderation and balance are key stewardship principles; any compulsive behaviors violate these principles.

3. Maintain your walk with the Lord by regular time spent in reading and studying the Word, and prayer. This is powerful protection against slipping into a harmful fad or becoming obsessed with a worldly concept of physical beauty.

4. Remember that your primary mission in life is to glorify God. Throughout Christian history, some sects have sought to do this by practicing rigorous self-denial or self-punishment, including extended fasting. Our view is that there may be a place for a day's fast occasionally, provided one's time and attention are intensively focused on the Lord. We see no place for self-denial as an end in itself.

5. If you are unhappy with your physical appearance, your present body fat level or weight distribution, use the principles explained earlier in this book to make positive changes. Ask your instructor for help. Few of us have mortal bodies that look exactly as we would like. Select clothing that accentuates positive features of your appearance, and minimizes those we perceive as negative.

6. Daily recommit your life in all its aspects to the Lord. Through study of the Word and prayer, seek His guidance and aid in dealing with feelings of helplessness and lack of control in your life.

We offer these suggestions as ways we think a Believer can avoid slipping into disordered eating behaviors. However, we recognize that for some, the roots of these behaviors may lie below the level of conscious thought, and that professional aid may be necessary for them to break the pattern.

If you have reason to think a friend or family member has an eating disorder, do all you can to get help for them. These maladies are very destructive to the body, and can have life-long effects on well-being. If you realize that you struggle with disordered eating, seek help through your student health service, your personal physician or your instructor. These problems can be overcome, but first they must be recognized and addressed.

Frequently Asked Questions about Weight Management

QUESTION: *What is "cellulite"?*

ANSWER: This is the term coined by the weight-loss industry for the dimpled-appearance of the skin overlying areas of subcutaneous fat deposits. In some people, adipose tissue is infiltrated by connective tissue, which sections the tissue into "pockets." This is hereditary; some peoples' adipose tissue is affected this way, while others' are not. To the dismay of many, there is no non-invasive way to "make these disappear."

QUESTION: *Does having excess body fat cause diabetes?*

ANSWER: The form of diabetes associated with being overweight is termed "non-insulin-dependent". That is, the individual is able to make insulin, but it is not effective in controlling the level of glucose in his/her blood. To varying degrees, inherited body chemistry likely plays a part, since this form of diabetes is often seen in several members of a family. The role of insulin is to transport glucose (the form of sugar the body uses for energy) into cells.

As to the relationship of body fatness to diabetes, it likely "goes both ways". In those who acquire excessive body fat by eating a diet high in starches and sugars, the body cell receptors for insulin become less sensitive. So, even though there is sufficient insulin available to transport glucose (sugar) into cells where it can be used, it doesn't readily enter cells, so the level of glucose in the blood rises. Although there is plenty of glucose available for cells to burn, it isn't getting into the cells. That, in turn, is read by the body as needing more food, which prompts the person to eat more, triggering release of more insulin. As this process goes on over time, cells' insulin receptors become less-and-less sensitive; the excess calories consumed are stored in adipose tissue. Body fatness increases, and blood glucose levels become abnormally high, over time resulting in a diagnosis of diabetes, as well as obesity. The adipose tissue acquired this way tends to accumulate in the abdominal region, where it is known to pose health risks discussed earlier.

We are finding this form of diabetes, previously seen mainly in middle-aged adults, occurring more and more among teenagers and young adults. That is why nutritionists and healthcare providers are so concerned about the high-sugar intake of so many school children.

QUESTION: *People who go on medically supervised very low calorie diets (consuming only a liquid nutrient preparation) for several months appear to be successful in losing excessive body weight; are these weight loss plans "healthy"?*

ANSWER: Everyone who does this inevitably loses weight, due to the significant negative energy balance created. There are some drawbacks though. After a few days, the body begins to break down muscle tissue as well as adipose tissue, in order to meet metabolic needs. This results in the kind of "muscle wasting" and weakness that people sustain in prolonged illness; without an intentional and persistent muscle conditioning program, this may not be restored. The body's metabolic rate drops, so that energy is burned at a slower rate; when the person returns to eating foods and has a normal intake of calories, more will tend to be stored as fat, since the rate of use has slowed. That explains at least partially the reason for the tendency of most people to eventually regain more pounds than they lost. Also, any plan that does not help people make changes in their approaches to eating and in the choices they make will not be successful in the long term.

QUESTION: *There is a lot of concern in the media about overweight children and teens; might there not be a true "epidemic" of obesity in those groups?*

ANSWER: We're not sure the term "epidemic" is appropriate, but there certainly is an increased number of over-fat children and teens. However, we believe, as mentioned earlier, that this is rooted in the inactivity typical of many school-age kids, as well as the ready availability of high-calorie/low-nutrient foods.

It seems there are at least three "critical" times during which excessive weight gain in youth is likely to result in adult obesity. Those are: a child's first year, the period between ages 5 and 7, and during adolescence. Important things parents can do during those years include:

1. Model good eating habits; children will tend to form the ones they see in their parents.

2. Limit the availability of snacks high in sugar and fat; have raw vegetables and fruit available for after-school and study snacks. If that is what is there, that is what they will eat.

3. Don't buy soda pop; that is the greatest "single offender" in kids' diets; it is sugar-water with artificial flavors, coloring agents, and often caffeine. Teach kids to drink water.

4. Fruit juices, though nutritious and "natural" are high in calories; whole fruit is a better choice.

5. Use fast-food meals for occasional outings; while cheeseburgers and fries, or pizza, aren't "bad," they are high in salt and fat. They pack a lot of calories in even small-sized meals.

6. Be as active as you can as a family; ride bikes, go hiking, do gardening and yard work together. It doesn't hurt for children to learn the satisfaction of work requiring physical effort.

7. Get kids outside, playing active, informal games. Activity doesn't have to be formalized. Children should play tag and other running games, play pick-up games of soccer, kick-ball, or baseball/softball. They should play hop-scotch, jump rope, and yes, climb trees too!

8. Exert every pressure possible on local schools to restore meaningful physical education programs to your schools; "recess" is not enough, and community-based youth sports do not meet the needs of all children.

QUESTION: *Are there prescription drugs that will help people to lose excessive fat?*

ANSWER: The prescription drugs now available for weight loss are not very effective, and have unpleasant side-effects in many people. The initial appetite-suppressing effect is short-lived, so unless the individual also undertakes an exercise program and some diet modification, success will be very limited. Also, these medicines are very costly, and are not covered by most insurance plans; we think it would be better for one to put the cost of the pills toward good walking shoes and/or a membership to the local YMCA or fitness club.

QUESTION: *Some people who are very heavy have had surgery to help them lose weight; is this a legitimate way to deal with being overweight?*

ANSWER: There are some individuals who suffer from "morbid obesity" for whom this is often the only treatment that may be effective. Morbid obesity is having at least 100 pounds of subcutaneous adipose tissue; it tends to limit ones ability to be physically active, and is associated with several significant health problems. This person typically has tried numerous approaches to weight loss without success; their size and weight limits their ability not only to exercise, but to work, to travel, or to do the things most take for granted. Desperate situations call for drastic measures, and this is one of those instances. Most surgeons accept only those patients for whom they believe this to be the only viable option. The typical procedure consists of placing surgical staples across the stomach, restricting the "pouch" available for receiving food to a very small size. Most of these surgeries are now done through very small incisions, but all carry risks; patients often experience chronic vomiting and/or diarrhea and nutritional deficiencies related to altered digestion and absorption of nutrients. Patients should only consider this option when its potential benefits clearly outweigh its risks.

QUESTION: *What is "metabolic syndrome"?*

ANSWER: "Metabolic syndrome" is a relatively new diagnosis; it refers to an individual having a cluster of biochemical "abnormalities" which have not yet progressed into "disease states". Those include high levels of triglycerides and low-density lipoprotein in the blood, hyperinsulinemia (higher than normal serum insulin levels), insulin resistance, moderately elevated fasting glucose levels, and elevated blood pressure. It tends to be observed in people with an excessive amount of abdominal fat. We might categorize these individuals as "pre-diabetic, pre-hyperlipidemic, and pre-hypertensive"; values are high, but not yet indicative of full-blown conditions requiring treatment. Prevalence increases with age, though it is being seen among young adults as well. It seems to represent a state of "warning" signs for problems to come, as well as an opportunity to make modifications in food consumption and activity level.

Bibliography and Resources for Further Study

Ainsworth, Barbara, William Haskell, et al. "Compendium of Physical Activities: Classification of Energy Costs of Human Physical Activities." *Medicine and Science in Sports and Exercise*, 71-80, 1993.

Ashwell, Margaret, and L.M. Browning. "The Increasing Importance of Waist-to-Height Ratio to Assess Cardiometabolic Risk: A Plea for Consistent Terminology." *The Open Access Obesity Journal*, 2011, Vol. 3, 70-77.

Brown, Judith E. *Nutrition Now*. 5th ed. Thomson-Wadsworth, 2008.

Compos, Paul. *The Obesity Myth*. Gotham Books, 2004.

Cooper Institute. "Cardiorespiratory Fitness, Body Composition and Cardiovascular Disease Mortality in Men." *American Journal of Clinical Nutrition*, 69:373-380, 1999.

Herzog, D.B. and P.M. Copeland. "Eating Disorders." *The New England Journal of Medicine,* Aug. 1, 1985, 295-303.

Hsieh, S.D., H. Yoshinaga, and T. Muto. "Waist to Height Ratio, A Simple and Practical Index for Assessing Central Fat Distribution and Metabolic Risk in Japanese Men and Women." *International Journal of Obesity*, vol. 27, 610-616, 2003.

Janssen, Ian, Peter Katzmarzyk, and Robert Moss. "Body Mass Index, Waist Circumference, and Health Risk." *Archives of Internal Medicine/* Accessed Oct. 14, 2003:_www.archintern med.com.

Manore, Melinda and Janice Thompson. *Sport Nutrition for Health and Performance.* Human Kinetics, 2000.

McArdle, William, Frank Katch, and Victor Katch. *Sports and Exercise Nutrition*. 3rd ed., Lippincott-Williams &Wilkins, 2009.

Nguyen-Duy, Thanh-Bin, M.Z. Nichaman, T.S. Church, S.N. Blair, and R. Ross. "Visceral Fat and Liver Fat are Independent Predictors Of Metabolic Risk Factors in Men." *American Journal of Physiology, Endocrinology and Metabolism*, Jan. 2003.,Vol. 284, E1065-E1071.

Robinson, Georgina, Megan Geier, Denise Rizzolo, and Mona Sedrak. "Childhood Obesity: Complications, Prevention Strategies, Treatment." *Journal of the American Academy of Physician Assistants*, 2011:www.jaapa.com.

Wajchenberg, Bernardo Leo. "Subcutaneous and Visceral Adipose Tissue: Their Relation to the Metabolic Syndrome." *Endocrine Reviews*, 21(6):697-738, 2000.

Wellens, R, W. Chumlea, S. Guo, A. Roche, N. Reo, and R. Siervogel. "Body Composition in White Adults By Dual-Energy X-Ray Absorptiometry, Densitometry, and Total Body Water.", *American Journal of Clinical Nutrition*, Vol. 59, 547-555, 1994.

Williams, Melvin. *Nutrition for Health, Fitness and Sport*. 9th ed., McGraw-Hill, 2010.

Chapter 12

Health and the Consumer: Stewardship of Well-being and Resources

Essential Terms

Alternative or complementary therapy

"Brand-name" drugs

Generic drugs

Herbal supplements/remedies

"House-brand" drugs

"OTC" drugs

Phytochemicals

Prescription drugs

Quackery

Objectives

Upon completion of this chapter, students should be able to:

1. Define and correctly use the terms listed.

2. Distinguish among the various clinical specialties, and identify the clinician most appropriate for a given kind of medical problem.

3. Explain the role of mid-level healthcare providers, i.e., physician assistants and nurse practitioners.

4. Explain the differences between "generic" and "brand-name" medicines, both prescription and non-prescription.

5. Explain why the consumer must be cautious when choosing to use nutritional supplements.

6. Explain why it is important that one list nutritional supplements and herbal preparations among other medicines when seeing a physician.

7. Discuss the health risks associated with consistently consuming a diet that is >30% protein.

8. List the "red flags" that should alert one that a particular remedy or treatment may actually be quackery.

Introduction

Most of us buy goods and/or services several times a week; we are "consumers." From time to time, the goods and services we purchase are health-related. Obviously we can be our own best health "advocate" by practicing good body stewardship.

However, from time-to-time all of us have occasion to seek help in managing an illness or injury to ourselves, family members, or close friends.

In the course of doing so, we may buy various over-the-counter medicines; we seek treatment from clinicians for illness or injuries, and we fill clinician prescriptions. We purchase health insurance to help pay for major health needs we may have. Most adults in America spend amounts ranging from a few hundred to several thousand dollars on health-related products and services each year. The intent of this chapter is to provide some basic knowledge that will help you to be a wise consumer in this area, and so be a good steward of the financial resources the Lord entrusts to you.

The chapter will cover the following:

> Clinician Services
> Prescription and Over-the-Counter Medicines
> Alternative and Complementary Medicine
> Health Insurance
> Evaluating Nutritional and Herbal Supplements
> Recognizing Health Quackery

Clinician Health Services

When you complete your education, and are fully "on your own," selecting providers of health services you may need is something you will need to do. Even healthy young adults, from time to time, have illnesses or injuries that require the services of a health professional. The best choice for most people is a "general practitioner" who will serve as your "primary care provider." If you have a chronic condition, like diabetes for example, it is essential that you become associated with a clinician as soon as possible after settling in a new area. Friends and co-workers are usually good sources of information on clinicians in your area. You can also contact the local medical society for information on clinicians in your area.

Your choice of health care providers may be dictated by your health insurance company, if you are covered by an employer-purchased coverage, or your own. If you are uninsured, your choice will be limited to those practices in your area that are accepting new patients, and your ability to pay for care received.

When you set out to find a "primary care provider" (family physician), you will find both osteopathic (D.O.) physicians and allopathic (M.D.) physicians. The academic and clinical training for M.D.'s and D.O.'s is now virtually identical. The requirements for certification and licensure are the same, so you may be assured that either is fully qualified. The only difference today between the two is that the osteopathic physician has had some training in the use of musculoskeletal manipulation in the treatment of some conditions. Most D.O.'s today rarely use it.

A preliminary visit to the offices of recommended practitioners is a good idea. You can learn such things as what providers are members of the practice, the hours for the practice, the insurances accepted, and the ease with which one can be seen for a problem. Many general practices now include physician assistants and/or nurse practitioners as well as physicians. That is advantageous to patients, in that it usually means that one can obtain an appointment in a more timely fashion.

Physician assistants and nurse practitioners are health professionals trained and licensed to diagnose and treat many health problems and injuries. They examine patients, order diagnostic tests, and prescribe medications. They are typically affiliated with one or more physicians, and may practice in urgent care centers or hospital emergency rooms as well as in physician offices. The professional "designators" or letters you will see after their names are PA-C for the physician assistant, and CNP for the nurse practitioner.

Questions to Ask at Your Preliminary Visit:

1. What insurances are accepted by the practice?
2. At which area hospitals do the clinicians practice?
3. Are appointment hours compatible with your work schedule?
4. What is the typical "waiting time" to get an appointment for an acute problem?

Of course, it is a "plus" if you can find a practice where at least some of the providers are Believers. It helps too, if clinicians and staff seem friendly, and willing to answer your questions.

Health Care Specialists

If you have a chronic health problem, that is, one that is ongoing and requires monitoring and treatment daily or frequently, you will need to become established with a specialty practice. For example, if you have asthma or other respiratory system problem, you need a pulmonologist. Often your "family" physician will make a referral to a specialist when he/she deems it necessary. Below is a list of medical specialists, and the kinds of problems they treat.

Allergists: treat symptomatic responses to numerous substances, from pollens to pets to peanuts and other foods

Bariatricians: specialize in helping patients cope with severe obesity

Cardiologists: specialize in the diagnosis and treatment of diseases of the heart

Dermatologists: diagnose and treat conditions affecting the skin and mucous membranes

Endocrinologists: diagnose and treat conditions arising from dysfunction of the endocrine system; mainly diabetes, thyroid dysfunction, and pituitary or adrenal dysfunction

Gastroenterologists: diagnose and treat problems arising from any of the digestive system's organs

Gynecologists: specialize in conditions of the female reproductive system

Hematologists: diagnose and treat abnormalities of the blood and bone marrow

Immunologists: diagnose and treat malfunctions of the body's immune system.

Infectious Disease Specialists: have expertise in the diagnosis and treatment of unusual and particularly virulent diseases caused by bacteria, viruses, fungi, or other microscopic organisms

Neonatologists: a sub-specialty of pediatrics; provide care to newborns with various life-threatening conditions

Nephrologists: diagnose and treat conditions of the kidney and renal system

Neurologists: diagnose and treat conditions arising from dysfunctions of or injuries to the brain, spinal cord or peripheral nerves

Obstetricians: provide prenatal care to expectant mothers, and deliver babies

Oncologists: treat malignant tumors, typically with radiation or chemotherapy

Ophthalmologists: diagnose and treat diseases and injuries of the eye

Orthopedists: correct or repair abnormalities of or injuries to bones, joints, cartilage and tendons; orthopedics is actually a subspecialty of surgery

Otolaryngologists: specialize in diagnosing and treating dysfunctions of the ears, nose and throat

Pediatricians: treat illnesses and injuries to infants, children, and adolescents

Podiatrists: (DPM) are licensed to diagnose and treat conditions of the foot and ankle; treatment may include surgery and/or drugs and physical therapy

Pulmonologists: diagnose and treat malfunctions of the respiratory system, like asthma or emphysema

Rheumatologists: diagnose and treat inflammatory conditions damaging the body's joints and connective tissue, which have their source in malfunction of the auto-immune system; rheumatoid arthritis is an example of such a condition

Surgeons: physicians who treat disorders by removing, repairing or replacing damaged or injured structures; general surgeons are those who perform various procedures, ranging from appendectomies to cholecystectomies (gall bladder removals), and the removal of superficial tumors on or just under the skin. Until fairly recent times, general surgeons set broken bones, removed tonsils, and performed just about all surgical procedures deemed necessary to patient recovery. Now, with the expansion of medical knowledge and technology, there are many surgical subspecialties. Below are some of them.

> Orthopedic surgery: includes repair of broken bones, torn cartilage or tendons as well as the replacement of joints

> Cardiovascular surgery: includes replacement of defective heart valves, the opening or by-passing of clogged coronary arteries, the surgical repair of aortic aneurysms, and grafts to restore circulation to extremities affected by atherosclerotic conditions

> Ear-Nose-Throat surgeons: perform tonsillectomies, repair malformed sinus cavities, correct abnormalities of the structures related to hearing, and remove growths affecting the larynx or vocal cords

> Neurosurgeons: surgically treat conditions affecting the skull or vertebral column, the brain and spinal cord, and peripheral nerves

> Ophthalmic surgeons: surgically treat diseases or injuries to the optical structures, like removal of cataracts, and repair of retinal injuries

> Plastic surgeons: remove skin lesions and perform restorative and/or cosmetic procedures to the skin and subcutaneous tissues primarily, but not limited to, the facial structures

Urologists: specialize in the diagnosis and treatment of the male reproductive system as well as the urinary system

There are several specialists whom you may not meet, but will see listed on the bill for a diagnostic or therapeutic procedure. These are the two you are most likely to notice.

Radiologists: specialists who read the various imaging studies that your treating physician may order; these include x-rays, ultrasounds, CAT scans and MRI's

Pathologists: specialists who microscopically examine tissue specimens to determine whether a growth or "tumor" is benign or malignant; and cultures of blood, urine, or other body fluids to determine whether pathogenic (disease causing) organisms are present

Your health care provider may also prescribe/suggest the services of various allied health professionals. Some of the most frequently consulted are the following:

Physical Therapists: provide rehabilitative exercise regimens and modalities aimed at restoration of normal joint and muscle function following surgery, musculoskeletal injury, or stroke

Occupational Therapists: specialize in assisting people to regain normal function and/or to function effectively with permanent disabilities

Speech Therapists: specialize in remediation of speech and swallowing difficulties

Chiropractors: may alleviate chronic musculoskeletal pain by manipulation of the spine, and/or use of modalities like heat, cold and muscle stimulation; chiropractic manipulation can be very helpful in treatment of some conditions, particularly chronic back pain; it has no place in treatment of conditions like hypertension, endocrine dysfunction, etc.

Dental Care Providers

Care of teeth and gums is a part of good body stewardship, and important to overall good health. Even though we brush our teeth regularly, and have a good diet, we may in time develop problems that require the services of a dentist. It is part of good stewardship to take care of dental problems when they occur. Decayed teeth provide a route by which harmful bacteria can easily reach the bloodstream, and cause major infections.

Cost and lack of dental insurance often lead one to ignore dental health needs. That is short-sighted, and is likely to result in more costly treatment "down the road." Don't ignore dental problems; treatment may be "budget-stressing" at the time, but cost will be greater as the problem progresses.

For general dental care such as cleaning, filling cavities, fitting dentures and perhaps pulling a tooth that can't be saved, search out a Doctor of Medical Dentistry (D.M.D.). This is the "general practitioner" of dentistry. He or she will examine, take x-rays of problem teeth, and refer to a specialist if necessary. Dentistry, like medicine, has "specialists." The major ones are shown below.

Oral surgeons: these are dentists who specialize in difficult extractions, the surgical repair of injuries to the teeth and oral cavity, and the placements of dental implants

Endodontists: specialize in the diagnosis and treatment of diseases of the gums

Orthodontists: specialize in the correction of mal-aligned teeth; these are the specialists who use braces and other appliances to bring individual's teeth and jaws into proper alignment

Typically, dentists have one or more *dental hygienists* in their practices. These are the "allied health" providers of dentistry. Hygienists are trained and certified in cleaning teeth, and assisting in dental procedures.

Medications: Prescription and Non-Prescription

Most of us, on occasion, use non-prescription medicines for minor problems. We take aspirin or acetaminophen (Tylenol™) for headache or muscle pain; we take antacids like Tums™ for mild stomach discomfort. Numerous preparations are available for coughs and the nasal stuffiness we identify with the "common cold." Those are just a few examples of real drugs that have been deemed "safe" for use without a clinician's direction or supervision. Since they are available without a provider's prescription, they are known as "over-the-counter" drugs or "OTC's." Just because they have been deemed safe enough to be used without having been prescribed by a medical practitioner doesn't mean that they have no potential for harm. Read labels; use them according to the directions given, and don't exceed recommended doses.

Consumers need to remember that OTC's are "real drugs" which have beneficial effects if used according to directions and for the right purpose. Before using an OTC pain reliever or cold remedy, read the list of ingredients. Avoid "doubling up" on drugs that have similar actions. For example, naproxen sodium, ibuprofen, and aspirin all have similar effects. They relieve pain and inflammation, but can cause GI irritation. So, use one or the other. The same is true for acetaminophen, the chemical name for "Tylenol." It is a major ingredient in many cough and cold preparations; avoid taking two forms of it at the same time. Large amounts of acetaminophen are associated with liver damage. Non-prescription anti-inflammatory drugs like ibuprofen and naproxen also should be used cautiously. Used on a regular basis or in larger-than-recommended amounts, they can cause kidney damage.

Another thing consumers should know about OTC drugs is that many are available in less costly "house brands," which are the same as their branded counterparts. For example, the aspirin tablet sold under the name of a discount store, or drugstore chain, is the same in content and effect as the one sold under a "brand" name. Read the labels before paying more for a "name."

Some of the most often used non-prescription drugs are shown below.

Table 12.1		
Generic Name for Drug	Uses for the Drug	Some Brand Names
Laratadine	Allergy symptoms; itching	Alavert; Claritin; Tavist
Laratadine/pseudoephedrine	Nasal or sinus congestion	Alavert D; Claritin D
Diphenhydramine	Allergy symptoms; insomnia	Benadryl
Pseudoephedrine	Nasal or sinus congestion	Sudafed
Ibuprofen	Anti-inflammatory; analgesic	Motrin; Advil; Nuprin
Naproxen	Anti-inflammatory; analgesic	Aleve
Acetaminophen	Fever reducer; analgesic	Tylenol

Drugs that require the prescription of a health care provider are those considered to require clinician evaluation prior to their being taken. Selection of the correct drug, in the correct strength, for the right symptoms for the specific patient is a huge part of the practice of medicine. That's why those licensed medical practitioners study so long and rigorously.

Many prescription drugs are available in both "brand" and "generic" forms. Generics are required to have the same concentration of active ingredients as the brand-name version. It is possible for inactive, binding agents to affect bioavailability; your health care provider is your best guide when deciding whether to use a generic rather than a branded product.

What about "Alternatives" to the Usual Forms of Medical Treatment?

Today, one hears and reads quite a bit about "more natural" treatments for health problems. In this context, "natural" usually means treating a problem using therapies other than drugs or surgery. Acupuncture, various forms of massage, and the use of various herbal preparations are offered as alternatives to our usual interventional and pharmacological therapies.

Acupuncture comes to us from traditional Chinese medicine. It is based on the theory that the body has numerous, but well-defined channels, or "meridians" along which energy flows. When the energy flow is smooth, the body functions well; when there is a blockage of the energy flow, it causes dysfunction of one or more of the body's systems.

An acupuncturist seeks to relieve such a blockage by stimulating prescribed points along one or more of the meridians by piercing the skin with very thin and very sharp needles. There are reports of chronic pain being relieved, and maladies like migraine headaches lessened in severity and frequency through use of acupuncture. Some allergy sufferers have reported dramatic relief of symptoms following acupuncture treatment.

Well-controlled, large studies of acupuncture's therapeutic value are relatively few, and the numbers of subjects small. Far from "dismissing" the value acupuncture may have, medical science continues to study it, and strives to understand its underlying physiology. American medicine has recognized the use of acupuncture as a means of treating chronic pain, though its use in the treatment for other conditions is under study.

Most states in the United States license and regulate the practice of acupuncture either through the state's medical board, or a separate board. Some states permit any licensed physician (M.D. or D.O.) to use acupuncture in treatment. Non-physician acupuncturists typically must complete an educational program accredited by the Accreditation Commission for Acupuncture and Oriental Medicine (ACAOM) and be certified by the National Certification Commission for Acupuncture and Oriental Medicine (NCCAOM).

Before seeking acupuncture treatment, it is essential that the cause of pain has been diagnosed by a physician, using standard diagnostic procedures. Patients should seek acupuncture therapy only from a licensed practitioner. Does it work? The most accurate answer at this time is likely "Maybe, for some conditions, in some patients." What is sure is that it should **NOT** be used to treat conditions plainly calling for surgery (such as a tumor) or those due to an infectious agent (bacteria, virus, or fungus).

Deep massage, or "acupressure" has some commonality with acupuncture, in that it's based on applying very firm pressure to specific areas of the body surface, again using charts of body meridians and points, corresponding to the body's systems. One form known as "rolfing" applies pressure to specific points in the palms of the hands that are believed related to specific organ systems. Another, "reflexology" takes the same approach to the soles of the feet.

To date, neither form of acupressure has been shown effective in relieving documented systemic disease processes. While therapeutic massage is licensed and regulated in nearly all states, these forms (rolfing and reflexology) are not. Anyone can buy some charts and open a practice. Our suggestion is that you avoid those practitioners.

Herbal medicine is the use of roots, leaves, bark, and flowers of various plants to treat bodily ills. Rather than being something "new," this is harkening back to the "beginnings" of pharmacology, since many of our medicines are derived from just such sources.

Sometimes people erroneously assume that, since these preparations are derived from plant sources, i.e., they are "natural," that they are also "safe." That is NOT an appropriate assumption. The consumer should also be aware that, although some herbalists may have knowledge of pharmacology, there are those who do not, and it's difficult to "tell the difference." Our advice is that one talk with his/her health care provider prior to taking herbal preparations.

Health Insurance

As a student, most likely you are included in an insurance plan your parents have. You should know the details of that plan, at least in terms of knowing the basics of its coverage. Of course, where you should initially seek care for illness or injury is the university clinic.

In a few short years, you will graduate and be "on your own." Most family insurance coverage for a student ends either at graduation, or upon attaining a certain age. Some will continue through graduate study provided one immediately enters a graduate or professional program. What is important is that you not be without a means of paying for necessary health care. One trip to an emergency room for an injury or an emergency appendectomy can put you several thousand dollars in debt.

How Americans should be insured for health care costs is a topic of political debate. Most working individuals have, in the past, had at least some insurance coverage through their employer. As the costs of providing insurance for workers have risen, many employers have reduced benefits and required that workers assume a greater share of the cost of coverage. The cost of all health care insurances has risen, and may continue to do so.

So, what will this mean to those of you who graduate three or four years from now? There are a few words of advice we can give you.

1. You literally cannot afford to be without some form of health insurance, at least for "major" injuries or illnesses. A broken bone suffered in a slip on the ice, or an inflamed appendix can easily accumulate thousands of dollars in medical expenses.

2. If you have employer-subsidized group health insurance available to you, be sure to enroll, and know the benefits it provides. Carry the card in your wallet.

3. If you're working at a part-time job, and do not have health benefits, search for the best coverage you can afford. You at least need to have a plan that will help with costs incurred for treatment of an injury or illness that may require surgery or hospital admission. As a young, essentially healthy person, you likely will be able to find a coverage you can afford. It will typically have a "deductible," which is the cost you would have to assume before the insurer would pay. Lower deductibles mean higher premiums, and vice-versa. You would need to decide what combination is best for your situation.

Nutritional Supplements: What A Consumer Should Know

These products include vitamins, minerals, and combination products purported to enhance physical strength and athletic performance, promote weight loss, slow the effects of aging, or similar claims. A key fact the consumer should know is that our Food and Drug Administration does not regulate these products beyond requiring that manufacturers list the product's ingredients on the label. So long as the product does not purport to treat a specific illness or medical condition, it is "outside" the tight control placed on medicinal products.

The Dietary Supplements and Health Education Act of 1994 states that "Manufacturers do not have to provide FDA with evidence that dietary supplements are effective or safe." When a supplement is marketed, the FDA would have to prove the product ineffective or harmful in order to restrict its sale or remove it from the market. Considering the number of medicinal drugs FDA must evaluate, together with the time and cost involved in researching products, it is not surprising that few supplements are banned. An exception to that occurred in 2004 when products containing the herb ephedra (also known as ma huang) were banned. Products containing the ingredient were marketed as aids to weight loss, but they were found to have harmful effects on the cardiovascular system.

Ephedra-containing supplements were banned because they were shown to be unsafe. However, it is usually the responsibility of the consumer to assess claims made for the effectiveness of supplements. Consumers must be knowledgeable enough to evaluate manufacturers' claims for a product, and must determine whether effectiveness is sufficient to warrant the product's expense. They must also realize that even supplements that are "safe" can have harmful effects if taken in large amounts.

Evaluating Dietary Supplement Advertising

Manufacturers of various types of nutritional supplements would have consumers believe that our food supply is somehow depleted of nutrients. That is untrue; the meats, eggs, milk, grains, fruits, and vegetables produced by American farms are as nutrient-rich as ever. It is in the storage, preparation, and processing that nutrient content is reduced. For optimal health, consumers need to purchase whole or minimally processed foods and prepare them properly, rather than turning to supplements.

Dietary supplements are widely advertised in print, on TV, and over the Internet. Much of the advertising for nutritional supplements is aimed particularly toward the athlete or fitness enthusiast. Some are designed to appeal to the older person who has become very health conscious as increased age has begun to cause changes in appearance and energy level. It is important that consumers know how to evaluate the claims they read and hear.

Guidelines for evaluating advertising for supplements:

1. Products purported to enhance strength, endurance and/or athletic performance tend to be "pitched" by well-known athletes, who supposedly use and endorse the product. Bear in mind that the individual is being paid handsomely for supporting the product, and that he or she may, or may not, have really taken the supplement. Remember also that elite athletes achieve success through a combination of their physical gifts and many years of training. It's not likely that any particular dietary supplement played a significant role in their success. So, don't be influenced by such testimonials.

2. Many supplements claim that research has proven the beneficial effects of their products. Rather than accept those claims at face value, the astute consumer should ask the following questions.

   a. Who did the research, and where was it done? Was it done at a university known for research, or at an "independent lab?" What are the credentials of the researchers?

   b. Who sponsored the research? A great deal of supplement research is supported by the company marketing the product; obviously, there is the possibility that the vested interest may skew results.

   c. Is the research that is claimed published in peer-reviewed professional journals?

   d. What was the nature of the research cited? Were studies conducted according to accepted research protocols? Were appropriate comparisons made?

3. Be aware that the cost of nutritional supplements often far exceeds that of simply eating a varied diet, with plenty of vegetables and fruits, along with protein and whole-grain foods. Dietary supplements made from freeze-dried concentrates of vegetables and fruits, although harmless, are very costly.

4. There is no "magic" pill, potion, or supplement that will bring about sustained and healthful loss of excess body weight. The only approaches to weight loss that have a track-record for success are those based on consuming a balanced diet of regular foods, limiting one's intake of "empty calories," and engaging in 30-60 minutes of age-appropriate exercise at least 4-5 days of the week.

The best advice: Use the resources you have to obtain a varied, nutritious combination of foods that you enjoy eating. Unless you are suffering from a nutrient deficiency or are recovering from an injury or illness that resulted in significant muscle wasting, supplements are not needed. Following are some reliable guidelines one can use in evaluating nutritional supplements.

Vitamins

1. The primary role of vitamins is to serve as catalysts in the body's thousands of biochemical processes. Only tiny amounts are needed for optimal function. Unless one is unable to eat, is pregnant, or has been found to have a deficiency, there is no need for supplemental vitamins. If psychologically one "feels better," taking a one-a-day multiple vitamin, that's fine. However, beware "mega-doses."

2. Vitamins A, D, E, and K are lipid-bound, and accumulate in the body over time. Excessive intake of any of those will cause harm. A normal diet affords an ample amount of these.

3. The rest of the vitamins are water-soluble. That means that the body extracts the amounts needed, and literally washes away the rest. So, extra B-vitamins and vitamin C are simply discarded in the urine.

4. In spite of product claims, controlled studies show that taking massive doses of vitamin C during the winter months will not "prevent" the common cold. Maintaining the immune system by eating a healthful diet and getting adequate rest is much more effective!

Minerals

1. **Calcium** is a major constituent of bones and teeth; it also, in minute amounts, enables nerve transmission and muscle contraction, and is essential to normal blood clotting. Again, if one is consuming a diet containing dairy products, and a variety of vegetables, intake is adequate for needs through approximately age 55. At that time an age-related loss of bone density may begin, which can be slowed by modest calcium supplementation. If one is unable to tolerate dairy foods, a supplement of 1000 – 1500 mg/day is sufficient. Mega doses of calcium, over time, may result in chronic fatigue and the formation of calcium deposits in the kidneys, liver, and other organs.

2. **Iron** is essential for oxygen transport in the body, and although needed in small amounts, is the mineral for which most deficiencies occur. Meats and fish are the best and most absorbable food sources of iron; other iron-rich foods include dark green vegetables, dried fruits like apricots and raisins, and whole grain cereals and breads. Iron is needed in only small amounts for optimal function, 18 mg/day for women and 8 mg/day for men. Excessive intake (>45mg/day) over time is harmful, leading to a condition known as hemochromatosis, which is life-threatening. If one chooses to be a

vegetarian or really just doesn't like spinach and other dark green vegetables, a daily multiple vitamin pill with iron is recommended. If one is diagnosed with an iron deficiency, supplemental iron should be taken as prescribed. Otherwise, just eat a healthful diet on a regular basis. There is no value, and potentially significant harm, in excessive iron intake.

3. Other minerals like magnesium, zinc, iodine, chromium, and copper are often touted as needing to be supplemented, if one is to be healthy. Again, while each of these is essential to the body's optimal functioning, a normal diet will provide them in sufficient amounts. Our grain-products, dairy foods, and vegetables contain them in adequate amounts. There is no value in supplementing them.

Phytochemicals: What Are They, and What Do They Do?

Phytochemicals are substances present in plants which are involved in many aspects of plant metabolism. Some are essential to energy production and storage; others are pigments, giving them color; still others afford them some protection from insects, molds, and other threats.

It has been long recognized that people whose diets contain lots of plant foods have less risk for developing cardiovascular disease, some types of cancer, and age-related eye conditions such as macular degeneration and cataracts. As scientists began to identify the host of different phytochemicals contained in plants, they wondered if those were the reason why fruits and vegetables are so "healthful" when consumed in adequate amounts. Retrospective studies suggested, for example, that cigarette smokers whose diets contained lots of beta-carotene containing vegetables and fruits had lower rates of lung cancer than smokers with less consumption of those foods. Was beta-carotene indeed a "protector" against cancer in smokers? Could taking beta-carotene as a supplement protect smokers?

Controlled studies, comparing smokers who took supplements of beta-carotene developed lung cancer at the same or higher rates than smokers who did not take the supplements. Researchers concluded that supplementation of a specific phytochemical is unlikely to have beneficial effects in humans. Rather, it's more likely that their benefits are realized in combinations, as they occur together in foods. That is, it's useless to isolate them, and package them as pills and powders.

That however does not deter manufacturers from doing so, and marketing "phytonutrients" to health-conscious consumers. One can purchase a variety of such products in health food stores and from internet sources. However, consumers should realize that there is really no proof of their value when consumed as supplements, rather than in foods. Their value lies in consuming them in the combinations in which they naturally occur—and that is in foods.

Herbal Supplements and Remedies

A variety of herbal products are marketed in supplement form with the suggestion that they may "remedy" a variety of problems. Some have a degree of benefit, while others may offer primarily psychological benefit-- that is, you think they will help so you feel better. Some can be harmful. All have the potential to interact with prescribed medications. If you take any herbal supplements, they should be listed as "medications" in information you give your health care provider.

Many people mistakenly assume that, because these products are derived from plants, and are therefore "natural," that they are also safe. That is a false assumption; there are plants that are deadly poisons. Moreover, consumers must remember that these products are not subjected to the quality controls and purity standards applied to prescription and nonprescription medicines. Their stated "benefits" do not have to be proven, and their side-effects profile is not required.

Selected Herbal Products

Red yeast rice—an herbal preparation made from rice grown with red yeast. It contains chemicals known as "statins," which act in the liver to reduce blood lipid levels. They work in the same fashion as the statin class of prescription drugs prescribed to lower cholesterol. Because they work in the same way, they have the same possibility for doing damage to the liver as prescription statins. Consumers should also be aware that they are not subjected to the same standards of purity and consistency as are prescription preparations.

Ginkgo biloba—made from extracts of flavenoids and terpenoids from the leaves of the ginkgo tree; some evidence suggests that it may improve memory and cognitive deficits in persons with age-related dementias. Health care providers need to know if patients are taking this, as it will interact with drugs prescribed for dementia.

Saint John's Wort—an herbal preparation made from the flowers of a plant that grows widely in fields and along roadsides throughout Europe and North America. An extract is made from its flowers and it is marketed as an antidepressant. It is known to interact with a wide variety of other medications, and again, should not be used without medical advice.

Saw palmetto—an extract made from the dried berries of the palmetto plants common to the southeastern United States. It is purported to relieve the frequent need to urinate caused by benign enlargement of the prostate, which is common in older men. Evidence doesn't support effectiveness.

Ginger—a tropical plant, with an underground "stem" or rhizome that is dried and used as a spice for baking and cooking, as well as a "remedy." It has been used to alleviate nausea and vomiting, as well as joint and muscle pain. Studies suggest that it has some value in relieving nausea and vomiting associated with pregnancy, and that it is likely safe if taken in small doses. It hasn't been found effective in treating joint pain and inflammation.

Garlic—usually sold as tablets or capsules made from dried, powdered garlic cloves, is marketed as a cholesterol-lowering agent, as well as being preventive for atherosclerosis, and hypertension. In controlled studies, garlic supplements have not been shown to lower cholesterol. There have been findings that suggest it may be slightly effective in slowing the development of atherosclerosis, as well as slightly lowering elevated blood pressure. Concerns center on its tendency to reduce blood-clotting, and its potential for interaction with other drugs.

Echinacea—a flowering plant whose leaves and roots are dried or expressed to make extracts purported to stimulate the immune system to ward off respiratory infections, and to lessen the severity and duration of their symptoms. Controlled studies have shown mixed results regarding Echinacea preparations; they may have some efficacy in alleviating symptoms of respiratory infections in children, although not in adults. Anyone with plant allergies, like ragweed, may be likely to have an exacerbation of allergy symptoms if they take Echinacea preparations.

Ginseng—is a root much used in Chinese medicine for nearly all maladies. It is most often recommended to boost general energy level and a feeling of well-being, as well as enhancing the effectiveness of the immune system. A host of side-effects are possible, depending on the actual ginseng content of the product taken. These range from itching and headache to nervousness, rapid heart beat, or blood pressure changes. The consumer must be aware also that the herbal preparation they purchase may contain other plant material, as well as pesticides and molds. This is a product the consumer should avoid.

Hoodia—is a cactus-like plant that is native to Africa's Kalahari Desert. It has been imported and cultivated in many other places. It is marketed as an appetite suppressant to aid in weight loss. The stems and roots of the plants are used to make extracts, and are also dried and sold in tablet or capsule form. Hoodia has not been studied in any reliable, scientifically sound manner, so neither its effectiveness nor its safety is known. Consumers should avoid using this product at this time.

What About Protein Supplements?

Protein supplements are second only to vitamins and minerals in the frequency with which they are used. There is also a great deal of misunderstanding about their role as part of a health-wellness promoting diet.

As discussed in the chapter on nutrition, protein is essential to tissue building and repair as well as the body's production of numerous compounds essential to normal function. Protein-rich foods include meat, poultry, fish, dairy products, eggs, legumes, and grains. Smaller amounts of protein are found in many vegetables and fruits.

The average adult needs 0.8-1.0 gram of protein/kg of body weight, so a person weighing 160 lbs. (72.7 kg) would need not more than 73 grams of protein/day. The average American, eating as most of us do, consumes 100-125 grams of protein daily. In fact, it is not unusual for us to consume 150-200 grams of protein. Some studies suggest that the athlete or very active person needs between 1.2 and 1.8 grams of protein/kg of body weight in order to build strength and increase muscle mass during training. (McCardle, Katch, and Katch, 209) Consequently, protein powder, shakes, and bars are highly promoted through any media likely to be seen by athletes and fitness enthusiasts. These products have become the basis of a multi-billion dollar industry. Always looking for any competitive edge, athletes and millions of athletic want-to-be's are enthusiastic consumers.

What should you, as a wise consumer, know about protein supplements? Can one consume too much protein? Will high protein consumption promote loss of body fat?

Nutritionists recommend that the diet should contain no more than 30% protein; that is, a person (a highly active one) consuming 3600 calories/day, should have no more than 1080 of those calories from protein. That amounts to 270 grams of protein, which can be easily obtained through food choices.

Too much protein does pose a risk to health. Nitrogen is the element unique to proteins; it is not contained in either carbohydrates or fats. Nitrogen must be processed and excreted in the form of urea; that is accomplished primarily by the kidneys. Flushing large amounts of urea, of course, causes a large amount of water to be lost as well, placing one at risk for dehydration which can lead to symptoms as simple as muscle cramping or as severe as heart arrhythmias and even death. Loss of calcium also occurs in the processing of large amounts of protein. Over time, that results in loss of bone density.

Another fact that consumers often don't consider is the calorie content of the extra protein being consumed. Protein contains 4 calories/gram; so, one must consider whether they are using enough energy in work and exercise to handle a lot of extra calories.

All that is meant to point out to consumers that protein supplements are not needed, even by those who are active, including athletes. Checking out the prices for the various protein powders, drinks, and bars marketed shows that they are costly; compare their per pound cost with that of boneless chicken breasts, or even steak... you may be surprised.

The only people who really need super-high protein intake, beyond the diet, are those who are recovering from an illness or injury that has produced significant loss of muscle mass. Others are well-advised to use their resources to obtain healthful foods.

If you are unalterably committed to "super" consumption of protein, you can do the following inexpensively.

1. To make an omelet, use 2 whole eggs + the whites of 2 more; add some low-fat cheese and you have a "super-pro" omelet.

2. Blend non-fat dry milk with 2% milk, nonfat frozen yogurt and fruit to make a high protein shake at a fraction of the cost of the marketed protein shakes.

3. Combine dry-roasted peanuts with raisins, dried apricots, and dried cranberries to make a tasty high protein snack.

4. A sandwich of peanut butter and low fat cheese on whole-grain bread provides both energy and a lot of protein in a relatively small volume.

Whey is the protein source most often used in commercial protein supplements; it is a by-product of cheese-making. Makers of supplements obtain it cheaply, convert it to a powdered form, add some flavoring, obtain "testimonials" to its value from some well-known athletes, and sell it at high prices. Our advice is "spend your resources on a balanced diet."

What About Energy Bars?

There are many products marketed as nutritious, quick high-energy snacks for the busy person who may need to skip a meal, or for athlete looking for an "energy boost." Many parents put them in school lunches, or have them available as an "after school snack." They range from the pricey "sport bars" marketed to athletes, to less costly granola bars made by the cereal companies.

None have any harmful ingredients; consumers just need to decide how much they want to spend, and whether they really desire to consume that many calories. All contain a combination of carbohydrates, protein, and fats, and all contain 170-230 calories. Some things for the consumer to keep in mind are the following:

1. These products are best used either as an occasional meal substitute, or, for the replacement of energy stores following rigorous exercise. Their carbohydrate content is not going to be absorbed quickly, due to the protein, fat, and fiber they contain.

2. The protein in "sport bars" is from one or more of these sources: soy, dried milk solids, or dried egg white. The usual protein sources in other snack bars are oats, nuts, and dried fruits like raisins.

3. Some, in both categories, contain coconut or palm oil. Those are saturated plant oils, and in the body, are the same as saturated fats from animal sources.

4. A significant amount of the carbohydrates in both are from high fructose corn syrup. Depending on the proportion of fructose to glucose that manufacturers use, HFCS may contribute to significant gain of body fat.

5. Many snack/energy bars contain peanut products; those who have allergies must be aware of that.

You can make your own high-energy trail mix less expensively than you can buy commercial energy bars. You can "fine-tune" your mix to suit your own taste; it will provide complex carbohydrates to replenish energy stores, plus protein, fiber, and the all the vitamins and minerals contained in the foods you choose contain, and none of the added sugars and fats.

You can make a tasty mix from a combination of dried cranberries, dried apricots, raisins, mixed nuts, and granola. You can add other dried fruits you enjoy; the proportions depend on your tastes!

Final Advice on Nutritional Supplements

God has provided us with a varied food supply consisting of both plants and animals. He gave us the choice of using animals for food, while assuring that everything needed for good health is available from plant sources. If we follow the guidelines developed by those whose career is the study of foods and the roles various foods play in our health, we don't need supplements.

The portion of a healthy diet that most of us are "short" on is vegetables and fruits; we should have five servings daily. If you don't usually get those five servings, then taking a multiple vitamin capsule daily is a reasonable thing to do. It does not need to be an expensive, "brand name" vitamin. Unless you have been diagnosed with a vitamin deficiency, avoid taking further vitamin supplements. The only exception is for those who choose to be vegans, or total vegetarians. Since vitamin B-12 is contained only in foods of animal origin, they will need to take a supplement to obtain that vitamin.

Likewise, a normal, varied diet provides adequate mineral intake. Unless you have a deficiency, mineral supplements are not needed. When you reach the age of 55 or 60, taking an additional calcium supplement is advisable, due to age-related loss of bone density. Your health care provider can evaluate bone density, and give a specific recommendation.

As a consumer, you have available a tremendous spectrum of nutrition-related advertisements, claims, and testimonials to the value of a wide variety of products.

There a few things to remember in evaluating what you read and hear from those selling nutritional products.

First, there is no combination of supplemental nutrients that will either cure or prevent disease that is superior to a healthful balanced diet of "real" foods. Second, be wary of taking herbal supplements; their purity and consistency may vary from batch to batch, and their effects may vary from person to person. If you have a physical problem, have it evaluated and treated by your health provider, rather than self-treating with an herbal preparation. Third, if you are an athlete, or a very active person, you may benefit from increasing the protein in your diet up to 30% of your total calorie intake; more will NOT make you stronger or faster. That means that if you consume 3000 calories/day, then 900 of those can come from proteins; you can obtain those from foods or commercial supplements. Do remember that protein calories "count," so don't take in a lot more than you're using, unless your goal is to gain weight.

Be a good steward, both of your body and its well-being, and the resources God has provided by utilizing your intellectual ability to weigh information and discern what "makes sense" in light of all the research-based knowledge we have. Be a steward who uses wisdom and discernment based on careful research and knowledge to be faithful with the Master's goods.

Identifying and Avoiding Health "Quackery"

Medical "quackery" refers to the marketing of treatments that are unproven, or even known to be false, by those who seek to profit from their sale. Quack remedies have been around as long as medicine has been practiced. False remedies may be medicines, as well as devices and treatments of various kinds. In the nineteenth century, salesmen traversed the country, putting on "medicine shows," and persuading the assembled crowd that the elixirs sold would cure just about any ailment. Since most of the "medicines" sold were alcohol-based, and many also contained laudanum (an opiate), aches and pains certainly were temporarily relieved. Today's counterparts use electronic media, but the messages are just as false as those of the "snake oil salesmen" of yesteryear.

Some "Red Flags" That Should Alert the Consumer

Beware when those who are selling a particular remedy claim that there is a "conspiracy" on the part of government or the medical profession to keep the product from the public. Our medical care system is not perfect, but it does not aim to "keep" cures secret, or to deny patients effective treatments.

Be skeptical of claims made for a "secret formula," or one "guaranteed to cure, with no side effects." Such a product just doesn't exist; well-researched drugs of proven efficacy don't always work for every patient, and a small percentage will have undesirable side effects, at least in some people. Quacks often present their products as "safe, natural" remedies, because substances used may be derived from a plant source. Laetrile, the name given a substance found naturally in the pits of apricots and other fruits, was touted as a cancer cure. Even though scientific medicine had rejected it as both toxic and ineffective, thousands traveled to Mexico seeking a cure, which they did not find.

Who Is Most Susceptible to Quackery?

Understandably, those who have an illness, like cancer, with a poor prognosis, are more open to consider unproven remedies. They may feel that "mainstream medicine" has failed them, and so will consider alternative therapies that offer hope. If they have the means to pursue alternatives, that is their choice. It is tragic, though, when cancer patients who have <u>not</u> exhausted available options reject proven therapies in favor of bizarre and ineffective treatments.

Others prone to turn to quack therapies are those with chronic conditions like diabetes or arthritis, and people who have, for whatever reason, developed a fear and mistrust of established medicine and the laws that govern its practice. Also, there are those who will not take a prescribed medicinal "drug," but willingly take "natural" products of unknown content and purity.

Examples of Current "Quack" Therapies

Chelation is a procedure in which chemicals are taken into the body, usually by mouth, which will bind to heavy metals, and hasten their elimination from the body, usually in the urine. It has been promoted as a "cure" for atherosclerotic plaques in the arteries. In fact, the only proven use for chelation is the treatment of lead toxicity. It will not dissolve arterial plaque. Moreover, the chelating agents used may be damaging to the kidneys.

Many products are touted as "anti-aging" agents, and they sell very well among those who "over-value" youthfulness. Preparations purported to contain "growth hormone releasers" are promoted with infomercials on radio and TV, as well as over the Internet. Aging is a natural process, and the rate at which signs we identify with age appear are in some part due to genetic heritage, and in greater part to lifestyle. Eating a healthful diet, avoiding harmful habits like smoking and excessive alcohol use, and exercising regularly are the best ways to "age well."

Colonic irrigation is at once the most dangerous, and most ridiculous, of quack remedies marketed. It is based on the premise that the colon harbors all sorts of toxic materials, and that good health depends on keeping it "flushed out." Infusing large amounts of fluid rectally can damage intestinal mucosa, and substances added to the fluid may be injurious to the mucosa. In any case, healthful function of the gastrointestinal tract is promoted by adequate intake of water and fiber-containing foods.

Copper bracelets, as well as magnet-containing wraps are promoted as effective in relieving the pain of arthritis. Studies have suggested that the magnetic field would have to be much stronger than that of marketed devices to have any significant effect. Copper has no effect beyond perhaps an ornamental one.

In Summary....

The consumer needs to use "common sense," as well as reliable sources, in evaluating any "out of the mainstream" therapy. Be wary of any remedy that purports to "cure" a condition that thus far can only be "controlled" by conventional therapies. Conditions like diabetes and arthritis are examples.

If any pill or potion is presented as being based on an ancient, "secret" formula, known only to a select few and sold only by mail, avoid it. Likewise, don't be fooled by undocumented testimonials from persons who supposedly have used the products; there is no way of substantiating their claims.

In short, if the treatment seems to be "bizarre" and offers results "too good to be true," in all likelihood, they are!!! Use the credible sources of knowledge available to you, and be a good steward of both the body and the resources God has entrusted to you.

Bibliography and Resources for Further Study

Barrett, Stephen. "Magnet Therapy: A Skeptical View." *Quackwatch – Your Guide to Quackery, Health Fraud, and Intelligent Decisions.* Accessed July 4, 2011: www.quackwatch.org.

Barrett, Stephen, and William Jarvis, eds. *The Health Robbers: A Close Look at Quackery in America.* Buffalo, NY: Prometheus Books, 1993.

Beik, Janet I. *Health Insurance Today – A Practical Approach.* St. Louis, MO: Elsevier/Saunders, 2011.

Burke, Louise. *Practical Sports Nutrition.* Champaign, IL: Human Kinetics, 2007.

Fugh-Berman, Adriane. *Alternative Medicine: What Works.* Baltimore, MD: Williams and Wilkins, 1997.

Juhnke, Eric S., ed. *Quacks and Crusaders: The Fabulous Careers of John Brinkley, Norman Baker, and Harry Hoxsey.* Lawrence KS: University Press of Kansas, 2002.

Manore, Melinda, and Janice Thompson. *Sports Nutrition for Health and Performance.* Champaign, IL: Human Kinetics, 2000.

McArdle, William, Frank Katch, and Victor Katch. *Sports and Exercise Nutrition.* 3rd ed. Philadelphia: Wolters Kluwer Health/Lippincott, Williams & Wilkins, 2009.

National Cancer Institute. "Laetril/Amygdalin." Last modified September 24, 2010. Accessed June 28, 2011: www.cancer.gov/cancertopics.

Walters, Peter, and John Byl, eds. *Christian Paths to Health and Wellness.* Champaign, IL: Human Kinetics, 2008.

Williams, Melvin. *Nutrition for Health, Fitness and Sport.* 9th ed. New York, NY: Mc-Graw-Hill, 2010.

Chapter 13

So...Now What?

We have reviewed a fair amount of basic physiology. We've gone over how mental and emotional stressors interact with physiological processes. We have discussed at length the impacts of personal lifestyle on well-being. Above all, we have attempted to convince you that we humans indeed have a God-given stewardship responsibility for the care of this intricate vessel in which we live.

While it's indisputable that we were formed from the dust, and will return to dust, our Maker has ordained a given span of time to be on the earth. In His sovereignty, He has not made all of us exactly the same; some have stronger muscles, some superior coordination, enabling great feats of athleticism, and some have specific physical challenges with which to cope. All of us are but a few pounds of organic and inorganic compounds plus a lot of water, yet we are the most complex entities in the universe.

In 1999 NASA built the first "artificial muscles," and staged the first "bionic handshake." Polymer strips responding to electrical impulses reached out and clasped; the resulting grip was barely perceptible in its force. Likely, God chuckled. (Swenson, p. 90) The point is that, as clever as we may become, we can make only poor attempts at duplicating God's handiwork. We live in wonderful bodies. What are we going to **do** about being faithful stewards of them?

Actually, perhaps this chapter is written mostly for you to read 15–20 years **after** you've graduated from college. Care of the body takes on new meaning once the invincibility of youth has worn off. So, imagine that you have discovered this volume in a box from the attic, have blown off the dust, and decided to take a look at one of your old books from college.

Conflicting Health Information: Navigating the Maze

There are few topics that get as much attention in the media today as health. Television specials, billboards, and scores of articles in magazines and newspapers invite us to lose weight, gain muscle, sleep better, cope with stress, etc. using methods ranging from reasonable to ridiculous. The internet has opened a "whole new world" to the purveyors of health-related information, and those who seek it. There is a lot of good information available; there is also a great deal of quackery (false health information). This can range from being not helpful, but at least not harmful, to being outright dangerous. We offer some suggestions for "navigating" the maze of often conflicting and confusing information.

1. Take note of the source for the information/claims you're considering. Do the people presenting the information have solid credentials? Do their ideas appear in a peer-reviewed publication of good reputation?

2. What type of support is given for the claims made? Does it consist of the "testimonies" of people who have used the products/methods, or are actual data given? If there does appear to have been an "experiment" how many subjects were there? What was the time period over which the study took place? (it takes time for possible "side effects" to appear). Were there appropriate controls in the experiment?

3. What is the relationship of the "researchers" to those who will profit from the sale of whatever the product is?

4. How bizarre or "far fetched" are the ideas presented? If an idea sounds "fishy" it probably is. For example: "Just take these capsules daily, and watch those pounds melt away without any exercise, while you eat anything you want" sounds like baloney, and it is! If something doesn't make sense, leave it alone.

Home Exercise Devices

Simply walking can be the greatest exercise in the world; interspersed with some recreational activities like tennis, racquetball or golf (provided you walk the course) it can be the backbone of your total exercise program. However, there are "bad weather days," and time constraints, so if your financial situation allows, home exercise equipment can be a sound investment.

A set of free weights, with plates varying from 2 pounds to 10 pounds is a good investment. If you are concerned about weights dropping on toes, there are some very satisfactory cable-tension exercisers that can be used to increase muscle strength. Check in your local fitness equipment store, and be sure to try them out before you buy. If you have a lot of money to spend, BowFlex makes an excellent home strength gym.

For aerobic workouts inside, it's hard to improve on a good quality stationary bicycle. You need to have a model that allows the tension (or resistance) to be adjusted, and for the seat height to be altered to fit users of different sizes. Don't buy a treadmill for home use unless you can afford one that costs close to a thousand dollars. Smaller models will not stand up under vigorous use, and represent poor investments.

Several devices are designed to simulate cross-country skiing, a great aerobic activity. Before you purchase one, try it, and talk to other people who have and use them. Some put a great deal of stress on the knee joints. For most adults, that is not a good thing.

Our advice is to pass-up the devices for strengthening the abdominal muscles. They are designed to rock, or roll, or both, propelled by the users abdominal muscles. Sounds wonderful, but those who use them do so vigorously for a few days, get very sore, and stash the exercise device in the closet or under the bed.

Probably the best advice regarding purchase of home exercise equipment is to be sure you thoroughly research the device you're considering, and talk with others who have it. A lot of American homes have treadmills (and other items) gathering dust!

The other option with regard to indoor exercise is to join a fitness or health club that has the equipment you need for a good exercise regimen. Go and look at the facility; talk to instructors, and to other members. Be sure that you check on the hours the facility is available, to be sure it will be available when you have time to use it. The drawback to joining a health club is that you do have to leave home to use it... if that will pose any kind of problem, it may not be the best move for you.

"Bedrock" Principles for Health and Fitness... at Any Age

Kenneth Cooper, in his book *Regaining the Power of Youth* cites what he terms "bedrock" or foundational principles for getting and/or staying fit and healthy. We offer a summary of these.

1. Get regular aerobic exercise at least 3, and preferably 5 days/week. Take opportunity to increase your exercise time by "accumulating" at least 30 minutes of aerobic activity in your work day.

2. Limit fat consumption to not more than 20% to 30% of your calorie intake most days. To the degree possible, choose those that are monounsaturated.

3. Do your best to avoid obesity, but don't be "paranoid" about your weight. Some of us will never be thin (particularly after 40), and there is research to show that skinny people who don't exercise are far more likely to die prematurely than moderately obese ones who do.

4. Take a folic acid supplement (vitamin B-9) daily; this is an "antioxidant" and gives some protection against cardiovascular disease.

5. Eat fruits and vegetables... raw as much as you can. Include the "cruciferous" ones (broccoli, brussels sprouts, cauliflower and cabbage) which contain beta carotene, a cancer-fighting substance.

6. Include fiber in your diet; use whole grain breads and cereals.

7. Retard bone loss by weight-bearing exercise and calcium supplementation (1000–1500 mg. per day.)

8. Drink water—eight 8-ounce glasses/day.

9. Don't use tobacco in any of its forms. Lung cancer may not be the consequence, but the tobacco user never is unscathed, assuming tobacco use has been long-term.

The authors add another couple of principles. They are:

1. Be careful about any herbal remedies or supplements you have opportunity to use... remember that simply being "natural" doesn't render something harmless. Ask your medical provider about any of these alternative medicinal products you consider; this is especially important for those who take prescription medications, due to interactions.

2. Be a skeptic where health products and/or remedies are concerned. Your watchword should always be: "Show me the study!"

Conclusion

All of us have God-ordained purposes for our lives; whether our ministries be large or small, they can only be accomplished through our physical beings. To do "our best for God's highest", these fleshly tabernacles have to be in the highest functional state possible. You know what to do . . . now get up, get going, and **"be a faithful steward."**

Bibliography and Resources for Further Study

Cooper, Kenneth. *Regaining the Power of Youth*. Nelson Books, 1998.

Cooper, Kenneth, and Tyler Cooper. *Start Strong, Finish Strong – Prescriptions for a Lifetime of Great Health*. Penguin Group, 2007.

Ettinger, Walter, Brenda Wright, and Steven Blair. *Fitness After Fifty*. Human Kinetics, 2006.

Jacobsen, Michael. *The Word on Health*. Moody Press, 2000.

Rubin, Jordan, and David Remedios. *The Great Physician's Rx for Health & Wellness*. Nelson Books, 2005.

Swenson, Richard. *More Than Meets the Eye*. Navpress, 2000.

Terry, Patricia H. *Made for Paradise – God's Original Plan for Healthy Eating, Physical Activity, and Rest*. New Hope Publishers, 2007.

Appendix A

Introduction to Cedarville University Fitness Center and Nautilus Equipment

In our fitness center, we have the Nautilus line of variable resistance exercise equipment. These devices, through a patented system of cams, levers and pulleys vary resistance that a muscle group works against throughout the range of motion. This allows the muscle to be "worked" in both the concentric and eccentric phases of the movement, causing the exercise to be more effective in increasing muscle strength.

The machines are very "user-friendly"; they are adaptable to persons of varying body sizes, and differing levels of initial muscle strength. They are equally useful for novices, regular exercisers, athletes, and senior citizens.

On the North side of the fitness center is a selection of Nautilus "2ST" machines. These are slightly easier to adjust for different body sizes, and offer 1 lb. incremental weight adjustments. Although they are helpful for a wide range of persons, they are particularly helpful to one just beginning an exercise program. These machines are arranged in a "circuit", that is it's set up for users to move from one machine to the next in order. Fitness center "etiquette" requires that, when several people are working in that area, everyone go in order rather than randomly choosing a machine.

On the South side is a selection of Nautilus "Nitro" machines. These are similar to the 2ST pieces, but have 5 lb. weight increments. Most of the machines on this side have counterparts on the 2ST side which work out the same muscle groups, but in a slightly different way. You may find that one of the Nitro machines suits you better for a particular muscle group than its 2ST counterpart, or vice-versa. That's fine; use the one that allows you to do the exercise in a way that is most comfortable and beneficial for you.

Nautilus equipment is designed to allow the user to concentrate on a specific group of muscles. Below is a listing of equipment in our fitness center, and the muscle groups it's designed to work.

You will note that, in many instances, while a machine focuses on a specific group of muscles, other muscle groups may be involved. The leg press, for example, emphasizes those muscles that extend the leg at the knee; hip flexors and extensors are also involved. The low back machines also give some work to the muscles of the abdomen and thigh.

You will notice also that some of the machines have seat belts attached to them. The purpose of the belts is to help the exerciser focus the exercise on the intended muscle group rather than "recruiting" other groups to help.

Upper Body	2ST-Line	Nitro-Line
Arms, Shoulders, Chest	Preacher Curl	Biceps Curl
	Vertical Chest	Vertical Chest
	Super Pullover	Super Pullover
		Pec-Fly
		Incline Press
Arms, Shoulders, and Upper Back	Compound Row	Compound Row
	Lateral Raise	Lat Pull-Down
Trunk		
Abdomen, Mid-Back	Rotary Torso	Abdominal
		Abdominal
Lower Back	Low Back	Low Back
Lower Body (Legs, Hips)		
Knee Extensors (Quadriceps)	Leg Extension	Leg Extension
	Leg Press	Leg Press
Knee Flexors (Hamstrings)	Seated Leg Curl	Prone Leg Curl
Hip Abductors, Adductors		Adduction/Abduction

Your instructor will give you an orientation to the equipment and its proper use. Each piece of equipment has easy-to-follow instructions on the machine itself, so if you forget what your instructor showed you, read. There are also workers in the fitness center who can help you.

Getting Started

Start by choosing 8–10 exercises, being sure that you have included something for all major areas of the body: upper body, trunk, and lower body. For example, you might choose:

Leg press	Large flexors and extensors of the hip; quadriceps
Leg curl	Muscles of posterior thigh (hamstrings)
Vertical chest	Arms, shoulders, chest
Preacher curl	Muscles that flex the elbow
Triceps extension	Muscles that extend the elbow
Compound row	Arms, shoulders, upper back
Abdominal	Muscles of abdominal wall; flexors of the spine
Low back	Extensors of spine; abdominal muscles
Hip Abduction/Adduction	Muscles that abduct and adduct the thigh

The workout includes something for all major muscle groups and works opposing muscle groups; that is, flexors and extensors, abductors and adductors.

Performing the Exercises

Adapting the Equipment to Your Body Type/Size

Each piece of equipment has on it an explanation of how to properly perform the exercise for which it is designed; your instructor will also have given you an overview of proper use for the various pieces. It is important that you make the adjustments in seat height, seat-back angle, etc. that are needed so that you can perform the exercise properly, concentrating on the targeted group of muscles. This will require some time and "trial-and-error"; you should allow yourself at least a full-hour for your first work-out session, as that will be a time of learning just how to adapt the equipment to your body size, and how to do the exercise itself. You should write down the machine settings that suit you for each piece you are going to use.

Determining the Weight to Use

Again, there is "trial-and-error" involved in selecting the appropriate starting weights for each exercise in your strength training program. Research has shown that the resistance should be such that it fatigues the muscle groups worked within 8–12 repetitions of the exercise. Consider the size of the muscle group an exercise targets; for example, the leg press works the largest, strongest muscles of the body. Your starting weight will be much higher than, for example, the biceps curl, which concentrates on just the elbow flexor muscles. When you can go beyond 12 repetitions with a given weight, it is time to increase the resistance.

Speed at Which the Exercise Should Be Done

An exercise can be done fast, at a moderate speed, or at a slow speed. When you lift a weight at a fast speed, you can't stop the motion; fast lifting speeds emphasize momentum and thus actually reduce the muscle's work. In addition, speed increases the risk of injury. Lifting efforts under two seconds are considered "fast". Lifting efforts of two to four seconds are "moderate" speed. This controlled effort de-emphasizes momentum, increases the work done by the muscle, and reduces risk of injury. A slow exercise effort is one done over four or more seconds. These minimize momentum and maximize tension in the working muscles.

Research has shown that the best results are from performing resistance exercises at moderate to slow speed. The targeted muscle group develops greater force and maintains it throughout the range of motion; there is less risk of injury to muscles and tendons because momentum is controlled.

Therefore, it's recommended that the lifting phases on an exercise be done to a two-count, and the lowering phase done to a four-count. The longer lowering phase causes the muscle to work just as much in lengthening as in contracting, and so maximizes the strength-development value of the exercise.

Number of Repetitions and Number of Sets for Each Exercise

If you use a weight that will fatigue the muscle group in 8–12 repetitions, you will make optimal strength gains. When you find that you can do 13 or more repetitions, it is time to increase the weight.

Research has shown that, for the average person, there is little additional benefit gained from doing more than one set of each exercise (Wilmore and Costill, p. 107). One set of 8–12 repetitions, done with an appropriate weight is just as effective as three sets. One set of each exercise lets you complete a workout efficiently; it also prevents over-fatigue and reduces muscle soreness. Competitive athletes training for sports like football and wrestling may gain from multiple sets.

Frequency of Workouts

When you do strength training, you are asking your muscles to adapt to greater demands than they are used to. They will do that, but it takes two-to-three days for those tissue changes to be made. Therefore, strength workouts should be done two or three days per week. Studies have shown that doing strength workouts three days/week will yield a slightly greater gain in muscle strength than a two-days/week schedule. You have to look at your overall time demands, and choose what is best for you

Muscle Soreness

When we do muscular work we're unaccustomed to, our muscles typically are "sore" a day or two after the effort. God made our muscles to be wonderfully adaptable to demands made of them. However, those adaptations involve some "remodeling" of tissue; in that process there is some breakdown of cell membranes, with the liberation of tissue enzymes that stimulate our pain receptors. It is not severe, and will resolve in a day or two. We can minimize muscle soreness by avoiding the temptation to "overdo" when we begin our training program, and to progress in the weights we're using at a deliberate pace.

Remember the fable of the tortoise and the hare!! Careful stretching of the muscle groups after the workout may also lessen soreness.

Warm-Up, Cool-Down, and Stretching

Doing at least ten minutes of some aerobic activity like walking/jogging on a treadmill, or using one of the bikes or elliptical machines in the fitness center increases the rate of blood circulation to your muscles and prepares them for work. At the conclusion of your strength workout, at least five minutes of aerobic activity at an easy pace helps to relax muscle groups that have been made to work harder than they are accustomed to working .

Stretching a muscle group after you have worked it helps it to transition from activity to rest, so that it feels relaxed rather than tight. Stretching the muscle group after it has worked is better than before work because the muscle tissue is warm, and more extensible. There is no one "correct" set of stretches; simply find a position that makes the muscle group feel stretched, and hold it for 20-30 seconds.

"Learning Curves" in Strength Training

You will find that early in a strength training program, you can progress to higher resistance fairly quickly. Your muscles aren't changing that rapidly, but they are learning how to apply force more effectively to the task you've given them. As you come closer to whatever their present force production capacity is, your rate of progression will slow. This is normal. The rate at which you progress is unique to you; don't be concerned if it's different from that of your friends.

Sequence of Exercises in Your Workout

There is no one order in which you must do the specific exercises in your workout. It's suggested that you work your largest, strongest muscle groups first, followed by medium and then smallest groups. For example, do exercises for the legs, shoulders and chest before exercises for the elbow flexors and extensors, i.e., leg press before biceps curl. If possible, it is a good idea to "pair" exercises, so that you work opposing groups of muscles. For example, follow leg extensions which work muscles of the anterior thigh with leg curls, which work those of the posterior thigh.

Appendix B

Assessing Your Cardiorespiratory Fitness

Assessing Your Cardiorespiratory Fitness:
1.5 Mile <u>Running</u> Test

A commonly used field test for cardiorespiratory or aerobic fitness is a timed 1.5 mile effort. To be a valid assessment, this test assumes you are healthy enough to complete it safely, and that running is an activity that your body is comfortable doing, that you have been doing efforts similar to this test 3-4 times a week for several weeks so that it is an appropriate assessment medium.

As you prepare to do the assessment, you should do some light jogging and stretching to make sure the muscles are well prepared for this level of activity. To be a valid assessment, the effort must have integrity. If you are somewhat of a novice runner, you should control the urge to start rapidly...save that for the last quarter mile. Pacing yourself well in the early part of the assessment adds to its validity as an accurate assessment of your cardiovascular system.

Once you have completed the run, be sure to continue jogging or at least walking for a few minutes to give the cardiorespiratory system an opportunity to make the shift from running hard back to resting over a period of time.

The following chart lets you know the estimated fitness category for your time, based on gender and age:

Time (minutes)						
Age (years)						
Fitness Category	13-19	20-29	30-39	40-49	50-59	60+
I. Very Poor (men)	≥15: 31*	≥16:01	≥16:31	≥17:31	≥19:01	≥20:01
(women)	≥18:31	≥19:01	≥19:31	≥20:01	≥20:31	≥21:01
II. Poor (men)	12:11–15:30	14:01–16:00	14:46–16:30	15:36–17:30	17:01–19:00	19:01-20:00
(women)	16:55–18:30	18:31–19:00	19:01–19:30	19:31–20:00	20:01–20:30	20:31–21:00

III. Fair (men)	10:49–12:10	12:01–14:00	12:31–14:45	13:01–15:35	14:31–17:00	16:16–19:00
(women)	14:31–16:54	15:55–18:30	16:31–19:00	17:31–19:30	19:01–20:00	19:31–20:30
IV. Good (men)	9:41–10:48	10:46–12:00	11:01–12:30	11:31–13:00	12:31–14:30	14:00–16:15
(women)	12:30–14:30	13:31–15:54	14:31–16:30	15:56–17:30	16:31–19:00	17:31–19:30
V. Excellent (men)	8:37–9:40	9:45–10:45	10:00–11:00	10:30–11:30	11:00–12:30	11:15–13:59
(women)	11:50–12:29	12:30–13:30	13:00–14:30	13:45–15:55	14:30–16:30	16:30–17:30
VI. Superior (men)	<8:37	<9:45	<10:00	<10:30	<11:00	<11:15
(women)	<11:50	<12:30	<13:00	<13:45	<14:30	<16:30

*< means "less than"; ≥ means "equal to and greater than"
From The Aerobics Program for Total Well Being by Kenneth H. Cooper M.D., M.P.H, copyright © 1982 by Kenneth H. Cooper.
Used by permission of Bantam Books, a division of Random House, Inc.

Assessing Your Cardiorespiratory Fitness: One Mile <u>Jogging</u> Test

Directions: For individuals more accustomed to jogging than running, the 1 mile jogging test may be a better assessment of cardiovascular function than the 1.5 mile run. In the 1-mile jog test, you are to self-select a steady, comfortable pace (recomended total mile times are <u>greater than 8 minutes</u> for males and <u>9 minutes</u> for females, with an ending heart rate of less than 180 beats per minute). You must jog the mile at the same pace throughout. As you approach the finish, find your pulse so that immediately upon crossing the finish line, you can count your heart rate for 10 seconds. Record your time in minutes and decimal seconds (seconds divided by 60) and heart rate in beats per minute (10 second count times 6). Using the following equation, estimate the body's ability to take in and use oxygen ($VO_{2\,max}$)

100.5 + (8.344 if male; 0.0 if female) − (0.164 × weight in kilograms) − (1.44 × mile jog time in minutes and decimal seconds) − (0.193 × ending heart rate in beats per minute) = $VO_{2\,max}$

Example: Jim does the 1 mile jog in 9 minutes and 24 seconds (9.4 minutes), weighs 75 kgs (165 lbs. divided by 2.2), and has an ending heart rate of 130 beats per minute. His estimated $VO_{2\,max}$ would be:

$$100.5 + 8.344 − (0.164 × 75) − (1.44 × 9.4) − (0.193 × 130) =$$
$$100.5 + 8.344 − \quad 12.3 \quad − \quad 13.536 \quad − \quad 25.09 \quad = \mathbf{57.92}$$

Example: Joan does the 1 mile jog in 13 minute and 30 seconds (16.5 minutes), weighs 50 kg (110 lbs. divided by 2.2)., and has an ending heart rate of 130 beats per minute. Her estimated $VO_{2\,max}$ would be:

$100.5 + 0.00 - (0.164 \times 50) - (1.44 \times 13.5) - (0.193 \times 130) =$
$100.5 + 0 \quad - \quad\quad 8.20 \quad - \quad 19.44 \quad - \quad\quad 25.09 \quad = \textbf{47.77}$

Males: (18-26 years old)		Females: (18-26 years old)	
<38	Below level for good health	<28	Below level for good health
39-43	Fair	29-34	Fair
44-51	Good	35-43	Good
52-56	Very Good	44-48	Very Good
57-62	Excellent	49-53	Excellent
63-69	Athletic	54-59	Athletic
70+	Nationally competitive	60+	Nationally competitive

Assessing Your Cardiorespiratory Fitness: One Mile Walking Test

Directions: For individuals for whom running or jogging is not appropriate. Walk a measured one mile distance on level terrain as fast as you can. You must only walk, and must try to maintain an even, best effort pace throughout. As you are approaching the finish line, find your pulse so you can begin counting your heart rate as soon as you finish. Count your heart rate for 10 seconds and multiply by 6 to get your heart rate in beats per minute.

Use the following formula to determine an estimate of the body's ability to take in and use oxygen ($VO_{2\,max}$):

88.768 + (8.892 if male; 0.0 if female) − (0.096 × weight in pounds) − (1.454 × walk time in minutes & decimal seconds) − (0.119 × ending heart rate in beats per minute) = $VO_{2\,max}$

Example: Jim does the 1 mile walk in 14 minutes and 24 seconds (14.4 minutes), weighs 165 lbs., and has an ending heart rate of 98 beats per minute. His estimated $VO_{2\,max}$ would be:

$88.768 + 8.892 - (0.096 \times 165) - (1.454 \times 14.4) - (0.119 \times 98) =$
$88.768 + 8.892 - \quad\quad 15.84 \quad - \quad\quad 20.9376 \quad - \quad\quad 11.662 \quad = \textbf{49.22}$

Example: Joan does the 1 mile walk in 16 minutes and 30 seconds (16.5 minutes), weighs 110 lbs., and has an ending heart rate of 110 beats per minute. Her estimated VO_{2max} would be:

$$88.768 + 0.00 - (0.096 \times 110) - (1.454 \times 16.5) - (0.119 \times 110) =$$
$$88.768 + 0 \quad - \quad 10.56 \quad - \quad 23.991 \quad - \quad 13.9 \quad = \mathbf{41.12}$$

The following table can be used to determine the fitness category for the $VO_{2\ max}$ value achieved:

Males: (18-26 years old)		Females: (18-26 years old)	
<38	Below level for good health	<28	Below level for good health
39-43	Fair	29-34	Fair
44-51	Good	35-43	Good
52-56	Very Good	44-48	Very Good
57-62	Excellent	49-53	Excellent
63-69	Athletic	54-59	Athletic
70+	Nationally competitive	60+	Nationally competitive

Appendix C

Target Training Heart Rates for 60%, 75%, 85% Heart Rate Range

MINIMUM TARGET HEART RATE (using 60% of heart rate range)

Resting Heart Rate	Age									
	16	17	18	19	20	21	22	23	24	25
50	142	142	141	141	140	139	139	138	138	137
51	143	142	142	141	140	140	139	139	138	137
52	143	143	142	141	141	140	140	139	138	138
53	144	143	142	142	141	141	140	139	139	138
54	144	143	143	142	142	141	140	140	139	139
55	144	144	143	143	142	141	141	140	140	139
56	145	144	144	143	142	142	141	141	140	139
57	145	145	144	143	143	142	142	141	140	140
58	146	145	144	144	143	143	142	141	141	140
59	146	145	145	144	144	143	142	142	141	141
60	146	146	145	145	144	143	143	142	142	141
61	147	146	146	145	144	144	143	143	142	141
62	147	147	146	145	145	144	144	143	142	142
63	148	147	146	146	145	145	144	143	143	142
64	148	147	147	146	146	145	144	144	143	143
65	148	148	147	147	146	145	145	144	144	143
66	149	148	148	147	147	146	145	145	144	143
67	149	149	148	147	147	146	146	145	144	144
68	150	149	148	148	147	147	146	145	145	144
69	150	149	149	148	148	147	146	146	145	145
70	150	150	149	149	148	147	147	146	146	145
71	151	150	150	149	148	148	147	147	146	145
72	151	151	150	149	149	148	148	147	146	146
73	152	151	150	150	149	149	148	147	147	146
74	152	151	151	150	150	149	148	148	147	147
75	152	152	151	151	150	149	149	148	148	147
76	153	152	152	151	150	150	149	149	148	147
77	153	153	152	151	151	150	150	149	148	148
78	154	153	152	152	151	151	150	149	149	148
79	154	153	153	152	152	151	150	150	149	149
80	154	154	153	153	152	151	151	150	150	149
81	155	154	154	153	152	152	151	151	150	149
82	155	155	154	153	153	152	152	151	150	150
83	156	155	154	154	153	153	152	151	151	150
84	156	155	155	154	154	153	152	152	151	151
85	156	156	155	155	154	153	153	152	152	151
86	157	156	156	155	154	154	153	153	152	151
87	157	157	156	155	155	154	154	153	152	152
88	158	157	156	156	155	155	154	153	153	152
89	158	157	157	156	156	155	154	154	153	153
90	158	158	157	157	156	155	155	154	154	153

MINIMUM TARGET HEART RATE (using 75% of heart rate range)

Resting Heart Rate	16	17	18	19	Age 20	21	22	23	24	25
50	166	165	164	163	163	162	161	160	160	159
51	166	165	164	164	163	162	161	161	160	159
52	166	165	165	164	163	162	162	161	160	159
53	166	166	165	164	164	163	162	161	160	160
54	167	166	165	164	164	163	162	161	161	160
55	167	166	165	165	164	163	162	162	161	160
56	167	166	166	165	164	163	163	162	161	160
57	167	167	166	165	164	164	163	162	161	161
58	168	164	166	165	165	164	163	162	162	161
59	168	167	166	166	165	164	163	163	162	161
60	168	167	167	166	165	164	164	163	162	161
61	168	168	167	166	165	165	164	163	162	162
62	169	168	167	166	166	165	164	163	163	162
63	169	168	167	167	166	165	164	164	163	162
64	169	168	168	167	166	165	165	164	163	162
65	169	169	168	167	166	166	165	164	163	163
66	170	169	168	167	167	166	165	164	164	163
67	170	169	168	168	167	166	165	165	164	163
68	170	169	169	168	167	166	166	165	164	163
69	170	170	169	168	167	167	166	165	164	164
70	171	170	169	168	168	167	166	165	165	164
71	171	170	169	169	168	167	166	166	165	164
72	171	170	170	169	168	167	167	166	165	164
73	171	171	170	169	168	168	167	166	165	165
74	172	171	170	169	169	168	167	166	166	165
75	172	171	170	170	169	168	167	167	166	165
76	172	171	171	170	169	168	168	167	166	165
77	172	172	171	170	169	169	168	167	166	166
78	173	172	171	170	170	169	168	167	167	166
79	173	172	171	171	170	169	168	168	167	166
80	173	172	172	171	170	169	169	168	167	166
81	173	173	172	171	170	170	169	168	167	167
82	174	173	172	171	171	170	169	168	168	167
83	174	173	172	172	171	170	169	169	168	167
84	174	173	173	172	171	170	170	169	168	167
85	174	174	173	172	171	171	170	169	168	168
86	175	174	173	172	172	171	170	169	169	168
87	175	174	173	173	172	171	170	170	169	168
88	175	174	174	173	172	171	171	170	169	168
89	175	175	174	173	172	172	171	170	169	169
90	176	175	174	173	173	172	171	170	170	169

MAXIMUM SAFE UPPER LIMIT (using 85% of heart rate range)

Resting Heart Rate	16	17	18	19	Age 20	21	22	23	24	25
50	181	180	179	178	178	177	176	175	174	173
51	181	180	179	179	178	177	176	175	174	173
52	181	180	180	179	178	177	176	175	174	174
53	181	181	189	179	178	177	176	175	175	174
54	182	181	180	179	178	177	176	176	175	174
55	182	181	189	179	178	177	177	176	175	174
56	182	181	189	179	178	178	177	176	175	174
57	182	181	180	179	179	178	177	176	175	174
58	182	181	180	189	179	178	177	176	175	174
59	182	181	181	180	179	178	177	176	175	175
60	182	182	181	180	179	178	177	176	176	175
61	183	182	181	189	179	178	177	177	176	175
62	183	182	181	189	179	178	178	177	176	175
63	183	182	181	180	179	179	178	177	176	175
64	183	182	181	180	180	179	178	177	176	175
65	183	182	181	181	180	179	178	177	176	176
66	183	182	182	181	189	179	178	177	177	176
67	183	183	182	181	180	179	178	178	177	176
68	184	183	182	181	180	179	179	178	177	176
69	184	183	182	181	180	180	179	178	177	176
70	184	183	182	181	181	180	179	178	177	176
71	184	183	182	182	181	180	179	178	177	176
72	184	183	183	182	181	180	179	178	177	177
73	184	184	183	182	181	180	179	178	178	177
74	185	184	183	182	181	180	179	179	178	177
75	185	184	183	182	181	180	180	179	178	177
76	185	184	183	182	181	181	180	179	178	177
77	185	184	183	182	182	181	189	179	178	177
78	185	184	183	183	182	181	180	179	178	177
79	185	184	184	183	182	181	189	179	178	178
80	186	185	184	183	182	181	189	189	179	178
81	186	185	184	183	182	181	180	180	179	178
82	186	185	184	183	182	181	181	180	179	178
83	186	185	184	183	182	182	181	180	179	178
84	186	185	184	183	183	182	181	180	179	178
85	186	185	184	184	183	182	181	180	179	179
86	186	185	185	184	183	182	181	180	180	179
87	186	186	185	184	183	182	181	181	189	179
88	187	186	185	184	183	182	182	181	189	179
89	187	186	185	184	183	183	182	181	189	179
90	187	186	185	184	184	183	182	181	180	179

Appendix D

Flexibility Assessment Activities

Following are four functional tests and one standardized test to measure the flexibility of several areas of the body whose adequate range of motion is critical to optimal body functioning. Proper warm-up should precede each test and the end position should be held for at least three seconds to help the results be accurate. Each of the functional tests should be evaluated using the following:

Complete comfortably

Complete with some difficulty

Needs work to complete successfully

1. NECK AREA: Lie on the floor on your back. Lift only your head, and, keeping your teeth clenched, attempt to touch your chin to your upper chest.

2. UPPER CHEST AND SHOULDER: Lie on the floor on your back. Clasp your hands together and attempt to flex your shoulders 180° so that your hands rest on the floor over your head and your arms are almost straight. The goal is a straight line from your trunk through your upper arms.

3. LOWER LEG (CALF): Standing with your feet flat on the floor and your knees locked, lift the ball of your right foot as high off the floor as possible. Have your partner measure if there is at least two fingers' width clearance between the ball of the foot and the floor. Assess both calves.

4. SHOULDERS: Put your right hand over your right shoulder to the upper back, and bring your left hand behind your back under your left shoulder and attempt to touch the fingers of your right hand. Reverse this procedure to assess the left shoulder.

The following standardized test measures flexibility of the lower back and the hamstring muscles (back of the thigh). The protocol described is for the Acuflex I Modified Sit and Reach Test which allows for variations in length of arms and legs. The Acuflex I tester (sit and reach box) is used to conduct this test and is available through companies like Novel Products (www.novelproductsinc.com) or FlagHouse (www.flaghouse.com):

SIT AND REACH TEST:

A. After properly warming up, remove shoes and sit on the floor with back, hips, and head against a wall, legs fully extended, and the bottom of the feet against the Acuflex I box.

B. Make sure the "L" shaped moving device on the reach indicator is perfectly even with the end of the reach indicator.

C. Place one hand on top of the other and reach forward as far as possible without letting the head and back come off the wall. The shoulders may be rounded as much as possible, but neither the head nor the back should come away from the wall. (This is the adjustment for arm length.)

D. Have your partner slide the reach indicator on the Acuflex I along the top of the box until the sliding device touches the tips of your fingers, making sure the sliding device is even with the end of the reach indicator. This is now the starting position for the test, and your partner must hold the reach indicator firmly in place for the duration of the test.

E. Lean forward, letting your head and back come away from the wall. Gradually reach forward three times, the third time pushing the sliding device forward as far as possible along the reach indicator. **Hold the final position for at least two seconds**. Be sure that your knees stay flat against the floor. Record the final number of inches reached to the nearest half inch using the scale on the left side of the reach indicator.

F. You may want to repeat this twice, taking an average of the scores for your final score. Use the chart below to get information about how you compare to others your gender and age.

Table D.1	Percentile Ranks for the Modified Sit-and-Reach (Inches) MEN		
Percentile Rank	Ages 15–19	Ages 20–29	Ages 30–39
99	21.2	23.5	20.8
95	18.5	19.3	17.4
90	17.5	17.9	16.3
80	16.3	17.3	14.9
70	15.5	16.2	13.9
60	14.5	15.3	13.3
50	13.6	14.3	12.3
40	12.6	13.8	11.5
30	11.8	13.0	10.5
20	10.8	11.8	8.4
10	9.0	10.3	7.0
5	8.5	9.3	6.7
1	6.5	5.5	4.1

Percentile Ranks for the Modified Sit-and-Reach (Inches) WOMEN

Percentile Rank	Ages 15-19	Ages 20-29	Ages 30-39
90	23.0	23.7	22.1
95	20.6	20.8	17.9
90	18.8	19.7	17.0
80	17.8	18.3	16.8
70	16.7	17.0	16.1
60	15.8	16.2	15.0
50	15.3	15.5	14.3
40	14.8	14.8	13.6
30	13.8	14.0	12.5
20	12.8	13.0	11.1
10	11.6	11.9	9.0
5	10.3	10.7	8.0
1	7.5	9.2	6.4

These norms were obtained from: Hoeger, Werner W., and David R. Hopkins. The Assessment of Muscular Flexibility: Test Protocols and National Flexibility Norms for the Modified Sit-and-Reach Test, Total Body Rotation Test, and Shoulder Rotation Test. *Rockton, IL: Novel Products, Inc., 1995, 14–15. Used by permission.*

Appendix E

Stress Assessments

Scale for Physical and Emotional Signs of Prolonged Stress

The following chart provides a list of common physical and emotional signs associated with prolonged stress. We may become insensitive to the signal they are designed to be for us. Reviewing this chart and jotting the number associated with each item on a piece of paper and determining a total can help you become more aware of the signals your body is giving you about stressors in your life. Again, remember this is not designed to be diagnostic...just to increase your awareness of signals your body is giving you. (Adapted from Allen and Hyde, *Investigations in Stress Control*, Burgess, 101-105)

Signs unrelated to known disease or illness	0 Never	1 Rarely; one or two times a year	2 Once every 2 or 3 months	3 Once every 2 or 3 weeks	4 Usually 1 or 2 times a week	5 Almost Daily
Impatient; easily irritated						
Tense; anxious						
Unable to relax						
Unable to concentrate						
Unable to sleep						
Unexplained fatigue						
Heart pounding						
Heart racing or skipping						
Throbbing headache						
Cold, sweaty palms						
Shortness of breath						
Nausea or vomiting						
Abdominal pain						
Diarrhea						

Appetite change (inc. or dec.)						
Headaches						
Muscle/joint pains						
Back ache						
Muscle twitches						
Eyelid twitches						
Hand tremors						
Itching skin						
Rash						
Brittle nails						
Unusual hair loss						
Excessive perspiration						
Dry skin						
Rapid eye blinking						
Dry mouth						
Frequent colds/ infections						
Stuttering speech						
Clenched teeth						
Totals						

EVALUATION SCALE: _0–30_: Moderate stress symtoms; _31–70_: Average for most; _71+_: Significant signs of prolonged stress responce; need to modify the stressors or develop better ways of managing your response to them.

Student Stress Scale

This is an adaptation of Holmes and Rahe's "Life Events Scale." This scale asks you to mark events that have happened in the past six months, and those you believe likely to occur in the next six months. Again, this is confidential, and is intended to help you to have a better understanding of the stressors in your life. Add up the point numbers designated for the events you checked. If the total is 300 or more, you have enough stressors that they may lead to a health problem. If your total is between 150 and 299, you have a 50-50 risk of health problems within the next two years. Those who score 149 or less have a 1 in 3 chance of a significant health change.

		Past		Future
1.	Death of a close family member.	____	100	____
2.	Death of close friend.	____	73	____
3.	Divorce of parents.	____	65	____
4.	Jail term.	____	63	____
5.	Major personal injury or illness.	____	63	____
6.	Getting married.	____	58	____
7.	Being fired from a job.	____	50	____
8.	Failed an important course.	____	47	____
9.	Decline in health of a family member.	____	45	____
10.	Unplanned/undesired pregnancy.	____	45	____
11.	Unhappiness with one's sex life.	____	44	____
12.	Serious argument with a close friend.	____	40	____
13.	Change in financial status.	____	39	____
14.	Change of academic major.	____	39	____
15.	Difficulties/disagreements with parents.	____	39	____
16.	New boyfriend/girlfriend.	____	38	____
17.	Increased academic workload.	____	37	____
18.	Outstanding personal achievement.	____	36	____
19.	First term in college, or in this college.	____	35	NA
20.	Change in living environment.	____	31	____
21.	Serious argument with instructor.	____	30	____
22.	Grades lower than expected.	____	29	____
23.	Change in sleeping habits.	____	29	____
24.	Change in social activities.	____	29	____
25.	Change in eating habits.	____	28	____
26.	Frequent car trouble.	____	26	____
27.	Change in relationships with family.	____	26	____
28.	Poor class attendance.	____	25	____
29.	Changing to a different college.	____	24	____
30.	More than one class dropped.	____	23	____
31.	Minor traffic violations (ticketed).	____	20	____

Total Past:_____ **Total Future:**_____ **Overall Total:**_____

Reprinted from Journal of Psychosomatic Research, Vol 11, Issue 2, Thomas H. Holmes and Richard H. Rahe, "The Social Readjustment Rating Scale, pp 213-218, Copyright 1967, with permission from Elsevier.

Appendix F

When Is a Serving a "Serving"?
How Your Food Choices and Portions
Look to a Nutritionist

A challenge, as we try to evaluate our eating patterns, is to know what nutritionists consider to be a "serving" of various foods. Most of us tend to consider servings as the amounts we put on our plates, and of course it varies with how much we like the food in question.

In order to look at our food choices as a nutritionist would, use the guidelines below. Food that comes in a retail package will have serving size information on the package. These guidelines will help in a restaurant or cafeteria.

Food Type	What Is Termed a "Serving"
Breads, cereals, rice, pasta	1 slice of bread or one small dinner roll 1/2 bagel, 1/2 of a large croissant, 1/2 doughnut 1 cup of dry cereal 1/2 cup cooked cereal 1–4" pancake; 1 waffle 1/3 cup granola 4 saltine crackers; 2 graham crackers 1 cup popcorn 1/2 cup stuffing
Vegetables	1 cup of raw leafy vegetables 1/2 cup of other veggies, raw or cooked 1/2 cup coleslaw; 1/2 cup potato salad 10 French fries 1/2 cup vegetable juice, such as V-8
Fruit	1 med. size apple, pear, orange, or banana 1/2 cup cooked, canned or frozen fruit 1/2 of 5" diameter cantaloupe 1 cup of watermelon (cut into cubes) 1/2 cup fruit juice 1/2 cup dried fruit (dates, raisins or other) 4 medium-size olives 1 medium-size tomato

Dairy Foods	1 cup milk or yogurt
	1/2 cup ice cream
	1 cup frozen yogurt or pudding
	1 cup cottage cheese
	2 oz. processed cheese (American)

Meats, Fish, Eggs and meat substitutes	3 oz. cooked meat, fish, poultry (a piece approx. size of credit card, and 1/2" thick)
	1/2 cup cooked dried beans
	1 egg
	2 tbsp. peanut butter; 1/2 cup nuts
	1/8 of 14" pizza

Fats, Oils, Sweets	1 tsp. butter or margarine
	1 tbsp. mayonnaise or salad dressing
	2 tbsp. sour cream
	1 oz. cream cheese
	1 tsp. jam, jelly, honey
	1 oz. chocolate
	2 medium sized cookies
	1 brownie, 2" x 2"
	1/6 of a 9" pie
	1/16 of a 10" layer cake

"Practical" guides to serving sizes:

A large handful is about 1 cup of dry cereal

An "average" closed fist is about a cup of raw vegetables

A deck of cards approximates a 3 oz. serving of meat

A 9-volt battery is about the size of 1 1/2 to 2 oz. of cheese

A 4 inch pancake is a little smaller than a compact disc (CD)

An egg is about the size of 1/4 cup of dates or raisins

Index

Body weight goal, 165–166
Bone
    composition, 83
    conditioning effects on, 89
    functions of, 79
    response to exercise, 84–85
    structure and flexibility, relation between, 102
    tensile and compressional strength, 84
Bone density, muscle strengthening influence on, 92
Bone health, importance of maintaining, 78
Bone mass loss after age 35, 154
Bone mineral density, preservation of, 85
Booth, Michael, 8
Brisk walking, 73
Bronchioles, 51
Bulimia
    clinical features of, 173
    compulsive behaviors associated with, 173
    signs of, 174
    suggestions for avoiding, 174–175

C

Calcium, 189
    content of bones and age, relation between, 153
    food sources of, 153
    loss with excessive protein intake, 193
    role in body's functions, 153
Caloric energy balance, 167
Calorie needs, daily
    by gender, age, and activity level, 142–143
    nutrient percentages and amounts for, 143
Campos, Paul, 161
Capillaries, 49
Capillary-alveolar interface, 51
Capillary networks, body tissues, 49
Carbohydrate foods
    complex. See Complex carbohydrate foods
    food sources of, 143
    simple and complex, 143–144
Carbohydrate intake
    low, skeletal muscle catabolism in, 146–147
    whole grains, vegetables and fruits, 145
Carbohydrates
    and body function, 145–146
    energy available from, 141
    storage in form of glycogen, 145
Cardiac muscle, 48

Cardiac output
    definition, 53
    distribution, 49–50
    increase in exercise, 53–54
Cardiorespiratory conditioning
    plan, 65
    purpose of, 59
Cardiorespiratory fitness. See Aerobic capacity
Cardiorespiratory system
    function of, 53
    purpose of, 46, 59
    role in body functioning, 4
    structure of
        airways and lungs, 51–53
        blood, 50
        heart, 46–48
        vascular system, 49
Cardiovascular conditioning
    benefits of, 67–68
    physical examination/treadmill test prior to, 66–67
    risk associated with, 66–67
Cardiovascular disease risk analysis
    questionnaire, 56–57
    risk factor categories, 55
Cardiovascular efficiency and aerobic exercise, 68
Cardiovascular fitness and physical fitness, 66
Carotid pulse, method for monitoring, 63
Cellular changes, muscle strengthening, 92
"Cellulite," 175
Central body fat distribution estimation, 163–164
Chelation, 196
Chest, 52
Children and adolescents
    health benefits of physical activity in, 9
    stress among, 121–122
Cholesterol levels and heart disease, relation between, 149
www.choosemyplate.gov, 169
Christ
    absolute and perfect representation of God, 24
    body importance in plan of God, 31
    parable teachings
        stewardship, 12–13
    spiritual body, 24
Christian, 2–3
    believers in Jesus Christ, 2
    characteristics of, 2
    God's will for life of, 27
    and his body
        confusion about, 31–34
        self concept, 20

D

Distress, 118
    impairing performance, 118
    and joyful stress, difference between, 118–119
DOMS. *See* Delayed Onset Muscle Soreness
Double knee to chest stretch, 111

E

Eating disorders
    anorexia nervosa. *See* Anorexia nervosa
    bulimia. *See* Bulimia
    motivations for developing, 172
Eccentric contraction, 95
Echinacea preparations, 191
Ectomorphs, 159, 162
Elbow, range of motion of, 102
Electrolyte replacement solutions, 69
Emotional health impact on body, 13
Endomorphs, 162
Endurance athletes
    iron loss among, 154
    physiological adaptation at high altitudes, 70
    regimens of diet and exercise, 145
    total body fiber type variations in, 83
Energy balance, 167
Energy bars, 193–194
Energy conservation system of body, variables influencing, 166
"Energy consumed – energy burned," internet sites for tracking, 169
Energy intake needs
    carbohydrate foods, 145
    for men and women, 169
    nutrient percentages and amounts for, 143
Energy requirement
    components, 168
    internet sites for estimating, 169
    for physical activities, estimation of, 169
    resting, estimation of, 168
Energy-storage processes, biochemical determinants of, 166
Ephedra-containing supplements, banning of, 187
Erythrocytes, 50
Eustress. *See* Joyful stress
Exercise. *See also* Physical activity
    adaptations to
      increased temperature, 54
      increase in cardiac output, 53–54
    blood pressure during, 53
    body response to, 42
    bone response to, 84–85
    and cardiovascular disease, link between, 55
    in cold weather, precautions for, 69

    duration, 42
      "Activity Pyramid," 61–62
      25–30 minutes, 61
    frequency, 42, 62
    and homeostasis, 42
    influence on bone tissue, 85
    intensity, 42, 46
      individualizing, 63–64
    joints response to, 88
    mode for aerobic conditioning, 61
    for muscle strength and endurance. *See* Muscle resistance exercises
    outdoors in cold weather, precautions for, 68–69
    oxygen needs during, 53
Exercise heart rate and heart rate reserve, relation between, 63–64
Exercise-induced muscle cramps, 97
Exercises for healthy back
    bench hip flexor stretch, 112
    bend over, 113
    curl down, 112
    double knee to chest stretch, 111
    modified Hurdler's hamstring stretch, 111
    pelvic tilt, 112
    single knee to chest stretch, 111
Expiration and intercostals, 52–53
External respiration, 53

F

Fat
    storage, factors influencing, 166
Fatigue and muscle strength, link between, 93
Fat intake
    limiting, 201
    making healthier choices for, 150–151
    recommendation for reducing, 150
Fats
    classification of, 148
    constituents of, 148
    energy available from, 141
    food sources, 148
    role in body, 149–150
Field tests for aerobic capacity, 60–61
Fitness club, 201
Flexibility, 115
    definition, 102
    factors affecting, 102–103
    importance in
      joints functioning, 103
      musculoskeletal fitness, 101
      warm-up and cool-down, 104

G

H

T

Technology impact on human lives, 119–120
    employment situation, 120
    muscle-work, 99
Temperature and flexibility, relation between, 103
Temptation of worry, 133
Testosterone
    effect on muscle mass, 93
    physiological effects on body tissues, 172
"Thermic effect of food," 169
Threshold stimulus, 42
Time management, 134
Tobacco use and cardiovascular disease, link between, 55
Torso twist (stretching exercise), 105
Training. *See* Conditioning
Training heart rate
    calculation formula, 64
    definition, 74
    determination method, 64
    factors influencing determination of, 63
    and workout intensity, 63
Trans fat, 148
Tricuspid valve, 48
Tylenol, 184

U

Underwater weighing, body density estimation using, 164
Unholy alliance, 20
Unsaturated fats, 148

V

Variable resistance isotonic exercise, 95
Variable resistance machines, muscle conditioning program using, 95
Vascular system
    arteries, 49
    arterioles, 49
    capillary beds in, 49
    definition, 49
    veins, 49
    venules, 49

Veins, 49
Ventricles
    functions of, 48
    right and left, 48
Venules, 49
Visceral fat
    measurement methods, 163
    as risk factor in dyslipidemia, 163
Vitamins
    as anti-oxidants, 152
    as co-enzymes, 151
    fat-soluble, 151–152, 189
    nutrient loss of, 153
    primary role of, 15389
    vitamin A, 152
    vitamin C, 152
    vitamin D, 152
    vitamin E, 152
    vitamin K, 152
    water-soluble, 151–152, 189

W

Waist circumference, 163
Waist-to-hip ratio
    central body fat distribution estimation using, 163–164
    standards, 163
    visceral fat estimation by, 163
Walking, changes in body to support, 3
Water drinking, frequent, 69
Water intake, 155
Water soluble vitamins, 151
    B-complex and vitamin C, 152
Weight-bearing exercise, 85
Weight management
    frequently asked questions about, 175–177
    myths about supplements for, 188
    suggestions for, 169–170
    very low calorie diets adverse effects on, 176
Weight selection, muscle conditioning program, 95
Whey, 193
Willett, Walter, 145
"Wisdom of body," 21, 141